The Second Handshake

The Second Handshake

by WILL FOWLER

Lyle Stuart Inc.   Secaucus, N.J.

First Edition
Copyright© 1980 by Will Fowler
All rights reserved, including the right to reproduce this book or any
portion thereof in any form.

Published by Lyle Stuart Inc.
120 Enterprise Ave., Secaucus, N.J. 07094

Published simultaneously in Canada by
General Publishing Co. Limited
Don Mills, Ontario

Manufactured in the United States of America

Library of Congress Cataloging in Publication Data
Fowler, Will, 1922-
     The second handshake.

     Includes index.
     1. Fowler, Gene, 1890-1960—Biography.   2. Fowler,
Will, 1922-   3. Authors, American—20th century
—Biography.   I. Title.
PS3511.093Z63 818′.5209   80-12679
ISBN 0-8184-0287-3

For their friendship, encouragement and whimsical belief that this wayward monk would not survive these many years, I dedicate this book to Hal Kanter, Jim Murray, Art Ronnie, Jack Smith, Al Stump, Walter Weschler and Robert Young, Jr.

Contents

*There are no fields of amaranth on this side of the grave.
There are no voices that are not soon mute, however
tuneful. There is no name with whatever tone of
passionate love repeated, of which the echo is not faint
at last.*

—Walter Savage Landor

1

Tit for Tat

This book is mostly about my father, Gene Fowler, and his many
famous friends I knew — people like John Barrymore, W. C.
Fields, Damon Runyon, and Jack Dempsey — but before we sail
into the mainstream of the book, let us take a moment out for a
brief sketch of my own life.

*　*　*

I weighed in at eleven pounds at Jamaica Hospital, Long Island,
New York, on August 29, 1922. And according to *The Book of
Days* (Lippincott), absolutely no one of any consequence was
born on this date during the past three centuries. However, it
must be pointed out that Edmund Hoyle, author of the book on
Games (1976), and St. John the Baptist (30 A.D.) both died on
August 29, the latter being beheaded as Salome dropped her sev-
enth veil — which was strictly *not* according to Hoyle.

Being a lady, my mother Agnes was with me at the time of my
birth. My father, however, was away in Salt Lake City, and as a
newspaper reporter for William Randolph Hearst's *New York
American*, was covering an execution.

In Salt Lake City, the man to be executed was given the choice
of death by firing squad or by hanging. Up until then, the execu-
tees had invariably picked the rifle route. But this critter, a mu-
nicipal judge convicted of incest and strangling his wife, chose
the noose because it would cause the state additional expense to
erect a scaffold. Following the execution, Pop wrote that the
Judge was not only hanged, but also "hung."

Tit for Tat

Not to be confused with Jamaica Hospital, we had a black maid from the island of Jamaica. She was Ethel, and her illegitimate daughter was named Mavis. There were times when Ethel would ceremoniously place Mavis and me in Pop's bed just before we were carried away for our night's sleep. Then there were days when Pop would roll us down Park Lane toward Jackson's Pond in a splendid perambulator to watch the toy sailboat races. One day racing car driver Barney Oldfield and wrestling promoter Jack Curley visited Pop in Richmond Hill. They sighted him coming out the front door with us in his arms. Oldfield was dumfounded as he saw one child (blue-black) and myself (cream white) in either arm. "Gene!" cried Oldfield. "What the hell! What happened?"

With his usual calm on such occasions, Pop said, "Well, you know, Barney. They tell me this happens every so often. I don't know about genetics — but aren't they wonderful, these kids? You'd never suspect they were twins, would you now?"

* * *

The day following my first birthday, my only pleasure was snatched from me: my mother, who had fed her three children at the breast, weaned me and took off for southern California to visit relatives.

I never got around to asking Pop whether he was celebrating or saddened by Mother's leavetaking. Anyway, he went out that night and took on a load of booze while in the company of Jack Dempsey, who was heavyweight boxing champion of the world. After downing a stirrup cup for the road, Dempsey knew that unless he had a rubber car Pop was in no condition to drive.

An hour later Jack pulled Pop's car to a stop at the front of our Richmond Hill home located on the Park Lane border of Kew Gardens. Jack, having grown up with my father in Colorado where the two youngsters used to run down wild horses, figured he'd better keep a close rein on Pop and stay the night.

When I began crying during the early morning hours, Dempsey, who slept only in his shorts, hopped out of bed to see what the commotion was about. He took me in his arms and tried to pacify me. The thing most obvious to me was Dempsey's nipple. Thinking it was my mother's, I bit it.

Dempsey was the first of many celebrities I would meet during my lifetime.

* * *

I had reached the age of five without being circumcised. When I was dragged off to Jamaica Hospital, I thought the true reason for the trip was to have my pecker cut off. No one could convince me I was going to have it trimmed. With a deathgrip, I clung to a brass rail outside the hospital. I damn near tore it from its foundation before I was wrenched loose.

* * *

At the age of six, following yet another execution my father was covering — this time the Ruth Snyder-Judd Gray electrocution at Sing Sing Prison — some classmates and I tossed rocks through the bay window of the executioner's home on St. Ann's Avenue. We resented Mr. Elliott receiving $300 for a double-header.

* * *

It was a few months after the stock market collapsed in 1929 when *Variety* bannerlined its noted head: WALL STREET LAYS AN EGG. It was the day before Christmas and Pop was home for a change, writing his first book, *Trumpet in the Dust,* an autobiographical novel, for publisher Horace Liveright.

I was seven, and Pop warned me not to hitch my sled to automobiles that would pull kids to the top of Park Lane. I considered I wasn't disobeying him if I hitched onto a *truck*. But the bakery wagon got off to a bad start, resulting in my being mashed between the machine and the cement curb. As a result, neighbors who helped hold me down on the living room sofa while I was chloroformed were shocked to learn I had so many blue four-letter words in my vocabulary.

Off again to Jamaica Hospital after a quick arm-setting. The place was becoming a home away from home. That night I informed all the kids in the children's ward that there was no Santa

Claus because I had seen my great-grandmother, Maria West, putting presents beneath the tree the previous Noël.

(At the time, Maria who could play the hell out of a bugle, was having a December love affair with ninety-two-year-old Daddy Ottens next door. Daddy had been a rivet boy in the Brooklyn Navy Yard during the Civil War. He had worked on the construction of the iron warship *Monitor,* which was to fight a stand-off with the Confederacy's *Merrimac* in 1862.)

* * *

When I was twelve, the entire family — Pop, Mother, granmother Catherine Hubbard, brother Gene, Jr., sister Jane and I — traveled to Europe on an ocean liner. We departed with one steamer trunk and one suitcase per person. We returned nearly three months later with five trunks and seventeen suitcases, and one of the latter exclusively contained stolen ashtrays. We were later formally requested by consulates of several countries never to return.

In Venice, while the merchants were robbing our parents in the front of the store, we kids were doing the same to them in the back. And in Egypt, we even talked Mother into stuffing a heiroglyphic fragment from King Tutankhamen's tomb beneath her dress. About to be found out, we put on an exhibition, shouting to the Arabs that they were attempting to defile a pregnant woman.

The Fowler tour de force erupted again when we arrived at the spot on the River Jordan where St. John the Baptist gave Christ a bath. Our guide warned us not to "make the Sign of the Cross." It would disturb the Mohammedans. It bothered the natives more than we had planned. I had taken an Arab boy and did the whole baptizing bit at the river's edge. The Moslems attacked! Sister Jane's knowledge of the high kick came in handy, resulting in several natives falling to the dirt clutching their groins. Pop and Gene grappled. Grandma Hubbard used the pocketbook-over-the-head technique, and Mother and our guide aided us in a hasty retreat.

I was nearly six years my brother's junior and going through a gullible time in life. This often made me the goat for his jokes.

Tit for Tat

While staying in the prime suite at the Excelsior Hotel in Naples, I took special interest in a nearly-two-foot-high bowl with a fountain nozzle at its center. Because of its size and shape, I considered it should have had a toilet seat on it. I questioned my brother about this. "That's not a toilet," he chuckled. "That's a drinking fountain, you nut."

I wasn't convinced. "But if it's a drinking fountain, why is it so low?"

Never lacking an answer, Gene said, "That's because the Italians aren't tall people."

This sounded reasonable, so I began to use the vessel as a drinking fountain.

"You'll drink bottled water like the rest of us," my mother informed me, after learning I was drinking from a faucet.

"But I drink from the fountain in the bathroom," I said.

After I showed Mother where it was located, she added more firmly, "You'll drink bottled water like the rest of us."

I was too embarrassed to tell her how I came to believe the bidet was what I thought it was.

*   *   *

I was thirteen when the Fowler family made its permanent home in Southern California. This was when I met the man whom I consider the world's greatest comedian, W.C. Fields. We both impressed each other well at our first meeting, and I was one of the two children he ever would like. The other was his trainer Bob Howard's son, Dick. He put his trust in me because I smoked black cigars and drank martinis with him.

This was the beginning of the magic years, which started when I received my learner's permit to drive a car. Since Pop had decided never to drive and drink at the same time, I became his chauffeur and was privileged to drive him to the homes and haunts of such greats as Fields, John Barrymore, Thomas Mitchell, directors Leo McCarey and Gregory LaCava, artist John Decker, Jack Dempsey, Red Skelton, Ben Hecht, Erle Stanley Gardner, Jimmy Durante and so many others. I was able to sit and observe these great personalities while they were off guard.

I knew then that something magnificent was happening which would never happen again.

* * *

At age seventeen, I had my first affair with a woman. It took place in the fabled Tijuana, Mexico, brothel, El Molino Rojo, which boasted one hundred cribs. And it only cost a dollar.

A small, well-figured lady of the evening had her eyes set for me. I knew "virgin" was indelible on me. Dressed in a skin-fitting gold sequined bathing suit-type outfit and wearing black net stockings, she refused all other male advances. I visited the bar to down a fifth straight brown tequila, waited for it to explode in my stomach, then turned and said to my companions, "Well, I don't know what you guys are going to do, but I'm goin' in!"

My beautiful lady in sequins leaped up and grabbed me by the arm. She escorted me to her crib, which was not too conducive to screwing, what with all the holy pictures and burning candles. She told me to remove my clothing. When I got down to my shorts, I stopped, then asked, "These, too?"

She nodded and unhitched the catches to her outfit in the area which so differentiates a woman from a man. Jesus! There it was! I had never seen one before. It scared hell out of me because it looked like General Grant with his teeth out.

I fully understood later when John Barrymore told me that "woman sits on the most powerful weapon in the world."

I did not, however, go headlong into this affair without taking precautions. No, siree. Before we locked into one another's arms, I wisely recalled my mother's sage warning: "Never remove your socks when in a strange place. You might catch athlete's foot." No, siree. She wasn't about to get me to take off my socks.

* * *

Following graduation in 1940, I began indulging. I strayed from my orchestration and composition studies with the late composer Ferde Grofé. Despite that first encounter, I was still not experienced in the ways of women. Then one day, while I was playing piano in a Fauré quintet at a get-together in a musical friend's home, forty-year-old Winifred Stoner and I collided. She was as statuesque and voluptuous as a Rubens model. She had recently divorced her seventh husband, and did not believe in alimony. She was the youngest person ever to be entered in *Who's Who* when she published her first book at the age of six.

That night, "Winnie," who continued to make her living as a writer, took me to a movie. As I drove her home afterward, she nonchalantly said, "If I'd have known it was going to be such a bad picture, we could have gone up to my place and knocked off a piece of ass." My head nearly went through the car's top.

I returned home late, but happy, that night. Our affair continued on nearly a daily basis for about six months. After I had lost about twenty pounds, I realized how Winnie had easily "wasted" seven husbands.

Twenty years later Winnie and I ran into each other at a bar. She was still a handsome person. She was visiting in the States away from a guest ranch she owned south of Mexico City, and had just divorced her eleventh husband. "Guest ranch," I thought. "That's Winnie's solution."

After a few drinks and cathing up on old times, I broached the inevitable question, "Was I any good at all in the saddle?"

She smiled, looking back through the years, and said, "Darling, you were a medical student."

Following a few intensive love affairs, I met Beverly Blanchard. So far, this one has turned out all right, although with five kids, I am more or less looked upon like a spare part in the machine of the family. Beverly and I were twenty when we wed, following my discharge during World War II from the U.S. Coast Guard where I drew full combat pay as our ship convoyed the local garbage barge out past Catalina Island.

During the early years of our marriage, I became an actor. My father refused to see me in any of my pictures, two of which were directed by Pop's friends William A. Wellman and Michael Curtiz. Fowler suggested I become a newspaper reporter. And anything Pop suggested, I did. But after making $250 a week as an actor, it was a comedown to make $34 as a reporter. "Subsidize me," I blackmailed. Pop did, at the rate of $50 a week.

My reporter days were the happiest of my life. I would show up for work even if I had pneumonia because I was afraid I would miss something. It was a great ego trip, too — to be "on the inside" of all the fast-breaking stories. Becoming a reporter was one of my father's best suggestions.

In 1952, I left the old *Los Angeles Herald and Express* where I had worked under one of the West Coast's finest city editors, Agness Underwood.

We called her Aggie, and cursed in her presence, but knew how far to go. We respected her as our special brand of lady. If we ever heard anyone on an opposition paper say anything derogatory about her, we would ask them to take back the slur. If they didn't, it would start a fight. I earned three hashmarks defending her honor. As for her barroom language, it was light tea, but properly used.

Aggie started her newspaper career as a telephone operator on the long defunct *Los Angeles Record* in 1926. A year later, an old man entered the city room claiming he was the first person to plant cotton in the State of California. No reporters were available so Aggie was ordered to interview the codger. Her story was so well written, she was given a by-line. She joined the *Herald and Express* in 1935 and became the West's first female city editor of a major newspaper in 1941. Today, at seventy-seven, she is retired and lives in Palos Verdes, California, where her six successful grandchildren visit her often. "When I hear them use the expression 'investigative reporter' on television today," Aggie told me, "I could throw a book at that damned tube! Hell, we were *all* investigative reporters! The only difference is that the ones like you and me were pioneers, and a helluva lot better at it. Today they pursue one story for a week or two. When we were young, we could do a couple of in-depth stories in a single day. Hell, you remember sometimes we even solved murders before the detectives did."

But in 1952 Agness Underwood and I were under the firebrand managing editor John B.T. Campbell. God, he liked a good reporter! You could get away with anything short of murder as long as you did your job well. But when I resigned to write for Red Skelton, Mr. Campbell would never speak to me again.

Tit for Tat

No one ever left John B. T. Campbell.

On the same day, now *Times Syndicate* columnist Jack Smith had resigned his position as a rewrite man in our lively bullpen. Mr. Campbell could not understand how both Jack and I could leave him for jobs that would pay hundreds of dollars more a week. (I think we were then making about $125.) Mr. Campbell later placed an edict on the bulletin board reading: "Jack Smith and Will Fowler are no longer allowed in the city room of the *Herald and Express* for good and just reasons." That's all. The following day the particulars of Mr. Campbell's edict drifted over to the boys in the city room of a tabloid-type newspaper, the *Los Angeles Daily News*. And although Mr. Campbell had never set foot inside the *Daily News*, an order in capital letters was nailed to their bulletin board:

MR. JOHN B.T. CAMPBELL IS NO LONGER ALLOWED IN THE CITY ROOM OF THE DAILY NEWS FOR GOOD AND JUST REASONS!

John Fenton Murray and Benedict Freedman were Red Skelton's veteran radio writers. We all had been hired for his TV show with a handshake, something New York Mayor Jimmy Walker said "went out of style years ago. In my day," he told me during the last year of his life, "you either kept your word, or you got out of town."

When Red's television show was still number one in the rating charts, it was switched from NBC to CBS. His entire production crew, including we writers, was discharged without notification. When I learned of this, I wrote an essay about Skelton in 1953 and filed it away for future reference. Now that more than a quarter century has flirted with me, then passed by, I find that what I had written was fair, honest and discerning. It is a study of the talented comedian and his private ways of acting and reacting when not in front of the cameras. To my knowledge, this view of the man has never been touched upon in print:

Tit for Tat

In the opinion of many qualified observers, Red Skelton is the foremost clown of the day, and perhaps one of the greats of all time. Many diverse explanations are offered as to reason or reasons for his endurance on television while others, also of genuine talent, have dropped from the vine. My father once told Red, "The television medium is a glass furnace which burns out the artist and burns up his material with pitiless despatch."

Several, indeed most of yesterday's comics are now on the sidelines, sitting out their million-dollar contracts, but unhappily out of earshot of audiences, forgotten by the fan magazines. Money does not take the place of their supreme sauce, laughter *that is heard or reported to them by their admirers.*

Skelton's past sporadic television ratings would shock a heart specialist. By all that has been written in the graf books, he should have been professionally dead a long time ago. Today, his ratings fly steadily high.

When Skelton hired me as one of the writers for his program, he was the Number One attraction among the funny men. I had been, among other things, a newspaper reporter. A pot of money, together with my inquisitive bent, caused me to leave newspaper work for the Skelton assignment. Contrary to the advice of several friends — among them my own father — I wanted this new experience, and got it. I wanted to learn, if possible, what relationship there might be between a fictional-type comedian and reality. I soon found that Skelton was a human paradox; earthy in many respects, and yet one who lived in a dream world.

Sometimes he invited those who worked for him to join him in that world. Again he almost commanded that they do so. Still again he might want to go it alone in that realm of fancy, retiring as it were behind a velvet curtain. I observed soon enough that the members of his court were in a highly talented state of flux. They came and went in platoon formation. Even the most stalwart among them had an air of uncertainty, as if they were in-laws. Other than their prescribed contributions to the scripts of the master, one and all of these generally gifted fellows had to be court jesters to the king of the

Tit for Tat

jesters, to keep him in a near-happy frame of mind.

There were others, also, who tried, or seemed to try, to keep him financially sound. But Red appeared to want that which he did not have at the time when his investors advised against carrying his money around in two suitcases. His passion for gadgets of all sorts may have been compensation for his deeper desires. His business coaches almost lost their minds over his wholesale purchases of cameras of all makes; his collection of automobiles, including a circus caravan and a pickup truck.

He never tried to conceal either his virtues or his faults, a sort of Diogenes in this respect. He can be winning, charmingly cordial, and sympathetic — subject of course to a change in his barometric pressure.

Secrecy is not his forte. Red Skelton does not know what diplomacy is, nor does he seem to care. If he appears petulant at times — as, indeed, he often does — or becomes downright quarrelsome with his intimates in front of strangers, it is because he does not know the difference between a private life and a public one. This can be either a curse or a blessing as the moment presents itself. He shares both his joys and his woes with anyone who happens by. And when there is a storm, and Red blows his cork, an eavesdropper who is hard of hearing thinks himself cured.

Whatever Skelton is, he is just that in spades, and no holds barred. He can sincerely believe his insincerity, because he is essentially a fine actor who enters into a part personally as well as professionally. It takes something of a hero to be his friend, but the friendship is both wearing and rewarding. If, in a moment of pique, he says something about your faults to a perfect stranger, you must be able to make allowances for the fact that a gifted child is having a tantrum.

He is Skelton, take him or leave him. And the public takes him. As a person, and not a genius, he perhaps has more former friends than a thriving mortician.

*   *   *

Murray continued on to be one of television's most respected comedy writers. Freedman became a professor of mathematics at Occidental College.

Following the Skelton experience, I sat around for a year, waiting for some lucky person to pick up this talented writer. It didn't happen. Damon Runyon was so right when he advised, "He who does not tooteth his own horn does not get his horn tooted."

A year later, I was approached by American Airlines' West Coast public relations director, Bill Hipple, to take over his Hollywood office which handled "tie-ins" with the news media, and supplied motion picture and television shows material, props and film to exploit the airline. Hipple gave me a free hand. We innovated most of the jimcracks others later took credit for. We had the initial complete modern airlines film library available to motion pictures and television. We constructed the first breakaway plastic jet stage mockup. We started the first television news coverage of arrivals and departures of famous personages, servicing the networks and local stations with film and news copy.

There wasn't much we didn't do — legally — until the 1959 television exposé when it was discovered that many stars and producers were on the take. Also, there were too many guest contestants appearing on high-priced quiz shows who seemed to know asnwers before the questions were asked. That was the end of my stay with American Airlines. Although they had nothing to do with the above mentioned, it was time for me to get out of this business.

The name Bob Cobb comes to mind. Cobb opened the first of his three Brown Derby restaurants in the 1920s. The Hollywood eatery is on Vine Street just south of Hollywood Boulevard. But beginning in the 1970s, following Cobb's death, the glamour, intrigue and infatuation with the Beautiful People had seen the fabled Hollywood drop to its knees for the ten count as it became the gold cap on a tooth that should have been pulled years before.

A sports lover, Cobb also owned the Hollywood Stars triple-A baseball team. He was as impeccable a dresser as Jimmy Walker. His hundred suits were tailored to trimly fit his thin, tall frame.

Tit for Tat

The only facet that remained old fashioned about his clothing was in the area of his pants. Instead of a zipper on his fly, there were buttons. Why? One day, while he still sported zippers, he made a hasty exit from the men's room when a painful tragedy occurred. He got his malehood hooked into his zipper locks. He was so well entrapped that it took a physician's scalpel to divorce him from the centipede of hooks. His tailors were busy for two weeks replacing Cobb's zippers with buttons.

When I visited Cobb's Hollywood Brown Derby a dozen years ago, he greeted me during the lunch hour. The booths were filled to capacity in the main dining room. They were occupied with folks of the entertainment world, most of whom were talking in the millions while freeloading on their company expense accounts.

While I was chatting with Cobb, a worn movie producer interrupted our conversation, starting to pump the owner's hand as he surveyed the tables like a hungry wolf. He was obviously seeking out a sucker who might back him to produce a remake of *Gone With the Wind*, or something of the like.

But for the inattentive, roving-eyed producer interjecting a "Wonderful," or "That's great," or "You don't mean it," the conversation was one-sided on Cobb's part until the latter mentioned, "I'd like you to meet Will Fowler." Then I found myself on the receiving end of a limp handshake.

Cobb went on, "Will is Gene Fowler's son."

The promoter stared at me. His exaggerated smile was followed by a now vigorous handshake. This was backed up with, "What a wonderful man Gene Fowler was! There'll never be another like him." Then, "You certainly are a lucky man to have been the son of Gene Fowler."

The initial flaccid handshake was routine to me. But, after being identified as the son of a famous author, I found myself on the receiving end of what I today refer to as *The Second Handshake*.

This has happened uncounted times. During these moments, I suffer in silent embarrassment. Perhaps this is why I am more comfortable with friends and still uneasy with strangers. My friends accept me for what I am, not for being Pop's son.

Being the son of Gene Fowler, I must admit, has had its advantages, except that Pop sort of usurped my youth.

My oft irreverent, but seldom irrelevant, father lived seventy years. During the last five, he had more or less deserted his craft. Whenever some luminary came to town, it was his habit to visit with Fowler at his Brentwood house at 12323 22nd Helena Drive, an address that playwright Charles MacArthur claimed was the combination to W.C. Fields' safe. There would be Secretary of Labor John Mitchell (Thomas Mitchell's nephew), Ben Hecht, Rube Goldberg, H. Allen Smith, John Steinbeck, William Faulkner, S. Jay Kaufman, industrialist billionaire Floyd Odlum, Pulitzer Prize poet Robert Hillyer, Eddie Rickenbacker, Grantland Rice, Walter Winchell, Jack Dempsey, Westbrook Pegler, Damon Runyon. . . .

Fowler had written books endearing him to these men who liked their prose rich, their nostalgia deep and their laughter uncontrollable. He was respected as a modern-day Twain. And oddly enough, in those days, men of this caliber of intelligence often circumvented the females in favor of a zestful, blithe evening of colloquy with their male companions.

I wish I had had the foresight to put down the forgotten phrases which rolled with ease from his tongue. He had a gift for word painting. "Man is an accident born of an incident. Forever is a woman's word. Success is a greased pig. Money was meant to be thrown from the backs of trains. Men who deserve monuments do not need them. Men are not against you, they are merely for themselves. I am a betrayed hobbyhorse."

The first I finally got around to noting was, "Hollywood is a place where you have a choice of riding in a Rolls-Royce or being run over by one."

Because of Fowler's gullible nature, he was talked out of writing W.C. Fields' biography. He was the only person given permission by the comedian, in writing, to do so. But Robert Lewis Taylor traveled to Hollywood from New York to ask that I introduce him to Fowler. I departed my Paramount Studios office with Taylor and headed toward Brentwood.

Fowler was living in an Italian villa at 472 North Barrington Avenue. A cluster of the then famous of Hollywood lived within a few blocks of one another. There were producer-directors Frank Capra and William Wellman, Nelson Eddy (who was our air raid warden during World War II), Deanna Durbin, the Andrews Sisters, John Payne and Anne Shirley, Cesar Romero, Fred MacMurray, Gary Cooper, Tyrone Power, Franchot Tone and Lana Turner.

When Taylor and I arrived at Pop's house, we found the squire outside dressed in his dirty garden clothes and straw hat. A rubberneck Hollywood sightseeing bus had stopped in front of the Barrington mansion. A lady passenger beckoned Fowler to her window. He removed his hat and asked what he might do for her.

"Tell me," the elderly lady asked, pointing to his baronial estate entrance, "does Lana Turner live in there?"

"Madam," Pop smiled, "do you think I'd be out here if she did?" Then he winked.

Following a two-hour visit, at which time Taylor learned that Fowler was in the midst of composing Jimmy Walker's biography, *Beau James* (Viking), Taylor asked permission to write the Fields book. Not wishing to be a dog in the manger, Fowler gave it. He went to his files and removed about two hundred fifty pages of notes, exclusively about Fields (and Pop's notes read like polished prose). "Here, Bob. Take these. They might help you some."

So many of these notes were put down in Taylor's book, *W.C. Fields, His Follies and Fortunes* (Doubleday), that many readers today think this book was done by Fowler.

In a sense, I still have the feeling that I am competing with my father, even though he's been dead for twenty years. Sometimes resentments well up in me, especially when a subintellectual pounces upon me with a no-think phrase such as, "Gene Fowler's son, eh? Well, I'll tell you, you can't write as well as your father did." My answer to this mournfully dull statement is, "Neither can you, you stupid son-of-a-bitch."

Do not misinterpret me. I am proud of my lineage. I revel in telling tales about Pop. It would just be more comfortable for me not to be compared to him in merit. I will admit, however, that in my youth when I was still uncertain of my talents, I parried for conversational openings in order to mention that I was Fowler's son so I might receive adulation or praise.

Following the above with the statement that I published a best-seller biography of my father titled *The Young Man From Denver* (Doubleday) makes me sound perfidious. But I had a point to make.

A short time ago I was introduced to a gentleman who said, "Oh, yes. I've heard quite a bit about you. You wrote that book."

"I'm afraid you have me confused with my father," I said.

"No, I mean *you*," he insisted.

*   *   *

When I first fell in love with my father, he was forty. We lived on Fire Island in New York State. There, if you had a musical ear, you could distinguish the wind tune from the sea tune. To a stranger, it might be just a noise. But to Pop and myself as I held his huge, gentle hand walking along the ocean front, it was a duet. This day the leaves of the huckleberry bushes were a warm russet, like the hair of my first girl. And the cranberries were plentiful in the hollows. There were many wonderful sights here. The best was my tall father as I looked up at him through the eyes of an eight-year-old boy.

Shortly before Pop's death in 1960, I had become news director for George Putnam at Hollywood's KTTV television studio. In addition to being news director, I also wrote, produced and directed a few documentary films. Here I drew upon my previous experience when television was young, and was paid only $100 a show by Procter & Gamble. The fifteen-minute vignettes in those days were shot in one day.

The first time Pop feared the Grim Reaper was knocking, he thought they were his last words when he looked up at Mother following a heart seizure and said, "Don't let the undertaker rook you."

But he chose to drive about and visit his three children on July 2. The last thing he said to me as he drove away from my Encino home was, "Eureka, perhaps."

Attempting to refresh his memory recently, a friend asked, "How old was your father when he died?"

"Seventy," I said.

"Well, that's a good long time for a man to live," he pondered.

"Not to a man who's sixty-nine," I said, not pondering.

*   *   *

My writing habits today have been thrust upon me by a dog at the top of the hill in my town of Tarzana, where Edgar Rice Burroughs created and wrote about Tarzan. The dog tirelessly barks between the approximate hours of midnight and six in the morning. He won't allow me sleep, so this is the time I spend writing. However, when I complete this book — or it abandons me — I am going to travel up the hill and bark at the goddamned mutt all day — so I can get some sleep for myself that night.

2

To Hollywood on a Rail

Somewhere in the vicinity of fifty years ago there was a sandbar just north of Santa Monica, California, with a sprinkling of beachhouses facing the Pacific Ocean. One of the handful of structures was uniquely fashioned after the upper decks of a ship. It belonged to screen star Lew Cody. He was one of Fowler's drinking companions and one of the first of the motion picture world to move to this then remote spot. During these days of Prohibition, one could not shout to a person in the next house because it was so far distant. Today, its buildings are hived tighter than freight cars on a spur siding, and folks of the movie — and, now, television — industry pay well over $1 million to own a house squeezed on a forty-foot lot. It is internationally known as the *Malibu Colony*.

But there was an earlier sandbar that attracted luminaries of the cinema and stage, which is still referred to as the original colony. This one braves the waves of the Atlantic. It is about forty-two miles long and usually a bit more than a half mile wide, stretched out like a basking lizard forming the Great South Bay to the south of New York's Long Island. Through the years its Saltaire lighthouse has beamed its rays navigationally marking the start or finish of history-making flights by Charles Lindbergh, Wiley Post, Howard Hughes, Amelia Earhart, Italo Balbo and his fleet of Italian bombers, the *Graf Zeppelin* and the ill-fated *Hindenburg*. Its days of glamour stretched between world wars. It is *Fire Island*. It was given its name by pilgrims of the seventeenth century. Indians who lived on the island kindled

To Hollywood on a Rail

huge fires which could be seen by the newcomers to this continent eight miles across the bay.

"Many seasons in the sun have gone since my Fire Island days," my father once wrote me. "The play which Wolcott Gibbs wrote about this long patch of sand is said to have expressed the true mood and the very life of Fire Island. His play began when my own Fire Island days left off." Pop had departed the Island in 1943. During the early days on Fire Island there were no roads, no automobiles, no electricity, no tap water, no telephones. But we did enjoy the luxury of indoor toilets. There was only one telegraph wireless from the Island to the mainland. We also happily boasted a lamplighter, a little old man known only as Mr. Klause.

Each day (Sundays excepted) telegrapher Charles Buelher would notify residents of Ocean Beach that noon had arrived (according to his gold pocket watch) by sounding the firehouse siren. The community had one doctor with offices in the firehouse. Since a fatal accident in the thirties, no bicycle riding was allowed on Ocean Beach. Cement sidewalks were coming in, replacing the boardwalks which daily infested our bare feet with splinters. An interesting diversion was to watch three-hundred-pound slabs of ice being unloaded from Captain Robinson's ferry, *The Traveler*, to supply our iceboxes.

In these days a few artists, actors, writers or other paid vagrants landed upon occasion at our primitive retreat. For the most part they were fugitives from the Fifty-Second Street cafés, transients from Broadway.

Fowler had much to do with the coming of the theatrical vanguard to the Island. During the heyday of vaudeville Pop revealed to a native New Yorker, comedian Joe Laurie, Jr., that such a place as Fire Island not only existed, but was also reasonably habitable, notwithstanding the circumstance that there were elevated boardwalks from which a drinking man was likely to fall on a dark night, getting his eyes and mouth full of sand, followed by a case of poison ivy.

During the hour long voyage, over a dogleg course from Bayshore, Mr. Laurie became mellow from salt air and bootleg rye. The scene at the village basin at Ocean Beach enchanted him.

The arrival of Captain Robinson's craft seemed the biggest event since the first coming of the Great Eastern to America. Mr. Laurie also observed that the welcoming committee of young ladies were taking advantage of the newer and more sensible style in bathing attire, an emancipation of body that confirmed the long-unproven theory that women had skin.

Mr. Laurie eventually bought a house built by the late Captain Noah Ackerly. Then everyone was a captain on Fire Island, just as now everyone there seems to be an actor, composer or book publisher. Captain Ackerly had been a deep-sea man. He wore gold hoops in his ears, had a beard whiter and longer than that of Johannes Brahms, and was chief of the Ocean Beach volunteer fire department.

Whenever somebody whanged the alarm (a great steel ring made of a piece of train track), Captain Ackerly would get off the scaffold or the roofbraces of his newest building project to go — not directly to the firehouse — but to his own house. There Mrs. Ackerly would draw an asbestos bag over her husband's beard, tuck in any stray wisps, and make fast the bag over his ears with gold hoops attached, and not before all was shipshape with his King Lear muff would the chief lope to the firehouse, thence to proceed with his laddies to the blaze itself. If a fire was remaining to be fought, there would be members of Captain Ackerly's audience usually seen on the other side of the proscenium arch, such as George M. Cohan, Jerome Kern, Fred Allen, Ed Wynn, George Jean Nathan and Sophie Tucker.

To the Laurie house, as well as to ours on Cottage Walk, the Broadwayites came on weekends or summer holidays. And soon the vaudeville hoofers, acrobats, monologists, comedians, playwrights and movie stars were on the loose all over the village. At our place, which was called *The Anchorage* (Island houses were not numbered, but "named"), there would usually be Ben Hecht, Charles MacArthur and Helen Hayes, Robert Benchley, Lucius Beebe, James Thurber or Damon Runyon. While staying at our cottage one summer, Robert Ripley conceived his idea for *Believe It or Not*.

Fanny Brice came over, fell in love with the place, and in turn imported the gallant Beatrice Lillie, and Bea's young son. The lad behaved with great restraint when the Fire Island brats (myself included) doubted that he was an authentic Lord Peel.

Fanny played hostess to numerous ex-Follies girls, and introduced Valeska Suratt and other faded divas to the Island. Georgie Jessel was a guest at the Brice house, a large one on the bay front, only a short way from the boat basin. He expressed wonderment as the ferryboat nosed into the slip, because he saw so many citizens pulling their little wagons. It convinced him that the place was a mental institution, and that the inmates played with toys. The islanders thought Mr. Jessel a bit nuts when he tried to find a taxicab to take him to the Brice home.

Billy Rose, then husband of Miss Brice, put in an appearance only on weekends. He was busy in New York most of the time, rehearsing plays or writing the lyrics of popular songs. Rose sometimes brought Jed Harris to the Island. They seemed to resent sunlight. If they arrived before the sun went down, Billy and Jed would dart indoors, as though pursued by creditors, draw the blinds, and not come out until the cool of the evening.

The Gershwins, George and Ira, followed the trickle of immigrants, and much of their historic opera *Porgy and Bess* was written on the Island. Indeed, that work was previewed, with George at the piano, at one of Brice's soirées. Jimmy Durante was there that night, and said, "It's great, but it's over my head."

I recall one Fourth of July when the night-living Durante was sleeping by day upstairs at Brice's. I was twelve, and slipped into the room to set off a nest of firecrackers under Jimmy's bed. The comedian leaped up with an asthmatic roar: "To the lifeboats! The lions is escaped!"

The following day, the Fowlers and the Brices had a date to take Durante on his initial deep-sea fishing trip. In order to get fourteen miles out to sea when the tuna were biting, it was necessary to start out in Captain Bink's fishing boat during the dark morning hours. Durante hadn't been up this early since he was a boy working in his father's Manhattan barbershop. As we walked along in the dark, Durante galloped over to a small tree and began to shake the hell out of it, crying, "If Durante don't sleep, the boids don't sleep!"

The sea was calm out by the light ship — until the ocean liner,

To Hollywood on a Rail

Europa, passed by. Its wake caused our boat to rock violently, and Durante became seasick. He was so ill it was necessary for Captain Bink to head back toward the Island. By the time we hit the inlet Durante was feeling better, but he was still rocky on his feet. Near shore, he spied a beachcomber walking peacefully. Jimmy pointed toward the sand. "See dat guy over dere?"

"Yes, why?" MacArthur asked.

Durante shook his head and whimpered, "How fortunate."

When we returned home that afternoon, my father noticed a letter on the mantelpiece with my crude printing on the envelope's face. It was addressed to body-builder Charles Atlas. He and Hecht opened my letter. They read one of the questionnaire interrogatives: "Do you have any secret habits?" Next to it, I had written, "Yes. I twist my neck." The two laughed long and loud. I had no idea that this question had sexual overtones.

In 1943 my father wrote to me:

> *I shall have finished the editing of the book about our great friend Barrymore by tomorrow. This is my last hour on Fire Island before taking the boat across the bay. I wanted to write to you from this place which has so many first-rate associations for both of us.*
>
> *I came here as a young man, shot with dreams, desires, and a modicum of whiskey. Now, I sit in my crow's nest overlooking the beach-grass, the sand, the water. And the sea is still the same, ageless and embracing. Only man charges, never the sea. The hurricane which drove across the island (I believe it was in 1937, but, as you know, I never am sure of years or even days — only nights) still can be evidenced by the scars in the dunes, and a faroff house or two bowing like decrepit actors to a perpetual audience. There have been shore-changes, but the waves roll in still the same. And all this reminds me of two things: Byron's apostrophe to the sea in* Childe Harold, *and my own lifelong philosophy of "What of it?" . . .*
>
> *Everywhere I turn in this large, empty house, I find reminders of a happy time when we were all young together. I can hear the laughter of my children. A whistle which you used as a life guard lies near me. I'd like to blow it. I think I shall. Let us stay young inside, for the*

To Hollywood on a Rail

*inside of us counts most, although the world passes judg-
ment only on our outsides. This may well be my last
journey here, so, until the boat comes, I shall look out at
the grass rippling in a West Wind, hear the locusts sing
of frost, and admire the autumnal complexion of the
poison ivy.*

While having our late afternoon dinner one Sunday, a long-dist-
ance phone call came in from Hollywood. An RKO Studio
executive was on the other end. He wanted my father to travel
west to write John Barrymore's first talking picture, *State's Attorney*. Pop agreed if the studio would stand the expense of
transporting the entire family to Hollywood. This was agreed
upon. Two weeks later, we traveled there by rail with our two
dogs and a parrot named Chester. We settled in Bette Davis'
house at the end of Canyon Drive, one mile north of Hollywood
Boulevard and three studios: RKO, Paramount and Columbia.

The first day he reported for work at RKO, Fowler was riding
a bicycle. The guard at the gate refused him permission to enter,
so Pop pedaled the two miles back home and composed his first
poem about Hollywood. He telegraphed the ten stanzas by night
letter to Ben Hecht in New York, suggesting he read it to the
boys at the Algonquin Hotel Round Table: such folk as Robert
Benchley, George S. Kaufman, Alexander Woollcott, Heywood
Broun, Marc Connelly and others.

Having just arrived in town, Fowler did not phone the studio
following the bicycle incident. It took RKO executives two days
to track him down. He was ushered through the gate by two
publicity men and informed that he was to attend a writers' conference presently in session. Before entering the conference
room, Fowler removed his pants. He opened the door to find a
dozen worried-looking men seated about a large table. Fowler
threw the trousers on the table, and before exiting said, "Have
these cleaned and pressed. I'll pick them up this afternoon."

Settling in his office, director Bill Wellman entered laughing.
"Your poem preceded you and none of the guys in the front office know how to take it. Ben Hecht wired it to me yesterday

and I had a hundred copies mimeographed. It should be all the way over to MGM by now." It follows:

HOLLYWOOD HORST WESSEL

> *The boys are not speaking to Fowler*
> *Since he's taken the wine of the rich.*
> *The boys are not speaking to Fowler —*
> *That plutocrat son of a bitch.*

For decades he stood with the bourgeois,
And starved as he fumbled his pen.
He lived on the cheapest of liquor,
And, aye, was the humblest of men.

> *And even though women foreswore him*
> *And laughed when he fell into pails,*
> *He went over big on the Bow'ry —*
> *The toast of the vagabond males.*

The wrinkles were deep in his belly,
The meat on his thighbones was lean.
Malaria spotted his features:
The stones that he slept on were mean.

> *Then Midas sneaked up to the gutter*
> *Where old Peasant Fowler lay flat,*
> *And the King of Gilt tickled the victim,*
> *Who rose with a solid gold prat.*

Gone, gone was the fervor for justice,
And fled was the soul of this man,
This once fearless child of the shanty
Was cursed with an 18-K can.

> *He hankered for costlier raiment*
> *And butlers who'd served the elite.*
> *He tore down the old family privy*
> *And purchased a Haviland seat.*

Oh, God, how this parvenu strutted,
And smoked only dollar cigars.
His jockstraps were lined with chinchilla,
His drawers were the envy of stars.

Ah, where was this once valiant spokesman,
Who gave not a care or a damn?
Alas, when they sealed his gray matter,
It weighed hardly one epigram.

The boys are not nodding to Fowler
Since he rose from the alms-asking ditch.
The boys will not cotton to Fowler,
That sybarite son-of-a-bitch!

* * *

The first of Pop's two internationally recognized romances was with Roumania's Queen Marie when that country's regal majesty visited the United States in 1926. At the time Roumania was in political upheaval and a dynasty was commencing its death rattles.

Marie, eldest daughter of Britain's Queen Victoria's son Alfred, Duke of Edinburgh, had just turned fifty when she made her grand tour of the United States. The first public test of her sense of humor came on the day she arrived in New York. Following a formal reception of the front steps of City Hall, Mayor Jimmy Walker accompanied Queen Marie in the rear seat of an open chauffeured limousine heading toward Pennsylvania Station. On the way, and from above in a building under construction, came the shout of a riveter:

"Hey, Jimmy! Did ya lay 'er yet?"

The Queen reacted to the question and turned to the Mayor to say, "You rule over some very droll and interesting people."

The Queen was to visit a large area of our country and was supplied with ten railway cars, each owned and custom-equipped by various railroad presidents. Along the way, Marie would be accompanied by ten elite newspaper reporters. The monarch, who radiated a ton of sex appeal, had private quarters in Northern Pacific's board chairman's car, the Yellowstone. It contained a large bedroom with brass bed adjoining a bathroom with tub and silver and marble fittings. The dining room sat six and had a soda fountain.

Fowler was one of the ten reporters who traveled with the

To Hollywood on a Rail

Queen. But at a few of the whistle stops the Queen would not appear. During each of these occasions, neither would Fowler.

One time, when Marie and Fowler were simultaneously present during a formal affair, Fowler's silk hat toppled from his head. Retrieving it, he fell flat on his face at the Queen's feet. He gazed up into her limpid eyes and said, "Please do not misconstrue this as humility, Your Majesty."

When the special train arrived at my father's city of birth, Denver, it seemed the entire population had turned up not so much to eye the Queen, as to get a glimpse of their hometown hero, Gene Fowler. Among the throng were two of his old pals, reporters Courtney Ryley Cooper of the *Post* and Harvey Sethman of the *Rocky Mountain News*.

Searching the crowd for a familiar face — just before Queen Marie was to make her initial appearance — Fowler focused on Cooper. His resonant bass voice boomed through the quiet: "Hey, Ryley! How's that dose of clap you caught down on Market Street?"

As H. Allen Smith reported in *The Life and Legend of Gene Fowler* (William Morrow), "Westbrook Pegler was one newspaperman who declared unflinchingly that Fowler kept Queen Marie horizontally occupied during many miles of the American tour." And Ben Hecht wrote in *Letters from Bohemia* (Doubleday) that "Marie fell in love with Fowler, but had to return Fowlerless and heartbroken to her throne."

Fowler's second international love affair took place in Hollywood in 1932 when he traveled to the West Coast — alone. When it got out, this romance became a national front-page scandal with roots in Havana, Cuba.

This year Fowler had written the screen play *Union Depot* for First National Pictures before returning to RKO to do the scenarios *What Price Hollywood?* starring Constance Bennett, and *Roadhouse Murder*. During this stay he met and fell in love with one of the most beautiful actresses ever to grace a motion picture screen. She had starred on Broadway with such stage stars as Leslie Fenton, in *Paris Bound*, and Rex Cherryman in *The Trial of Mary Dugan* and in films with Ronald Colman, in *Condemned*; Clive Brook, in *East Lynne*; Laurence Olivier, in

To Hollywood on a Rail

Westward Passage; Leslie Howard, in *The Animal Kingdom;* and William Powell in *Double Harness.*

She was acclaimed by George Bernard Shaw. Eugene O'Neill wanted her to star in his *Strange Interlude* and *Mourning Becomes Electra.*

Born Dorothy Walton Gatley on August 7, 1902, at Fort Sam Houston, Texas (an army post near San Antonio), she came to be known throughout the theatrical world as Ann Harding.

After moving to Chicago, Dorothy's mother had the child photographed at Marshall Field's. The pictures came out so well, the studio photographer offered Mrs. Gatley free pictures of her daughter if she would give him permission to display them in the store's front window. After this was granted, the news drifted back to Dorothy's father, professional army Captain George G. Gatley (who eventually became a general). He was so taken back by this in his Victorian moral restraint that he refused ever to see his daughter in a play or, later, on the screen. His objective voice at every turn of her career was antagonistic and uncompanionable.

Taking the bit in her mouth, as it were, Ann Harding became the producer and casting director of her own Detroit stock company while appearing in *The Esquimo, In a Garden* and *Bluebeard's Eighth Wife.* She also acted as the company's business manager.

During that time, Miss Harding married a man thirteen years her senior. He was stage actor Harry Bannister. The wedding took place at the Little Church Around the Corner in Detroit on October 22, 1926. She was twenty-four.

Mesmerizing the actress, Bannister commenced to run her professional life. In Hollywood, he even created a costarring role for himself opposite his wife in the motion picture *Her Private Affair,* for Pathé in 1929. As time bore on grimly, Bannister became insistent with studio heads that he take over the seat as director of his and Miss Harding's costarring picture, *The Girl of the Golden West.* This was awkwardly loutish, in the judgment of front office executives. They ordered Bannister never to show up at the studio where Miss Harding was working.

After Pathé raised her salary to an unheard-of $5,000 a week, the Bannisters purchased a choice piece of acreage atop the Hollywood hills, where one could view the whole of Los Angeles to the south and the mountains to the east. There they had built the Hollywood home-of-homes.

Constructed on a four-story level, the house boasted a tennis court atop the building. Directly below, inside the massive-walled structure, runs a gallery the length of the tennis court. There is a swimming pool and a theater. Everything was done on a grand scale, especially the master bedroom with huge fireplace. The staff of servants included a security guard, hired following a threat to kidnap their baby daughter, Jane.

As Bannister continued to run Miss Harding's life, their marriage came to an impasse. They could no longer resolve marital difficulties. The actress finally issued a public statement:

> *Due to Harry's constant and generous effort to forward my interests, often at the expense of his own, he is gradually losing his identity, becoming a background for my activities, and looked upon as "Ann Harding's husband." We have decided to cut the Gordian knot so he can set forth on his own. When we were married at the Little Church Around the Corner, we agreed to stay married as long as we both loved each other. A quick divorce now seems to be the only solution to a situation which has become untenable.*

Miss Harding established her Nevada residence in Reno, and after six weeks was given an uncontested divorce and custody of their daughter in April 1932.

Shortly thereafter, however, Bannister filed suit in Los Angeles Superior Court. He pleaded that the Nevada ruling be invalidated. Outside the courtroom, Bannister informed reporters he was going to offer "sensational evidence" that Miss Harding, now his ex-wife, was "an unfit mother," and he intended to acquire custody of their daughter.

At this point in time a close reporter friend informed Fowler that Bannister had seen love letters my father had written to the actress and that he — Fowler — was to be named by Bannister as his ex-wife's suitor.

Pop told his friend that he was aware of this, and that Bannister had already contacted him. "Bannister was threatening to break up my marriage and show copies of the letters to my wife," said Fowler. "I'll tell my wife *myself!* Then I'm going to go out and beat the living hell out of him!"

This threat reached Bannister's ears. He disappeared.

As time for the initial court appearance grew near, Ann Harding seemed to live in fear that her daughter would be taken from her. In due respect, Fowler engaged defense attorney Roland "Rich" Woolley.

Woolley reassured Fowler that, in Miss Harding's case, there no longer were any marriage vows to uphold "because her Nevada divorce is legal. But as for yourself, Gene . . . well . . ."

Because Bannister was unavailable to Woolley for a deposition, which might expose him to further unanswered questions, the lawyer advised Fowler to "stay out of sight. Give this story time to cool off in the newspapers."

Fowler had just signed with Paramount to write a screen play for French star Maurice Chevalier. It was titled *The Way to Love.* The author called his agent: the man who revolutionized the star system in Hollywood, Myron Selznick. A most understanding man, Selznick arranged for Fowler to work on the scenario away from the studio. Fowler took passage on a tramp steamer leaving the port of Los Angeles for New York via the Panama Canal and Cuba. "When Fowler reaches New York," Selznick assured Paramount's production head, "he'll have a first draft of the screen play completed."

The day after Bill Wellman finished directing Ann Harding and Richard Dix in *The Conquerors* at RKO, my father told me that Miss Harding had learned when he would arrive in Cuba. She was escorted by actor Alexander Kirkland and his secretary, Marie Lombard. They took a plane heading in the direction of Havana. Wellman was aware of the romance and told me he had tried without success to dissuade Fowler from pursuing the actress.

All hell broke loose when Fowler's ship arrived in Havana. The day before, Kirkland had hired a Cuban skipper to take Miss Harding, Marie Lombard and himself for a sail outside the Havana harbor. While a few miles offshore, a tropical storm bore down on the sailboat, and the boat capsized. For fear his passengers might drown, the Cuban skipper swam for shore and help. But he was killed by sharks. By sheer good luck, English yachtsman Captain J.L. Waggill, who happened to be carrying passenger George Andrews, a representative of the U.S. Embassy in Havana, spied the capsized boat. The three were rescued and taken to shore. All would have been hushed up, but for the death of the Cuban captain. It became, instead, an international incident after one of Waggill's crewmen leaked it out about the rescue, adding that Kirkland and the two women rescued were "nearly nude." The news that one of the women was Ann Harding made it hot copy for the press. The radio wireless began sending out bulletins. The next day, newspaper representatives from the States were swarming into Havana.

"What they didn't know," my father told me, "was that I had arrived in Havana the afternoon following the disaster. I contacted Ann, and stayed up with her all night, rubbing cocoa butter on her severely sunburned back."

The Cuban government claimed "three Americans were responsible for the death of one of our citizens." They demanded reparation, and Fowler considered that the most expeditious action was to telegraph his bank in New York for a draft of $10,000. Authority for the draft arrived. Fowler turned over the money to government representatives. They were mollified and Fowler was assured the dead man's family would be taken care of. (How much ya wanna bet?)

Some days later, Fowler's ship arrived in New York on schedule. Both Mother and Maurice Chevalier were present to greet my father. But Fowler was not aboard. He had stayed on in Havana to make sure everything would remain square with the Cuban government. Reporters, anxious to speak with Fowler, settled for an interview with my mother.

"Are you aware of Mr. Fowler's . . . friendship with Ann Harding, Mrs. Fowler?" one reporter asked.

"Of course I am," Mother smiled. "But I'd like to be on record as saying that I am patient with those who say they are in love with Gene. But I'll be a tiger if they interfere with his talent.

Pop telegraphed Mother to ask if she wished him to return home. She wired back:

> FIRST RETURN TO HOLLYWOOD AND FINISH YOUR PIC-
> TURE. THEN GET THE WOMAN OUT OF YOUR SYSTEM.
> LOVE, AGNES.

Fowler did this, and in that order. But gossip columns kept taking pot shots at the Harding romance, and he decided to vacate Hollywood. He was fully aware how much he had hurt his wife. Regaining a semblance of intelligence since his glands had taken over, he telegraphed again:

> HAVE JUST PASSED FROM A RATHER FUNNY YOUTH INTO
> ANOTHER AGE — A KIND OF CHANGE OF LIFE. WHEN YOU
> SUGGEST I DO NOT LIKE BEING MOTHERED, YOU ARE
> CRAZY. I DOTE ON IT. THANK YOU FOR BEING SO PATIENT
> . . . SO TIRED OF HOLLYWOOD AND ALL IT MEANS.

Mother wired back:

> DARLING BOY: WELCOME HOME. HAPPY YOU ARE COMING
> TO ME. HAVE BEEN DYING ON THE VINE. LET'S FORGET
> EVERYTHING AND START ALL OVER AGAIN.

Before departing, Fowler dropped a farewell note to a friend on the *Hollywood Reporter*. The latter thought it so noteworthy, he published it:

> *I leave for Fire Island to be with a grand entourage of*
> *goats, a parrot, two dogs, a frog, three utterly incorrigi-*
> *ble brats, and a wife, who gives me her word of honor*
> *that I never have bored her . . . . It is a fine thing to leave*
> *without bitterness or screaming, as I am afriad so many*
> *have done. In my days of romance (Chapter X, Breast-*
> *ed's Ancient History), I made it a practice to shove off at*
> *high tide. In romance or life, Fowler takes parachute*
> *jumps . . . .*

To Hollywood on a Rail

I doubt if any Hollywood writer ever received better treatment than I. And as to the pay, I should be arrested for taking so much. And still I cannot stomach the game. It may well be conceit, or perhaps a dash of paraonoia, but Fowler refuses to send his talent walking the streets, winking at intellectual boatswains, or letting uncouth chefs make an avocado salad of his bosom.

Many of the finest men I know live and thrive here. To them, greetings. Here also are credit-grabbers, but-tock-surveyors and fabulous fakers. Why not? Every man to his game. There are handicaps, also, that would defeat any sincere artist; such as the stupidity of censor-ship and the timidity of the local overseers of the indus-try . . . . Fowler will not continue to contribute the stories that start with great health and end up with diabetic sugars.

It is not all Hollywood's burden. Let us admit that civ-ilization has foozled; that men are popeyed with fear. Until they quit singing "Mammy" songs while simulta-neously kicking their mothers in the teeth, I shall have no faith in them. Until there is not one single hungry child in the world, I shall not admit to our humanity.

And as for the basket-weavers and peanut-munchers of the land — the boys who are supposed to be the movie audience — I am not sorry they get such a poor product from our punch-drunk cameras. My only regret is that the pictures are not worse.

So, following eighteen months in "the industry" during which he had composed five screen plays and turned out three books — and carried on a torrid love affair — my father departed Holly-wood until he would once again be enticed back by Paramount at another embarrassingly high salary to write *Shoot the Works*.

During his year of self-imposed exile from Hollywood, Fowler would write a saga of Western Empire, a story of the West dur-ing its days of growing pains — an era of pioneering, strikes, murders, wars and intrigues — with two colorful and dominant czars enthroned amid scenes of historic import: F.G. Bonfils, a Corsican and descendant of Napoleon, and his partner, H.H. Tammen, of Dutch blood, who for forty years were the rulers of the Rocky Mountain region in the roles of publishers of the *Denver Post*. The book was *Timberline* (Covici-Friede). A single chapter from the saga was purchased to become a Broadway musical comedy hit and, later, a motion picture box office extravaganza, *The Unsinkable Molly Brown.*

Shortly after he celebrated his seventieth birthday, my father telephoned me. He was distraught and asked that I "get over here right away. I've just gone through an emotional experience I haven't quite gotten over yet and I'd like to talk with you."

I speeded over the Sepulveda Pass from Encino to his home on Helena Drive. I hurried down to the workroom my brother and I had built for him. There I found him sitting at his workdesk, peering out over the hill facing east toward Bundy Drive, and sipping on a glass of Vat 69 scotch. He seemed almost serene now that the whisky had begun to take effect. I asked what had happened.

He explained that he had been down at the Beverly Wilshire Hotel waiting for Thomas Mitchell to show up. "Tommy and I had recently formed the most exclusive club in Beverly Hills," he said. "It's the *Beverly Hills Great-grandfather Club*. Mitchell and I are the only members."

"For God's sake," I repeated, "what happened?"

A sadness came over him. "While waiting for Tommy to arrive," he said, "a gentle hand was laid on my shoulder, and I heard a woman's voice say, 'Hello, darling.'

"I turned around. It was Ann Harding. I stood up, faced her, placed my hands on her shoulders and said, 'But I'm an old man now.'"

In later years, attorney Woolley told me that his copies of the love letters were returned to Miss Harding. "I'm sorry you never got to read them, Will. They were a thing of beauty; something no one today would ever be capable of composing. They were more than love letters. They were letters, love letters to the world. It is a loss in these days that find it impossible to share with a world which so desperately needs love."

Perhaps the letters shall remain an inscrutable mystery. And that, too, might be good because in mystery itself there are things unsaid and unseen — but imagined to a greater extent.

3

The Monster

At least in our age, it is the public's general impression that John Barrymore was the greatest actor America ever produced. When I was young, some still held that Edwin Booth was better. So it may be, but I always go by what I have personally witnessed. My father unequivocally claimed that Enrico Caruso was the greatest tenor of all time. I never heard Caruso except through the low fidelity records of his time. Therefore, it is my opinion that the Swede Jussi Bjoerling held top spot in this operatic category.

At my present age — fifty-seven — I am amazed that Jack Barrymore was only sixty when he died. At the time, I was not quite twenty and looked upon the actor as being an older man. On this side of the fence now, I have revised my thinking and remember him as a middle-aged man who wore out his body all too soon.

I first met John Barrymore in 1935. At that time my father referred to Jack's physical and mental state, later recorded in his Barrymore biography, *Good Night, Sweet Prince* (Viking):

> *Now at an ailing fifty-three, Barrymore began to pay at the usurious rates demanded of a man of public name and of middle years when he does not conform to the gospels of exemplary behavior. Condemnation by others went unnoticed by him; he seldom read the newspapers, and listened to warnings not at all. He forfeited his material belongings. He lost in health. But his spirit remained essentially young and unconquered.*

The Monster

When Jack began drawing his highest salaries as a cinema actor, some press agent had it ballyhooed that he was "the world's greatest lover." In later years Barrymore confided to me that this had always rankled him, conspiring to make him feel inferior whenever he went to bed with a strange woman.

But this occasion in 1935 found Jack knocking on the door at 727 North Bedford Drive in Beverly Hills. The house was owned by Marion Davies, and Marion, who had always had a soft spot in her heart, if not elsewhere, for Fowler, offered to *give* him the large home. He refused, just as he had turned Marion down the time she offered to give him a weekly newspaper she held title to, "just to get you back into the business you always loved," where he could again smell fresh printer's ink.

This day found The Monster between bus accidents. (He referred to his four unsuccessful marriages as bus accidents.)

We called Barrymore The Monster because of his almost morbid interest in medieval history, and he especially liked to sketch several ancient torture machines and gibbets.

Jack had departed his fifty-five-room Tower Road home high in the hills overlooking Beverly Hills this day to request a drink. He was unaware, however, that my mother did not allow spirits, other than cooking sherry, on the premises. Therefore, my sister Jane was assigned to mix The Monster a cocktail. In the kitchen, she brewed things together, such as Tabasco sauce, Worcestershire sauce (both in great quantities), a raw egg (which became fried two seconds after it was dropped into the glass), a tablespoonful of pepper, lemon juice, baking soda and ice.

Thirsty, Jack gulped it down. His reaction was something out of one of his screen roles of *Dr. Jekyll and Mr. Hyde.* First came the smile to all those about him. Then he retched and rattled. His eyes seemed to want to pop out like those of a rock cod rudely reeled up from the bottom of the sea. He leaped up, snorted, clutched his throat and created a sort of violent Martha Graham choreography on the spot before shouting, "Jesus Christ! I'm in the house of the Borgias!"

A few years later found Jack courting a young lady. When I met him at the Santa Fe train station in Pasadena, I viewed the unattractive lass. "I hope to hell you're not going to marry her,"

I said.

"Why not?" Jack elfinly smiled. "It *fits*."

When I vacationed in Fire Island, Jack and I kept in touch by letter. By this time he had married his fourth wife, actress Elaine Barrie. I had purchased some stationery that could impair a person's sight if he gazed at it too long. It was dark pink with a field of small white crisscrosses. Since his marriage, Jack had been socially quarantined from his male companions; therefore, we wrote often. Disenchanted while appearing with his wife in a buffooning play, *My Dear Children*, he wrote me from Chicago on the thirty-fourth and final week of its run. He had earlier written that his audiences came to watch him make a fool of himself as he departed from his role to converse with and curse them. But this letter reflected his dream to escape his bonds and be once again with his reliable friends:

> *Your missive and the amazing stationery on which it was couched arrived as I was finishing a matinee. As I was waiting for Elaine, who was doing one of those mysterious things ladies do in Ladies' Rooms. After I had gladly perused your letter, I tried to play tick-tack-toe on the writing paper and am almost blind and completely groggy in consequence!*
>
> *I have news which may or may not warm your crusader's heart. Elaine and I are going to fly to New York in about three weeks. If the movie that I start Wednesday is finished by that time. Anyway, it will be soon and we will foregather and resume our libidinous relationship!*
>
> *At present I am on the* Carta Blanca *wagon: a Mexican beer (alleged!) of piffling alcoholic content! So I will be in fine fettle for a reunion!*
>
> *Soon I trust we will all be tending our flocks together on the Grampian Hills! where the cows really come home.°*
>
> *Write me again soon. We have found a house which if we can only get it — as the owner is in Mexico probably*

° The original working title for *Good Night, Sweet Prince* was suggested by this letter. It was *The Grampian Hills*. These are the mountains that divide the Highlands from the Lowlands in Scotland.

> *getting shot in the fanny — in which there will be a murder's room with a concrete base where you and I and those of the cognoscenti of whom we approve (I need sincerely say an excessively attenuated roster!) can cavort and have our being undisturbed! It will also have a swimming pool that will wind tortuously under overhanging trees. AND a pool table, *at which we will fleece the neighboring bumpkins!*

Now, disenchanted following a few years of wedlock, Jack and his wife moved out of the Tower Road estate, down the hill to Bellagio Road. This move was summoned because, to complicate matters, Jack was in legal receivership.

In September 1940, Errol Flynn telephoned our house to tell me that there was continued uneasiness going on in the Barrymore home, and suggested that someone should "rescue him." This handsome and outgoing guy was having his own problems with the women, too. And he was increasing his daily alcohol intake.

When my father arrived home that evening, I broached this problem to him. He was between writing books. He suggested we drive down the hill to artist John Decker's house on Bundy Drive and pick him up before attempting to rescue Barrymore from his fourth bus accident.

Decker, who abided with his madonna-like wife, Phyllis, was at home. Fowler had helped the artist locate this small house at 419 North Bundy Drive. The rental was $35 a month. I understand it was recently sold for about $200,000.

Very late that evening, a maid answered our doorbell ring at Jack's house. After we were escorted into the living room, she returned to bed. Then Barrymore sort of emanated. "Welcome to the Halls of Montezuma," Jack whispered.

"We have come to take you away," said Decker.

"The walls have ears," Jack again whispered. Then, in a loud voice, he continued, "No thanks. Haven't had a drop in weeks. Anyway, it's past midnight, you know." And, in a stage aside, "Get me the hell out of here."

*Of all the luxuries Barrymore enjoyed, he never did own his much-wanted pool table.

The Monster

We told him to gather his worldly chattel and we would be on our way.

"I'd better not go upstairs myself," Jack cautioned. He summoned his male nurse, Karl Stuevers, and urged him to repair quietly above and get him some getaway garb.

Among the clothing Karl gathered was a Tyrolean hat. Barrymore traipsed out to the garden. There he plucked a sprig from an olive tree he had had transplanted from Tower Road. The tree was supposed to have been older than Christ. He said, "Who the hell *isn't* older than Christ?"

After he wedged the sprig in his hatband, Jack suggested "we take this noble plant with us." The tree was never moved, but we did uproot Barrymore from one of his many uncomfortable stations in life.

As I drove along the street, Barrymore was so elated to have been freed that he thought of other things besides his mounting problems. A light shone from one of his neighbors', W.C. Fields', upstairs window. Jack pleaded that we stop at the comedian's home, "considering he, at least, must be up to the bathroom . . . or a triple martini for sleep."

"We're taking you home," Fowler insisted.

Finally arriving at Decker's studio, Barrymore found a red velvet chair. He snorted, then offered that he wished a divorce, "immediately."

We — Barrymore and I — survived the evening until the last dark hours were upon us. Decker put to bed, Jack and I strayed to my house on Barrington Avenue. My father, who had left us hours earlier, had warned me, "From this night on, you are to take up with our durable friend whenever your brittle and aging father leaves the field. Don't ever return him to the place where we found him tonight. Tower Road is where he belongs."

After handing Barrymore a half-full bottle of cognac I had previously hidden, and after sharing the first few drinks with him, I suggested I take a nap, a short snooze, before the sun was up. This was all right with Jack because he had recognized our parrot, Chester. At the time, Chester's vocabulary consisted only of "hello," "okay" and "Polly wants ——."

This dawn the actor was to teach Chester two new words. He

The Monster

perched himself before the bird and steadily stared her in the eyes, then began to repeat the two words over-and-over-and-over. Entranced, Chester returned his stare.

At about five o'clock I woke from my nap, and Jack requested that I return him to his Tower Road home. We inspected the acreage as the sun began to rise. When we entered a large and long-deserted aviary, Jack asked me if I had always wanted something and never gotten it. "Yes," I said, "a pipe organ."

He stared at the many vacant perches in the long wall upon which he had expertly painted a fresco translating nature. Among birds and animals, he had rendered a figure of himself representing Peter Pan clad in green and playing a flute. "I always wanted a pool table."

Jack was drowsy now, so I put him to bed, then lay down on the only sofa in the house. It was old and beaten. I went to sleep.

The following morning my father entered the breakfast room at home dressed in his bathrobe. As was his custom before sitting down to toast and coffee, he would remove the cover from Chester's cage. But there was no Chester. The cage had disappeared.

My grandmother entered carrying a pot of coffee. Pop asked what had become of the bird. I was later to find out that when Mumsie removed the cage cover and said, "Good morning, Chester," the parrot repeated the two words Barrymore had taught him some hours earlier. The second word was the acceptable "you," and the first was an Anglo-Saxon expression that galvanizes the personal pronoun.

I didn't return home until late that evening. My bedroom was next to that of my parents, so I was quiet when I came in. If they were asleep, I didn't want to awaken them. Instead, I could hear Mother talking to Pop. "I'm beginning to take offense at Barrymore keeping our son up until all hours of the night," she said. "Maybe John can stand this kind of life, but I don't think we should have Will following in his footsteps."

I knocked and entered to say goodnight. My mother looked at me and gasped. "Do you see what I mean? Just look at him."

My father *did* carefully look at me, then said, "My God, Will, you look terrible. What's the matter? Are you sick?" Then, to

Mother, he remarked, "I guess the younger generation *can't* take it."

I had forgotten to remove the makeup Barrymore had fashioned on my face which transformed it to represent a death's head.

* * *

In 1939, Barrymore was the prime guest star on radio's *Rudy Vallee Show*, which was aired out of the National Broadcasting Company's studios at the northeast corner of Vine Street and Sunset Boulevard. Jack's memory was becoming bad, and when he was reading from the script his mind often wandered. When he was unable to find his place, he would pick someone out of the audience and make some remark, such as, "Well, what the hell are *you* looking at, you lunatic bastard?"

Following each of these broadcasts, the radio board of decency outfit would pounce upon the *Rudy Vallee Show* producers. "Tell that Barrymore fellow to clean up his act," they would complain. The producers would look repentant at the same time that they were hoping to get away with Jack's outbursts. They made the show's ratings soar.

One night I drove my father and Jack to the broadcast. And, sure enough, he lost his place in the script when he heard a young lady burst out in laughter. Jack looked at her over his reading glasses and said, "Don't you think you should be in bed, m' dear? Perhaps with me?"

After the show, Vallee asked us if we would like to follow him up and take a look at the estate he had purchased the year before. We drove up Laurel Canyon to the top of the small mountain range that divides Hollywood from the Valley, then turned to the east on Mulholland Drive. The view was spectacular in these days before the smog. One could see ranges of lights for miles.

While guiding us through the house, Vallee described the unique appointments of each room. To each of Vallee's descriptions, Fowler began saying, "I know, I know." Then he went on to add a few appointments the crooner had forgotten to mention. "You sound as if you've been here before," said Vallee.

"I have," said Fowler.

This was the estate Ann Harding had sold to Vallee.

* * *

Early in 1923, Lionel Barrymore announced to his brother that he was going to marry for the second time. But when he told Jack the lady was actress Irene Fenwick, the younger brother frowned and attempted to talk him out of the notion. Lionel would not be moved. In desperation, Jack said, "She's not a good woman. She'd never live up to your moral standards."

"And who the hell are you to make such a statement?"

"Jesus Christ," Jack blurted, "I've even gone to bed with her myself!"

Lionel was rocked by this. He glared at Jack, then left the room, slamming the door behind him.

After Lionel married Irene Fenwick, he remained cool toward his brother. And as the years passed, Jack's statement wore deeper into Lionel's mind like a poison. Eventually, he stopped speaking to his younger brother altogether.

But in 1932, Metro-Goldwyn-Mayer teamed John, Ethel and Lionel to costar in their only picture together, *Rasputin and the Empress*. Lionel started conversing once again with Jack, but reservedly and only when necessary.

When Jack's health began to fail in 1940, Fowler conducted a long telephone conversation with Lionel. After he hung up the receiver, my father told me to get in the car "and drive me out to Lionel's home in Chatsworth."

We picked Lionel up in the San Fernando Valley, then headed back toward Tower Road. Lionel had not been there for many years and was appalled to see the condition of the once lavishly furnished fifty-five-room home, which consisted of the *Little House*, the *Big House*, and the *New House*, the last of which was built when Jack married Dolores Costello.

Lionel could still walk, and the three of us entered the Little House where we discovered Jack slumped in a worn overstuffed chair.

When the brothers met, a great smile came over Jack's face. He stood up and said, "Well, hello, Mike!"

The Monster

"Hello, Jake," said Lionel.

These were nicknames the brothers had had for one another as boys.

Magically, Lionel's bitterness disappeared. He no longer held his grudge against Jack and seemed to forget what his brother had said about his now late wife.

The afternoon was also magic to me as I listened to the brothers and my father talk about old times.

*   *   *

I often like to think of the Point of View. By that I mean the philosophies or opinions of anybody, anywhere, as recaptured in accordance with the moment when the Point of View was the scale pan upon which the feathers of civilization were permitted to be weighed.

By means of association of ideas, I think back upon my own small epochs; that is, the unstable phases and periods of fad and mannerism and sermonizing, and of social compulsions which I survived in a somewhat confused fashion.

For example, in times of peace, war is inveighed against. Mothers' clubs are formed, and all manner of diabetic oratory is hosed upon the innocent earth. And then, quite suddenly, when war descends like a huge flyswatter on many flies, the orators unscrew their adjustable nozzles and commence to spray everyone and everything in behalf of the glories of conflict. If any poor fellow has overslept the last day of peace and dazedly comes to, amid the crashing of the new fashion, War, and if he dares to speak before being emotionally prompted, he is directly hustled off to prison. He is branded a traitor and hanged to a telegraph pole. And the poor mothers, who innocently believed yesterday's babble, are at once denounced, defamed, and, in a manner of speaking, their hair is shorn and their clothes are ripped off. They are whipped, proclaimed as spies, helpmates of the enemy, cunning old harlots, until, again, this time wearily, but suddenly, too, the glutted male beasts of the bloody day lie down to lick their own wounds, after having soundly thrashed one another, and strewn guts and bones all over the earth. And once again it is the fashion to decry "War"! And all the old girls once again receive flowers on Mother's Day.

Association of ideas brings me to a study of the life — not of man — but of the mighty racehorse, Secretariat.

"Here was a great fellow," sportswriter Jim Murray told me. "He was bred and born at Virginia's Meadow Stud Farm and won racing's elusive Triple Crown. He won many victories, not perhaps of his own will, but at that of the owner, Mrs. Penny Tweedie, who prided in his strength and speed, and at the artistry of the jockey who held a bat over the fleet stallion's withers."

This horse won to the roars of many throngs. He was not raced to death, as are most young horses. He was retired in his youth to a field of Virginia grass, never to want for food or to neigh for affection.

Now what else happened to Secretariat? What was it, from our Point of View, that leaves his nobility untarnished? I shall tell you. The finest females were brought to him, possibly more than a thousand. No gossip columnists wrote about these snorting times. No divorces or alimonies were involved. No one's pride was hurt. No pistol shots resounded. *But,* if the fillies and mares, fewer in number, had been women, and Secretariat had been Jack Barrymore, the Point of View would be laid down as a horse of another color.

I sat alone with Jack and his male nurse Karl in the Little House. We were about to drive to Hollywood and Grauman's Chinese Theater, where Barrymore was scheduled to place his footprints in a block of wet cement as did many others before him.

Anyone else would have been elated at this opportunity. Jack, instead, sat limp and hunched forward in his chair. He spoke little. His jaw hung loose and he stared into nothingness.

When it was time, Karl and I led Jack to the car. In his silence, he appeared like one of Bela Lugosi's zombies. We drove east on Sunset Boulevard heading toward this honor which was to be paid Barrymore for his latest picture, a lampoon on the life of an aging actor, *The Great Profile.*

I was concerned about Jack's condition when we arrived at the

The Monster

Grauman Chinese parking lot. He asked me where he was, and where he was going. I explained it to him all over again. "Well, let's get the goddamned thing over with," he said.

As the actor stepped from the car, a fan shouted that Barrymore had arrived. A roar came from the crowd. It was as though he had received a shot in the arm. He straightened up at once, then bulled his way through the throng, laughing and joking. His audience had caused the transformation.

After he had placed his footprints in the wet cement, a publicity man suggested he imprint one side of his face, The Great Profile, in the muck. Barrymore, cooperative, assumed the position. The artist pressed Jack's face into his pallet, the cement. A collection of photographers' flashbulbs exploded. Jack rose to his feet and shouted so all could hear, "My God, they're trying to bury me before my time!"

When we settled in his sitting room after Karl had gone to bed, Barrymore was in a talkative mood. He had forgotten where he had been that evening. He began reciting lines of the title character in Shakespeare's *Richard III*. "I know Richard was your favorite character of all time," I said, "but why did you like him so much?"

"Because he was a villain," Jack snorted. "And I always loved to play the villain because I understood him."

"How to you mean that?"

"Well," said Jack, holding his glass as though it were his dearest possession, "the villain always thinks he is right. Or at least he justifies himself *to* himself. Perhaps this is because he has to live with himself and consequently cannot live with a wrong person."

He philosophized that the remainder of the world might think the villain entirely wrong, or even put him in jail or destroy him. "But he who lives with himself must view that self as a just and persecuted person. In other words, the villain shows himself and is all the more effectively bad and menacing when he goes on his way to perdition or elsewhere, and takes innocent or stupid people with him."

Jack's mind would now switch from one subject to another, one having nothing to do with the other. I now heard him speak of Lionel with warmness. He seemed anxious to tell me how his brother had become the most popular man in a certain Atlanta brothel.

After I freshened his drink, Jack said that as a young man Lionel was playing in a stock company in Atlanta when John Hay was Secretary of State under Theodore Roosevelt, about 1904. Lionel had read in the newspapers that the Secretary's son, Del Hay, was arriving there as a representative of his father and the State Department to appear in the parade that was to open the convention of the Daughters of the Confederacy.

"General Joe Wheeler was also coming to represent the army," Jack said. "Young Hay and Lionel were pals. They hadn't seen each other for a time, so when they met, the first thing they did was proceed to the nearest saloon and drink to both their fathers' health until it came time for the parade." Another thought came to his mind. "Speaking of drinks, I think I've run out. I have a couple of bottles of warm beer hidden from Karl under the kitchen sink. Would you get me one, me bucko?"

I pointed to his glass on the table. "I just made a drink for you, remember?"

He didn't remember, but said, "Oh, yes," then continued on with the tale about Lionel and the Atlanta prostitutes. "When it was parade time, Lionel and young Hay were plastered, and at a spur of the moment, Del invited my brother to ride with him and General Wheeler in the carriage of state at the head of the parade. Lionel wondered if that would be the thing to do, but his friend insisted that all he needed was a high silk hat, which was obtained for him. So, as wobbly as they were, they managed to get into the carriage."

Jack described the parade passing along the streets and said that young Hay frequently raised his hat in response from one side of the carriage, and Lionel would do likewise from the other. No one knew who was who in the carriage other than General Wheeler, but it made no difference.

"They went down Peachtree Street, bowing and hat-tipping," Jack went on, "and Lionel chanced to look up at a balcony of a certain hotel to see a prosperous madam, surrounded by her household of comely girls." Following a rasping laugh, Jack continued. "When their eyeballs made contact, Lionel's hand, holding the silk hat, froze in midair. The madam gave a double-take, then turned to her girls and said, 'Look! Do you see what *I* see? It's Lionel Barrymore!' The girls confirmed their employer's identification."

Somehow, the parade made a circle and returned down the same street. This time, the madam and her girls cheered and called out Lionel's name. This did not go well with General Wheeler.

"After the parade," Jack said, "Lionel was not permitted to buy anything of any kind in the palace of masculine holiday in Atlanta. And when he modestly attempted to explain the situation and to say he had been in the state cab quite by accident, they knowingly smiled. And, by the Seven Muses, Will, it was rumored about the brothels of Atlanta that Lionel certainly was doing some kind of great secret work for the government, or else he wouldn't have been placed in such a position of honor."

Lionel experienced an enjoyable season in Atlanta.

* * *

The last trip Jack was to take with me occurred when I drove him, John Decker and his wife, and my father to Camp Baldy in the California mountains. It was January of 1942 and the weather was foul during the off-season. The rain came at us in sudden cloudbursts, making it necessary for us to stop at several cocktail lounges along the way. It took hours but we finally reached Camp Baldy.

As Pop and I assisted Jack to bed, he seemed to enjoy listening to the storm without. "The rain," he said, "beats upon the door with the persistence of an unpaid madam."

* * *

On May 19, 1942, Jack prepared in the late afternoon to leave for a radio rehearsal on *The Sealtest Hour* show with Rudy Vallee. Karl had departed the payroll, and Ehrling Moss was the actor's secretary-attendant. Before he left the house, Jack scribbled on a pink writing pad, "I have a rendezvous with death." He tossed the note on the nightable and was off to the studio. Jack did not ask Moss to stop at Ella Campbell's English-style eating house for his usual Pimm's Cup. He was cold and wrapped his camel's-hair coat tightly about him.

Following the rehearsal at NBC, Jack staggered down the hall looking for his dressing room. On the way, he bumped into a group of sightseers. An anonymous person spoke up: "Look, that's John Barrymore. He's drunk again." Jack glared at him, then went on his way to find an unlocked door. He entered the room and threw himself on a couch. He did not know it was the dressing room of the young actor John Carradine, who had always held up Barrymore as his idol.

Earlier, Jack had phoned Fowler who had asked how he was feeling. No matter how ill he was, Barrymore always came back with, "Never better." This day, for the first time Fowler could remember, Jack said, "Frankly, Gene, I feel like hell."

Now Carradine, who had been working on *The Edgar Bergen and Charlie McCarthy Show,* entered his dressing room to discover Jack asleep on the sofa. He was startled when Barrymore sat up to greet him. "Well, hello, Jack," he managed to say. "How are you?"

"Never better," Jack replied.

Not knowing what to say, Carradine eventually mentioned that he had opened in a play the night before doing the role of Louis XI.

While talking about Carradine's talents, Jack broke into a fit of coughing. Then he collapsed.

Dr. Hugo Kersten, who had been treating the actor for the past few years, was summoned. Barrymore was admitted to the Hollywood Presbyterian Hospital. His immediate illness was diagnosed as pneumonia of the lower right lung, although the primary cause of his physical problems was cirrhosis of the liver.

Counting the day he was admitted, it would take eleven more for Barrymore to die. He had never gone under the surgeon's knife, but on the second day, it was necessary that a trocar be inserted into his abdominal cavity that had swelled to three times its normal size and was endangering his heart. This was done under local anesthetic and twelve quarts of fluid were taken from the abdomen; the patient felt better.

The Monster

On the third day, a gastric ulcer appeared on the scene. The blood pressure sought new low levels. Bulletins were issued and newspaper reporters set up a death watch.

On the fourth day, Fowler suggested to Dr. Kersten that "perhaps a little alcohol might help the sinking actor." Five percent alcohol was added to the previous supportive intravenous treatment and Jack rallied to his old liquid friend.

There was an interlude during this tense time which was treated gravely by Fowler. But, looking back over the years now, it sounds comedic. A stranger had entered the waiting room where Decker and Fowler were sitting with reporters. "I am a healer, cried the stranger. "Just give me three minutes with Mr. Barrymore and I will cure him!"

There was a moment of silence until Fowler arose, snatched the seemingly demented fellow by the scruff of his collar and threw him down the stairs, calling after him, "Physician, heal thyself!"

Lionel had taken up residence in the hospital to be near Jack. Their rooms were adjoining. He asked for Fowler to come sit with him. "The last time you and I met in a hospital," said Fowler, "*we* were the patients." He was referring to 1939 when the two were treated in Los Angeles' Good Samaritan Hospital, Fowler as the result of an automobile accident with director Leo McCarey, and Lionel for a posterior ailment. Fowler entered Lionel's room in a wheelchair and said, "Doctor Gillespie, I presume."

Lionel was sitting in bed, rocking to and fro, grimacing with pain. Fowler asked him if his physician might not give him medical relief. "There's only one thing that would help," Lionel replied, "and that would put me right back again on the needle."

Fowler knew that Jack's older brother had become addicted to morphine back in 1925 when he was undergoing the agonies of arthiritis irritated by a venereal disease.

Lionel disclosed to Fowler that about a year earlier he had decided that he must make a break. "I sat in my living room with a wood fire going," the actor recounted, "and a greater one burning in my soul. I sat staring for five hours at a cabinet where I kept my syringes, needles and supply of the drug. I knew that in

The Monster

two minutes I could obtain a temporary release from my agony. But I sat there fighting as hard as I could. Finally I rose, took the drawer from the cabinet and threw its contents into the fire."

* * *

On the morning of the eleventh day, Jack roused from a coma and called for Fowler. At bedside, the author leaned over to hear Jack ask, "Tell me, is it true that you are the illegitimate son of Buffalo Bill?"

Fowler left the room and telephoned Jack's eldest child — by Michael Strange — Diana. "You"d better get down here to the hospital right away to see your father."

"I'm sorry," said Diana, "but I have a very important appointment."

"So has your father," said Fowler before hanging up.

An old friend, a priest, Reverend Father John O'Donnell, visited Jack. After a few minutes, he went to talk with Lionel, then returned to Jack's room where the dying actor was given the last rites of the Roman Catholic Church.

At 10:20 P.M. only Dr. Kersten was in the room when his patient whispered, "It's so beautiful." He immediately passed on — perhaps to his Grampian Hills.

John Decker then entered the room to render a deathbed sketch on a sheet of brown wrapping paper supplied by the hospital.

* * *

During his lifetime, Jack had admitted to taking "about twenty ounces of liquor a day" between the ages of twenty and sixty. This means his liver and kidneys had been visited by 293,000 ounces, 10,000 quarts, 3,200 gallons, or 640 barrels of alcohol.

The autopsy report gave the cause of death as bronchial pneumonia, congestion and edema of the lungs, and cirrhosis of the liver. Other pathological anatomical diagnoses were chronic nephritis, ulceration of the esophagus, arteriosclerosis, chronic dermatitis and chronic gastritis.

The body was removed to Pierce Brothers Funeral Home on Washington Boulevard where my father and I spent the entire night in attendance.

Some years later, Errol Flynn claimed to have stolen the body from another mortuary on Sunset Boulevard, fifteen miles to the north of the actual location. This was one of Flynn's many tall tales. The fable saw its genesis in Flynn's book, *My Wicked, Wicked Ways*. Some years following its publication, the impulsive actor confided to writer-producer-director Robert F. Slatzer that he had dreamed up the story "while in my cups. Anyway, I have to give the public all the sensationalism they demand of me." He added that he was sorry he had given birth to the lie.

Bitter about how Hollywood had treated one of his greatest friends in the final decade of his life, Fowler wrote a touching article for the newspapers, then, having gotten it out of his system, decided against offering it to them. Here it is, after nearly forty years of resting in a file marked private and confidential, written when he was unaware that he would soon become the actor's Boswell:

The wreck that once was John Blythe Barrymore touched shore last night. Like many another man of huge talent, he came upon days that were spears in his side. Yet he never complained. This great man, now that he has gone, will be acclaimed by all the shallow notorieties, who, during the artist's later years, were significantly absent from his audience, and blind to his needs. His few faithful friends, together with his gifted brother Lionel, were with him at the end.

This greatest Hamlet of our time — perhaps of all time — did not go into the evening of his sixty years with any whimpering, nor did he ask any quarter of this life or the next.

His Hollywood stock had fallen so low that producers and other mugwumps of the celluloid industry regarded him as a poison. On one night he was politely urged from a night club upon the excuse that his credit was nil. It might interest some of the choosey Powhatans to

The Monster

know that Mr. Barrymore retired to his Tower Road home and learned that Winston Churchill, the Prime Minister of England, was a guest of Franklin Delano Roosevelt at the White House. He asked a servant — which the creditors grudgingly had allowed him — to call Mr. Churchill. This was done. The Prime Minister of England not only answered the telephone but talked for a half hour with this great man, recalling old times in London when Mr. Barrymore had occupied Whistler's house and when his name was emblazoned upon the dramatic pages as the foremost Shakespearian actor of the era.°

It seems so strange — or is it strange? — that an artist shunned by the myopic peasants of his neighborhood should enjoy an intimate and personal conversation with England's spokesman an hour after he had been put out of a cheap bistro.

Perhaps anyone of Hollywood's leading lights would have given thousands of dollars to have enjoyed this privilege, and need we say, bragged about it the next day among their poison ivy set.

But this man never quarreled with the idiosyncrasies of his fellows. He forgave, he forgot. And he will be forgiven himself, but never forgotten.

A great many persons of the present generation knew this magnificent character only by means of his regrettable buffooneries over the radio. For the stinking compensation of a few dollars a week he appeared at the microphone, quite often ill, in fact, dying, and permitted himself to be lampooned for the enjoyment of the peanut munchers of America.

Because he was so forthright by nature, as many of our greatest artists have been, and because dishonesty was without his wish or nature, he was misunderstood, abused, ridiculed and resented. The bold and plain fact, however, is that he was perhaps the finest mind within a

---

° This came when Barrymore performed *Hamlet* in 1925 in London's Haymarket Theatre. At the end of the first night, to which his wife, Michael Strange, was escorted by George Bernard Shaw, Jack made his fifteenth and final bow carrying a saxophone.

hundred years of our history and undoubtedly was the greatest actor since Garrick.°

The harpies now will gather to pick his bones. Scullion minds will bring to bear their pudding brains to write plays, books and pamphlets concerning this sweet genius. He was a hard man to kill and undoubtedly he will squirm in his urn as his infamous commentators pour him into story and play and seek to dramatize themselves against the heroic mural of this man's full life. Well, let them!

He lived every moment of it. He had seen many things, indeed he had seen everything. He had done many things. Yes, he had done them twice, thrice and again. He drank life as if it were a wine and he would be the last to suggest that many regret his having been born and his having died.

He knew fame and he kicked it in the pants. He loved women and women loved him. He was victimized by some of these skirted charmers but he always knew it. He did not suffer that disease which is not listed in the medical literature — ignorance.

He was fully aware at all times of life, its pleasures and its penalties.

When the present generation has been weathered by time, by war, by stupidity, it may well be that several of our loud statesmen will have been forgotten. — History does not dote upon its warts. — But out of it all there may survive, as in the case of Garrick who had Goldsmith, Johnson, Boswell, and, in art, Sir Joshua Reynolds, to immortalize him, a paragraph by a writer or a portrait, perhaps by his faithful and almost equally talented friend John Decker, to give the future a picture of this great man.

Gifted beyond all measure in talent and in physical aspects, John Barrymore never once was less than gener-

---

°A deputation of very old gentlemen visited Barrymore in his dressing room following his sixtieth performance of Hamlet. They represented the Edwin Booth organization and urged Jack not to play more than ninety-nine performances. The master, Booth, had played one hundred. Shouting that they were still living in the past, Barrymore said, "I will perform it one hundred and *one* times!" And he did.

The Monster

ous nor was he ever conceited. Those who knew him learned that he was a very humble Man, a very gentle man. God rest him.

W.C. Fields was grumbling as his chauffeur drove the comedian, my father, John Decker and myself toward Calvary Cemetery in the celebrated sixteen-cylinder Cadillac with its fully equipped bar in the back seat. "The time to carry a friend is when he's still alive," Fields snorted. He was perspiring in his woolen black suit. They were to be pallbearers. I was designated as an honorary pallbearer.

More than two thousand people elbowed one another to find a better view of celebrities arriving at the Catholic cemetery where Jack's Requiem High Mass was to be celebrated. Finally making it, the deceased's daughter, Diana, arrived hanging on to Lionel's arm. The female member of theater's Royal Family, Ethel, was in the East, ill and unable to make the funeral on time.

Other honorary pallbearers were Edward Sheldon, Charles MacArthur, Herbert Marshall, Roland Young, Thomas Mitchell, Alan Mowbray, Ben Hecht, Arthur Hopkins, George M. Cohan, Herbert Bayard Swope and Bramwell Fletcher.

Only one of Barrymore's four wives was present. She was his fourth, Elaine Barrie. She was late. Dolores Costello was also home ill.

Some of the other entertainment world's luminaries present were Louis B. Mayer, Clark Gable, Errol Flynn, Fredric March, Ian Keith, Spencer Tracy, Norma Shearer, Harpo Marx, Anthony Quinn, Rudy Vallee, Earl Carroll, Jack LaRue, John Carradine, George Cukor, Edmund Lowe, Joan Davis, Raoul Walsh, William Powell, Ronald Colman and Cecil B. De Mille.

Following the obsequies, the original passengers piled back into Uncle Claude's Cadillac. As the car slowly nudged through the throng, a small boy put his head in the back window and thurst a pencil and pad at Fields. "Gimme your autograph!" he cried.

Fields shouted, "Back to the reformatory, you little nose-picker!"

The Monster

Traveling the outer streets now, Fields unlocked his bar and asked, "Would you gentlemen prefer a beer or a martini?"

"Both," replied Fowler.

Fields ordered his chauffeur to double-park while he filled the glasses. While pouring, a motorcycle officer pulled alongside to gaze at the proceedings in the back seat. "Just wadda you think you're doing there?"

Fields stared back at the policeman and replied, "We are sitting at the crossroads between art and nature, trying to figure out where delirium tremens leaves off and Hollywood begins." Then, to his chauffeur, "Drive on." As we pulled away, Fields cried back to the officer, "Sorry there's not enough, or I'd invite you to join us. Come to think of it though, I never bribe a peace enforcement officer. *Auf Wiedersehen*. And twenty-three!"

* * *

Back at the cemetery's Barrymore family crypt, two workmen busied themselves freeing the marble slab that sealed Jack's niche. When it was opened, they discovered a casket was already there. It contained the body of Irene Fenwick. It had accidentally been placed in the wrong niche. It seemed as though she had been waiting there for Jack all these years.

* * *

Immediately following Barrymore's death, Fowler was requested by Pascal Covici, then an executive editor for Viking Press, to write Jack's biography. "Don't you think it's a little too soon?" Fowler said. "It's like an old man marrying a beautiful young tart the day after he was widowed."

"It won't be by the time the work is ready for the presses," Covici reasoned.

This convinced Fowler. He went to work on a book which would eventually be titled *Good Night, Sweet Prince*.

* * *

I had told John Decker that it was my practice to read aloud to my father each new chapter draft he had written in order that he might get the "sound" of it. I added that I had just read what Pop had written about Barrymore's final collapse. When I said it

The Monster

occurred in John Carradine's dressing room at NBC, the artist became annoyed, complaining that Carradine had not yet reached his professional stature — such as that of John Barrymore. "Can't Gene just mention that Jack collapsed in *a* dressing room without using Carradine's name?" I said as much as "what the hell's the difference?" and even after I told Decker that Pop had left for Fire Island this very day to work on the book in a place where he loved to be alone and write, Decker kept after me. Eventually, I promised I would pass on his suggestion in a letter, though I had second thoughts about the idea. I kept my promise and mentioned it when I wrote next to my father.

Four days following the Decker aggravation, I received a letter from Pop:

> *. . . about the mention of Carradine in my book, don't bother too much about it. He was an eyewitness, the most accessible one, to Jack's actual moment of collapse before Barrymore was taken to the hospital. It was a dramatic moment. In literature, or in a court of law, an eyewitness is acknowledged to be an important factor, whether he be the King of England (I believe Edward VIII was King at the time he was allowed on a witness stand) or an organ grinder. In matters of record, one does not ask, "Is the man a friend, a great actor, a person of sweet nature?" but first of all, "Did he see the happening? And what did he see?" The other matters are subordinate to the dramatic or important moment itself. In reporting an event (in the newspapers, or in court) one gives (is bound by procedure and ethics to do so) the source of his information. One does not say "Barrymore caved in in the dressing room of a certain actor who is of such lowly professional standing as not worthy of mention in this work." No! One says, the collapse occurred in the dressing room of John Carradine. Then we know where we are, and who is present. The fact is the fact. We cannot, nor should we try to alter the fact, no matter who likes Carradine, or who doesn't. You would not expect your friend and musical orchestration teacher Ferde Grofé to foreswear and refuse to use the Key of G merely because some contemporary and mediocre writer*

The Monster

of sing-song trivialities pitched his crappy pieces in that key. One takes information from the devil!

4

His Hamlet

Following publication of *Good Night, Sweet Prince*, which was then the best-selling theatrical biography of all time, actor Orson Welles loudly criticized Fowler for writing a book about John Barrymore — and ignoring his *Hamlet*.° The purported exclusion of Jack's *Hamlet* attitude in the book was a constant burden to my father. Fowler declined to write about Barrymore's innermost thoughts while playing the part, mainly because of the actor's feelings while projecting his thinking into the brain of a second person. Because Ethel and Lionel were still alive when the book was written, Fowler found it impossible to make these most sensitive revelations to the public, or to his friends — it was a matter of conscience.

Of the several criticisms he received on this subject, Fowler remained mute to all — except one. This came from the distinguished New York physician Harold Thomas Hyman, author of many medical books, including an encyclopedia on medicine, which he was then writing. He wrote to my father at length about *The Hamlet:*

> *You have built the book, as I see it, up to and away from* The Hamlet. *You have faithfully recorded the reaction of many people to* The Hamlet. *You did not, however, make clear, at least to me, just why the Barrymore* Hamlet *was*

°Actually, Fowler mentioned *Hamlet* thirty-eight times in *Good Night, Sweet Prince.*

*so important and why it is as vivid to me today as when I
saw it so many years ago. . . . I almost got the impression
that you had not seen it yourself and, hence, were unable
to evaluate its importance.*

Not the least of Jack's achievements in his Hamlet *was
his psychoanalytic concept of many of the incidents.
Part of this was his extraordinary intuition, but part,
which you fail to mention, were his many conferences
with Pearce Bailey or Edward Zabrinski. For example,
the bedroom scene with his mother was deliberately
played for* incest. *This was in keeping with his concept of
the role of the Ghost, whom he regarded as his father
image and a villain — not with the affection which you
have stated.*

*I hope you will forgive my bluntness in calling these
things to your attention but I am sure you, as an artist
and a biographer, could not wish a friend to be other
than frank.*

Before he would answer Dr. Hyman's letter, my father gardened
for two days. He had to think deeply about the reply because he
felt it would have a historic importance "some years after I have
gone." The answer, to my knowledge, represents the most ana-
lytical expression my father had put to paper. It explores the
depths of John Barrymore's conscious and subconscious minds,
and, further, at last informs us just why it was impossible to go
into Jack's "thinking" *Hamlet* while he, Ethel and Lionel were
still alive:

*It ordinarily is a sad, and, for an author, futile horseplay
to try to explain a published book. To attempt to add to
or subtract from it now would be rather like an accused
surgeon telling the coroner why he had amputated a
healthy right leg when it was the left one that was gan-
grenous.*

*I wouldn't discuss my own recently born work with
most persons, partly because I am done with it, thank
God! I am not like Lot's wife. Then, also, there are not
many Hymans to be met with on the pier after the ship
has sailed and the crowd has dispersed.*

His Hamlet

You have been good enough to read the book intelligently and comment upon it from the standpoint of an articulate practioner.

You must bear in mind that the project itself, from my standpoint at least, was primarily reportorial, the only sphere perhaps in which I might claim any eminence by nature or by training. Perhaps you will permit me to postulate these two facts: I am neither a psychologist nor an expert on the drama. In respect to the former, I have, of course, read more of the authorities than the average layman; but, inasmuch as I am essentially a person of intuitions — with a slight dash of the creative impulse — I always have deliberately sought to keep memory's filing cabinet free of too much textual persuasion by the servants. Whenever I get deep, I get dull. . . .

My views on psychoanalysis in general could not by any stretch of the imagination be regarded as more than the babblings of a layman. However, we have had occasional examples of laymen finding out certain facts without benefit of Krafft-Ebing or Professor Alonzo Doakes, Jr. I cannot dismiss my impression that a great deal of mental therapy has accomplished about the same sort of thing as does the psychoanalyst's couch. And before all of these, in point of chronology, the mind-over-matter Hymns of Akhnaton of Egypt, who was described by Breasted as "the first individual in history," had their innings. I also believe that the age-old philosophies of the Hindus managed to achieve, and for a whole race, a serenity that offset neuroses. There is a whiff of plagiarism about Freud.

I think that, notwithstanding the brilliant pioneers among the P.A.'s, there are abroad many well-intentioned burglars, as well as an army of burbling charlatans who have made a cult of what really should be a sound and beneficial science. There are too many dramatics practised in this cult, and too many "hams" with medical degrees in one hand and jingle bells in the other.

. . . How then can I pontificate on the Oedipus Rex phase, when I have neither a diploma nor even a set of phonograph records containing the Freudian corre-

spondence school course? How also can I, who seldom go to the theatre (except backstage to drink with my pals) present myself suddenly as a rival of the late Archbishop Alexander Woollcott? Except for one short season, during which I was assigned to sit in for Alan Dale while he was having his prostate removed, I probably have not been a member of a playhouse audience for more than one hundred times in my life. (Yet I saw seven of Jack's Hamlets.) I have known numerous actors and actresses, not a few of them intimately. But the theatre itself seems to me so puny as against the hourly drama of life itself, that for me at least it becomes an anticlimax. How can it be otherwise for one whose theatre had been the court room, the operating chamber, the Death House at Sing Sing? Selah.

The audience for the most part seems to me, the reporter and observer of the realities, a drooling, program-rattling, asinine mass of strangers, who have paid a stud fee to enjoy a vicarious hump. True, I am interested in the better literature of the theatre, but largely as literature, just as I am interested in people of the theatre mainly as people.

My only recourse in dealing with these persons in my book was not to project my own verdicts. To do so would have been presumptuous indeed, from any professional standpoint. Ergo, I brought into my narrative a gallery of expert witnesses, just as an attorney for the defense does in a capital case.

Even to my lay eye, however, it was apparent that the incestuous motif was solidly lodged within the Barrymore Hamlet. Still, I ruled out his pre-play conferences with psychoanalysts. I had to do so for two principal reasons: first, all the competent testimony, gained at some pains by me, pointed to the fact that Margaret Carrington was his principal and only real adviser in regard to this role. And even she merely dispelled the smokescreen and opened the channel through which he moved into navigable waters and by virtue of his own intuitions and first-hand experience with incestuous situations!

You must remember that this man had one outstanding faculty — to make anyone *to whom he spoke or lis-*

His Hamlet

*tened feel that that person was the only one in his imme-
diate confidence, the only one to be entrusted with the
helm. I sensed this fact early in my long acquaint-
anceship with him. And he knew that I was wise to this
artful dodge. He even made Einstein (believe it or not)
think that he understood the broad elements of his theo-
ries, just as he made Jack Dempsey think that he knew
every nuance of pugilism. So, when any of your confreres tries to tell you that he shaped Jack's Hamlet, do
not laugh too loudly, but please believe me, they are talking via the sphincter muscle.*

As to his hatred of his father, *I, as a layman, would not
presume to debate that point with the scientists. It may
be argued that he hated his father because of* a fear that
his sire had passed on to him a blood-taint, or bequeathed
some other curse that promised eventual mental disinte-
gration. *It may be said that a hatred arose from the experience wherein Jack (and this is between physician and
patient) was* taken to bed by his beautiful stepmother and
given the works! *These two "situations" are imbedded in
the text,* if you look for them.

*I think that it might well be understandable why I
could not elaborate on these elements. It is an easy matter for a biographer, say that of Lord Byron, to leap back
across a century or more to record and appraise his illicit,
incestuous passages with Augusta.* It is quite another
thing to discuss actual *(or "circumstantial")* incest indulged in by a man only a few months, *or at most, two
years* dead. *How, for example, would you, if you were
writing for public circulation the life of the brilliant Libman, deal with certain of his, shall we say, "eccentrici-
ties" and their probably impact on him and on his
work?* °

*There not only are libel courts, but there is a greater
court, in which the biographer and friend must decide
whether or not to hurt the living or degrade the dead. I
had to make such a decision several times. For example, I
chose to "let lie" the Thaw case (so often discussed in*

° A homosexual, Dr. Libman was a renowned internist physician who
had died a short time before the writing of this letter.

*print, but never with the real, amazing background re-
vealed) in which* Thaw shot the wrong man, Stanford
White.°

*I am in possession of most of the incestuous evidence
in Jack's* Hamlet *case. But there was yet another reason,
aside from matters of public policy, why I did not feel
competent to evaluate this evidence — scientific pov-
erty.*

*As an indication of Lionel, the brother's sagacity and
wealth of mind, I quite understand what he said to me
while I was gathering material from him:*

"Too bad we are not all dead; then you would be free to
write a real story."

*Jack concealed from me little if any of the tragic
thread that was woven into the golden cloak of his genius. In fact, he was quite frank in discussing certain* dark
urges *he had had, such startling revelations as I do not
wish to discuss in a letter.*

*I eventually, as reporter, had the choice — even as a
non-psychologist — of describing fully his affair with a
woman who afterward became the wife of his brother,
and I assure you it is something that Dostoyevsky could
have cast into a great novel. The employment of this
grim saga would have made my book undoubtedly a sensational, and perhaps even a valuable case-history contri-
bution; but it also would have crucified Lionel, a great
person and my friend.*

*The choice was easy for me here. I decided to jettison
any claim as an outstanding author, and remain merely
what I am.*

°Just after the turn of the century, millionaire playboy Harry K.
Thaw suspected his wife, Floradora girl Evelyn Nesbitt, of committing
adultery with the architect Stanford White. Sensational newspaper
front-page stories said Thaw caught the two in a kissing embrace on
the roof of the original Madison Square Garden (a structure White
built). He shot White to death. At the time, Thaw was unaware that
John Barrymore was the man who was having a torrid, but on-and-off
love affair with Miss Nesbitt. The court found Thaw not guilty. He
died insane. Miss Nesbitt died in the 1960s, an old, forgotten woman
who lived in a small Hollywood apartment.

His Hamlet

The facts, the implications, as well as this letter, *may prove your point that he hated his father.*

A *certain hesitation caused me to leave out many revealing anecdotes in which I myself participated. I am so God-damned weary of reading the works of glib exhibitionists, who put themselves in such a fine and important light at every turn, that I did not choose to be enshrined in that category.*

Here is something I left out, *Harold, partly because* I did not want my book barred from the libraries, *nor did I want to destroy my protagonist's character utterly in the opaque and intolerant public mind. I think you will be interested in it, inasmuch as you are a connoisseur of Hamletiana. I also think it was one of the shrewdest questions ever asked by a reporter of an actor. I shall first state most of the queries I one day put to Jack in this regard, as nearly as I can record them, and then give you the gist of his answers, together with the one direct quote that I distinctly remember verbatim. My son, Will, was there with me at the time.*

QUESTION   *Do actors have a subconscious, or an unconscious, when they are on the stage reciting? By that I mean . . .*

BARRYMORE   *(interrupting)   I know perfectly well what you mean, you inquisitive police reporter bastard! Does the actor think beyond the line he is saying? Does he have a mind within a mind, or rather a mind within another mind?*

QUESTION   *Yes, would Barrymore on the stage, when reciting, say a Shakespearian line, and at the same time think as Barrymore, as Shakespeare, or, let us say as Hamlet?*

BARRYMORE   *It all depends upon my mood during a particular performance. If I was "into" the part (which I was during the first weeks at least) I thought as Hamlet.*

QUESTION   *All right. Could you now, years afterward, recreate the subconscious flow of ideas, associations — or let us call them backdrop thoughts — while you were declaiming in the presence of your stepfather, whose name escapes me?*

BARRYMORE *Yes, I could, and, if you will wait until we have this can of beer, I shall do it. If the dear old schoolteachers, who used to come to the Sam Harris theatre, knew what was going through my mind while I was saying my lines, well, they would have run screaming into the street, either to escape what was going on, or to hunt a sailor!*

QUESTION *Now give me, not* Hamlet *externally, or merely in a thespic Shakespearian scene, but repeat as nearly as you can Hamlet's stream of consciousness or unconsciousness, the associations of ideas, etc., when in the presence of his step-father on the stage.*

BARRYMORE *It wasn't merely when I was in the presence of my step-father. It was* most *of the time. The thing I like best was the second soliloquy, which closes with my determination to put on the play for the king. That is the soliloquy I remember best, and I can best remember what went thorugh my mind while reciting it.* . . . "That dirty, red-whiskered son-of-a-bitch! That bastard puts his prick in my mother's cunt every night!"

Now, in like language, he held forth for perhaps two minutes on his own jealousy of his mother when she was in the arms of a hated step-father. *The language was obscene, yet one began to forget its actual filth as against the powerful and unique performance.*

This was a remarkable insight into the mind of a great Shakespearian actor, and perhaps it is deplorable that a psychoanalyst could not have had the advantage of following this up and setting down the date in scientific form. However, I doubt very much if Jack ever would have given this evidence to a scientist, especially if he thought that it was being recorded even mentally.

It seemed that he would answer anything I asked him, because neither of us knew at the time that I ever would employ it as a literary or reportorial font. And, indeed, I never have used this episode which I now give to you for your files.

His Hamlet

I saw beyond the shattering violence of these words, and, with a reporter's intuition, found at least part of an answer that satisfied my frequent curiosity as to the subordinated thoughts of actors while speaking their lines.

All this may, I concede, substantiate your position that Jack hated his own father. It may well be that his stage step-father was a symbol that replaced a symbol, and that he had had similar thoughts about his own father when Maurice was alive.

If I had the answer to "what made Barrymore tick?" or his Hamlet "live?" I also could tell you what sleep is, and what electricity is.

Jack told me that he had entered actually into the character of perhaps but three of his many roles, and by that he said he meant he held the thoughts of these characters while playing the parts, instead of thoughts of his own. He said that he had usurped the character-mind of William Falder in Justice, *but to a lesser degree than in two other instances. He thought that he had come most fully into the character-mind of* Richard III. *He himself placed* Hamlet *second, not only as to the quality of performance, but also as to the amount of subconscious surges experienced during th rendition. Indeed, he added, he was "more of Richard than of any other character" he ever played. I do not agree with this, of course, nor indeed, may you.* Perhaps he was so closely akin to *Hamlet,* by force of circumstance and mental similitude, that the naturalness (to him) of the part outweighed the conscious striving he had exercised in preparing for his short-lived Richard.

I may say, as a rambling addenda, that while Jack was giving the private Hamlet *second soliloquy, translated by him into obscene and ghastly, incestuous terms, it became a most startling and compelling performance. The man's whole manner changed.* He seemed to be staggering beneath the reality of an unholy burden. *He revealed to his listeners* the hidden urges.

I must admit that I at once had recourse to a double whiskey (which I refused to share with Barrymore, a fact that caused him to denounce me for "coming in on a pass and occupying an aisle seat under false pretenses").

His Hamlet

Thank you again for your fine letter, which by no means was interpreted by me as an adverse criticism. After all I am not a supersensitive dolt. Now go back to your lancets and pills

Dr. Hyman seemed literally poleaxed by Fowler's letter. He wrote:

I have never been more highly complimented than by your extraordinary letter of recent date. Were it not so highly personal, I should return it to you and ask you to publish it. It is a document that unites the combination of integrity and facility of expression which you possess as a person and as an artist, though you will probably smile at my use of the term.

I am so completely persuaded that you are right about the Barrymore matter and I am wrong that I am now, in retrospect, somewhat awed at my audacity in presuming to express any opinion to you.

I shall indeed look forward to spending some time with you when you arrive in town. I would like very much for you to read the Chapter I have written on Psychiatry. . . . I think you will find that our experiences and opinions have been very strikingly parallel. If you are not coming soon, I will mail the manuscript to you.

5

The Molasses Mauler

In envy lives a shining mark, and success attracts a coterie of shitheels — with here and there a well meaning fellow.

I believe this befits all from kings to movie stars to world boxing champions. It certainly pointed out an underlying dilemma for Jack Dempsey after he defeated Jess Willard for the heavyweight championship.

"My troubles all seemed to start then," Jack said. Dempsey discovered he had accumulated so many back-patters and well-wishers that he purchased the Barbara Hotel in Los Angeles in order to supply them with living quarters.

It was not until after he lost his championship to Gene Tunney in 1926 that Dempsey became "The Most Popular Man in the World" for a period of ten years.

When a man met Dempsey to recapture a fleeting moment when the two talked last, he expected the fighter to remember him and everything the two had spoken about. This makes me think that the price of success can be a very dear price. When I see men who have so-called fame, they seem to pay such a drastic penalty for it, not in terms of dollars, but in time. And time is the greatest of all currency. Each man has a certain amount of capital called time, and hardly anyone budgets that capital. It may hurt if you take away a man's property, or even his wife, his mistress or some chattel — but if you take a man's time away, there is no substitute. Nobody can give you the hours or minutes that are wasted or of which you are robbed.

But as we get older, we become filled with little fictions, and eventually we believe them. Then they come into the realm of memories. An old man's memory is like an often-darned sock, a sock you're too poor to throw away. You keep darning and darning, and finally the sock becomes *all* darned, and it's not the sock it was. This leads me to wonder at what point in such a hypothetical case, the sock — meaning memory, in this instance — ceases to be the original sock and becomes all darning. I try not to get my remembrances crooked, but finally it happens with most of us — if we live that long. In my memory I find grace notes and figments that become barnacles, perhaps, on the main hull of legend — and old men (one of which I am becoming) don't like to go into drydock and get their bottoms scraped.

I remember that Dempsey was born in 1895, in the town of Manassa, located in the southern part of Colorado. It is located in a kind of hollow, or valley, you might say, with mountain peaks fourteen thousand feet and over to be seen. Manassa is west of Trinidad. In the winter it is very bleak. Blizzards sweep down from the Great Divide on this settlement which is now a town. This was a Mormon settlement. In fact, the *Dempsys* (the way their name was spelled until Jack changed it after becoming champion) had joined a Mormon migration and settled here instead of traveling on to Utah.

Jack's father Hyrum, a tall stringy chap who had been a schoolteacher in Virginia, brought his fiddle and his wife. They arrived in a covered wagon and settled with another group of Mormons in Manassa, which had a population of about four hundred.

In January, when the blizzards come down with fine twirling and smothering, devastating fury, the Dempsy family was away from home. They had been snowed in in various places.

Jack's mother, Mary Cellia Smoot Dempsy, alone at home, was several months pregnant with Jack. And out of this white hazard late one afternoon there emerged a smallish kind of fellow with a pack on his back. He was a peddler, and in those days, about the outlying districts of the west, these peddlers would come, carrying on their backs long boards with shelves. They were like a notions store in miniature — needles, thread, perhaps a few books, bolts of calico, pans and soap and things that were more or less necessities, but still luxuries.

This old fellow had been caught in the blizzard and, as quite often happened, had been lost. He saw the Dempsy farmhouse and knocked on the door.

Mrs. Dempsy was reading by the light of a kerosene lamp while worrying about her absent flock. She was seeking comfort in the Mormon Bible when the knock came. She answered it to find this snow-covered peddler. His hair was matted with ice. He released the shoulder straps of his pack and said. "Would you mind if I slept in the barn tonight? I'm lost and I'm afraid I might freeze to death."

"Come in," she said. "Have you had anything to eat?"

"'I wouldn't bother you for anything to eat," he said, stamping his feet, "if I can just sleep in the barn."

"No," said the pregnant woman, "I'm going to have you sleep in one of my boys' rooms and you'll be warm, and I'm going to make you some coffee and something to eat."

The next morning, the peddler wished to give Mrs. Dempsy something from his somewhat scant stock. Having noticed the night before that she had been reading the Bible, he said, "I only have one book, and I don't think it's a very good book for you, but it's the *Life of John L. Sullivan*."

Even though Mrs. Dempsy refused, the peddler left the book when he departed.

After he had left, Mrs. Dempsy noticed the frontispiece, with the belligerent-browed Boston Strongboy pictured flexing biceps.

By the time the storm had lifted and Hyrum and the children dug through, arriving to find she was all right, she had completed reading the Sullivan book.

"You know, I didn't think I'd like this book," she told her husband. "I'm kind of against fighting. I don't think it's a good thing for a boy."

Hyrum agreed.

"But," she said, "if this child that I'm carrying is a boy, after reading this wonderful book, I would like to have him grow up to be like John L. Sullivan. He drank, and I hope our boy will never drink, but otherwise there's something about him that's wonderful and warm and fine and human, and I would like that boy to be like John L. Sullivan."

* * *

Jack's first fight took place when he was seven years old. He fought a boy named Freddie. And Freddie's father was present. They were brawling like hell. Freddie was tough. Finally the old man shouted to his son, "Bite him! Bite him!" Freddie turned to bite Jack, and left an opening. Jack sank a hard right hand to Freddie's jaw. That was his first knockout.

* * *

There is only one fight in the record books wherein Jack Dempsey was apparently knocked out. It occurred in Salt Lake City in 1917 when Jim Flynn "KO'd" Jack in one round. Nat Fleischer, in his *The Ring Record Book and Boxing Encyclopedia,* points to this knockout as being "questionable." To back this up came a letter to me from Fred M. Mazzulla, an authority on the city of Denver and the history of its whorehouses for sixscore years.

"I have discussed this with Jack, with his then manager (Fred Fulton) and Ralph Carr, and several others," Mazzulla wrote.

"Jack, as you know," he went on, "was married to Maxine [his first wife], and Maxine was sent to Salt Lake City to get her away from Jack while he was training in Ouray and Montrose. Jack got lonesome for Maxine and went to Salt Lake to see her."

According to Mazzulla, this was in 1913, and Jack approached the local boys in order to promote some work.

"He was told he would be paid $50 to 'carry' the local boy for four rounds to make him look good.

"Instead, Jack [because of Maxine's urging] put the local boy away in the first round. The local boy was Jim Flynn."

The next morning, Jack found himself in jail charged with vagrancy.

"It seems as though Jack had let the Salt Lake City bettors down," wrote Mazzulla. "They had lost a lot of dollars in bets which they had put down on Flynn. Before the judge, Dempsey was given his choice of thirty days in jail for vagrancy or a $100 fine — or get out of town.

"Needless to say," said Fred, "Jack left town."

"Four years later Jack was booked to fight Jim Flynn. Again, it was to take place in Salt Lake City.

"Before the fight, Jack's manager, Jess, told him the local boys were now betting heavy on *him*; that they were the same S.O.B.s who had run him out of town four years before. Jim Flynn knocked out Jack Dempsey in the first round this time. This was Jack's way of getting even with the bastards."

* * *

Jack always believed he was the best fighter in the world. This was not vanity, but self-confidence. "If my own mother was in the ring with me," he told me, "I'd knock her out."

Jack finally won his way to fight champion Jess Willard, the man who defeated "the undefeatable" Jack Johnson. The fight took place on July 4, 1919, in Toledo, Ohio. But Dempsey's father was miles away in Provo, Utah, standing with a queue of acquaintances and well-wishers in front of the telegraph office. The only means of instant communication then was the telegraph. Telegraphers would receive the fight, round by round, type up the minute-by-minute results, then display same in the front window.

"You know, he shouldn't have gone into this ring," Hyrum said to his friends standing in front of the Provo telegraph office.

"Well, Hyrum, how long do you think he'll last?" a neighbor asked.

"If Harry [his name for Jack] wasn't so game, I don't think he'd last fifteen seconds. My God, that Willard can kill an ox! They say he's as big as a mountain. I just hope he gets out alive, that's all. I think that he may last most of the first round. I don't think he'll go more than that. It's no disgrace for him to get licked, except he's crazy to get in the ring with Willard."

It turned out that Dempsey almost killed Willard in the first round. He broke the champion's jaw; in fact, Dempsey became so wild he didn't hear the bell, and Willard, who had been knocked down seven times, was on the floor and out, he thought.

The Molasses Mauler

But Willard had been counted out *after* the bell rang. The referee had not heard the bell.

Dempsey left the ring, thinking he had won the fight. He later told Fowler that after one goes through an effort like that, especially thinking he had won a $10,000 side bet, and has to return to the ring, "that's one helluva strain."

Willard was tight on the pursestrings. He did not believe a manager was entitled to a cut on the winnings, and he had entered into this fight without one. Actually, *if* Willard had had a manager, this advisor would surely have claimed the fight by default when Jack left the ring following the first round.

Unfortunately for Willard, Dempsey returned, and the battered champion lasted only the next two rounds. He was so dazed and beaten and slaughtered that his seconds threw in the towel.

During this brutality, bulletins were hastily posted in the Provo telegraph window. Hyrum became so excited that at the end of the fight, he, who had predicted his son's early demise, began jumping up and down, yelling, "What did I tell you! What did I tell you! I *told* you Harry'd win!"

After the fight — as is always the case — the corner of the loser is a most sparsely populated spot. Everybody gathers about the winner, slapping his back. The winner walks to his dressing room through a great flying wedge of fans. But the poor loser? No one bothers with him. Not even Willard's seconds cared to administer to the fallen man's wounds. But from nowhere emerged newspaper reporter Charles MacArthur. A sensitive man, MacArthur, who was later to marry America's Lady of the Theater, Helen Hayes, saw this beaten giant stumbling along, bleeding, his face out, his jaw broken and dropped. Charlie guided Willard to his dressing room. The two were alone. None of the press was there to record Willard's feelings.

The contest had been hard for Dempsey, and he had been hurt by the giant. He was led to a nearby hotel in order to spare him an all-night clamor of big-time Charlies and gentlemen who wished to get on the gravy train.

Along about midnight, Dempsey roused from sleep. His jaw hurt. During the first round he had been hit by Willard so hard with a right uppercut that he thought he might lose the fight.

Lying between sleep and wakefulness, Jack finally rose and went into the bathroom, looked in the mirror. He noticed some dried blood. He had been bleeding from his mouth and nose, and felt torrid pain in his neck. He had lost his memory of what had occurred that afternoon. He thought, *Well, I was knocked out*. He couldn't recall winning. He seemed to be suffering from amnesia. He walked downstairs. The night clerk was on duty, nodding over a magazine. Dempsey slipped around to a side door so he wouldn't have to face the clerk.

The streets were deserted, except for a newsboy on the corner. Jack told him he'd like a paper. The boy didn't recognize him at once.

"Who won the fight?" Jack asked.

The boy stared up and said, "Well, hello, champ! Jesus Christ, can I shake your hand?"

Dempsey thought he was kidding. "Champ?" he asked.

"Yeah," the newsboy smiled. "You're Jack Dempsey, ain't ya?"

"Yes, I'm Jack Dempsey." He looked at the headlines:

NEW CHAMPION DEMPSEY
KNOCKS OUT WILLARD

Jack only had a dollar bill in his pocket. He gave it to the boy. He went back to the hotel and walked past the night clerk, popped the bell used to summon the bellboy, and went up to his room.

* * *

Jack's original name was William Harrison Dempsy, but he had named himself after the "Nonpareil," a renowned fighter born in 1862, from County Kildaerh, an Irishman who had retired undefeated.

After our Jack had taken on the name and spelling of the Nonpareil, one of the latter's daughters wrote to the new champion, reprimanding him for daring to take the name of her sainted father.

The Molasses Mauler

A thoughtful, diplomatic person, Dempsey replied to the lady. He said he had taken that name because it was such an illustrious one, and he admired the history of the man who had died the year that he had been born.

That squared it with the lass, and the two became close friends thereafter.

The eighth of eleven children, Jack was fond of his parents and sent them money or gifts as his winnings came in. But his father always seemed to be in deep need of a new icebox about every month. This puzzled Jack but, with no questions asked, he'd send along the iceboxes. It seems that the old man would receive his new icebox, then a fair-weather friend would admire the contrivance, and Hyrum would give it away — the same with all kinds of other things Jack had sent him over the years.

* * *

Tex Rickard was the most prominent promoter in boxing during the twenties. The proposed Dempsey-Luis Firpo battle in 1923 was a match especially to his liking. Firpo was a colorful, powerful, but clumsy fighter. He was extremely strong. He was almost six feet three inches tall and trained down to about two hundred and fifteen pounds on the day of the fight. Firpo had been a drug clerk in Buenos Aires, and then he became champion of the Argentine. At the time, Jimmy De Forest was training Dempsey.

Firpo was green and wished to have a bit more fighting experience when he traveled north to the United States. But Rickard informed his manager that Firpo would either have to get in and fight Dempsey then, or not at all. So the Wild Bull came to Atlantic City to work out near the seashore. Dempsey went over to Uncle Tom Luther's hotel at Saratoga Lake, eleven miles from Saratoga Springs.

Dempsey always trained hard. He liked outdoor life, but would become surly during training.

On a few occasions, Dempsey did get out of shape. His other trainer, Jerry "The Greek" Luvadis, helped get him back in shape. Luvadis was devoted to Jack. He used to rub him down and brag that Dempsey received more mail than any screen star. He was the first to call him "the Champ."

The Molasses Mauler

The Dempsey-Firpo fight was held at night in New York, and again Jack was uncertain of what had happened. Right away he waded in before seventy-five thousand people — Dempsey remembered that. He hit Firpo, but Firpo didn't seem bothered by it. Dempsey had a weaving style. He would come in low and weave his head. But the old story about how he began his fighting life with a great right hand and no left hand is bunk. His left hand was always good. And the story that his manager strapped his right hand to his side and had him fight his sparring partners with only his left was also pure bunk.

Jack knocked down Firpo five times, but he himself was in a daze because he had been hit hard in the first round. Every time Firpo got knocked down, he'd bounce up. Most of the fight was missed by the audience because in the excitement everyone stood up. The noise was overwhelming.

"I wish I could see the fight pictures again," Pop told me. "There were seven knockdowns in the first round, and I know Dempsey stepped over Firpo once."

Near the end of the round, Firpo was down for seven seconds, but he got up and pulled one right hand from the floor with his whole body behind it. Dempsey told Fowler he saw it coming, but it was so slow that he paused to marvel at the slowness. It caught him right on the jaw, knocking him through the ropes into the lap of a sportswriter. His crashing body wrecked one typewriter and almost everyone else.°

Firpo was knocked out in the second round.

As short as it was, the fight took its toll. Jack suffered an injury to his lower back from the fall. It bothered him for years. In fact, he made several trips to the hospital for corrective surgery. The last time, at Johns Hopkins, it was necessary that his coccyx, the vestige of his tailbone, be removed. During the surgery, Dempsey was given no anesthetic and had to be restrained during the thirty-minute operation.

° At least a score of people claim to have pushed Dempsey back into the ring, including comedian Milton Berle. But sportswriters have established that it was sports cartoonist Hype Igoe.

Unfortunately, Pop designed our summer home at Fire Island using the back of a large shingle as an architect's board. As a result, the house was far larger than expected. Our neighbor to the north, a Mr. Lannigan, never got to see the sea or the midday sun again. He was forced into a perpetual shadow, and never spoke to my father again.

During the construction of this huge summer hideaway, Fowler ran out of money.

The solution for this was to promote a fight. Jack Curley teamed up with Fowler to discover a fighter from South Africa named Johnny Squires. "The worst fighter in the world," said Curley. Nonetheless, Squires was pitted against "Fighting" Johnny Risco.

Fowler telephoned Dempsey, who was living in his bad investment, the Barbara Hotel. He asked his boyhood friend if he would referee the fight. With no hesitation, Jack said yes.

The fight drew $60,000, mostly because fans wanted to watch ex-champion Dempsey referee. It turned out to be a good one, though, with Risco winning a ten-round decision. And, unheard of, Fowler paid Squires' fare back to South Africa.

* * *

"Playful" is a small word when attempting to explain Dempsey. To his friends, he can be a horror with his strength and jokes.

On one occasion, Jack got the late wit Harry Hershfield in a tub of trouble with his friendly habit of biting men on the shoulders.

"This really happened," Dempsey said. "I was up at the studio one day [this was when Jack was making movies], and I went in and got my arm around Harry. I bit him in the neck. He finally got me off, but I suppose when his wife saw him putting on his pajamas, she saw him with all these teeth marks. Then his wife accused him of having some woman biting him."

"So what happened?" I asked.

"Well," Jack said, "Hershfield called me on the phone. He was almost crying. 'Come on over,' he said. I told him I couldn't. 'I'll give you a thousand dollars,' he said. 'My wife's going to divorce me!' I said, 'That so?' Finally, I had to go up to Hershfield's place and do the biting thing all over again; had to bite him in the same places to show Harry's wife the teeth marks matched. He's been greatful to me ever since. Harry said, 'You saved my life, because my wife was going to divorce me.'"

Following this incident, Fowler dubbed Jack "The Molasses Mauler."

* * *

When World War II broke out, Dempsey, in his late forties became a commander in the Coast Guard. He traveled the earth to help keep up the men's morale. Shortly after Jack received his commission, a superior officer said, "Now, Mr. Dempsey, will you show the men here your sextant?" Puzzled, Jack asked, "In front of all of them?"

Jack's daughters Barbara and Joan continually wrote to their father. In one mail he received a letter asking, "Papa, everyone else has captured a Japanese soldier. Why can't you?"

The opportunity presented itself at Okinawa. Jack's request to accompany the landing crews had been refused by his commanding officer. He sneaked into a landing barge anyway and became an assault member of the invasion.

On the beach, away from the main force of intruders, Dempsey found himself alone. But he had to capture a Japanese soldier for his daughters.

There was no one else about when Jack spied one of the enemy. He took after him, and Jack told Fowler that this man ran "faster than anybody I've ever seen in my life."

"Jack was out of wind," said Fowler, "but he finally nabbed this guy. He was so excited that he didn't notice at first that the enemy was an old man."

Jack was embarrassed, but had his photo taken with this fellow anyhow. He even mailed the picture to his daughters.

* * *

Although they lived only a few blocks away from one another, Dempsey and W.C. Fields never got around to visiting each other. One day, while Pop and I were at Dempsey's Los Feliz home, Fowler said, "Let's look in on W.C. right now."

"You go ahead," said Jack.

"I guess you're still mad at him because of the joke he played on you last month," said Fowler.

"God," said Dempsey, "I hope it won't get in the newspapers."

Quite early one morning Barbara and Joan's governess had awakened Jack to tell him something shameful was happening in the swimming pool. A naked man was bathing there.

The ex-champion leaped from his bed and ran down to the pool where, indeed, he discovered a man bathing there — in the nude. "Hey! What do you think you're doing there?" Jack cried out. "Get the hell out and get your clothes on! But quick!"

"Leave me alone," the bare swimmer replied as the sun began to lighten up the mountains in the east. "I'm not hurting anybody."

"For the last time," Dempsey warned, "get out, or I'll come in and throw you out!"

"Aw, go to hell!" came the answer.

Dempsey leaped in and belted the man a few times until he discovered — "Good lord, what will people say if they find out I hit a midget?"

"They'll think you're trying a comeback," Fowler laughed, "by easy stages, of course."

*   *   *

Back in 1947, Dempsey decided to throw a big party at his Los Feliz home. There must have been close to one hundred in attendance. I recall arriving early and going upstairs to visit Barbara and Joan in their sitting room suite; I played the piano for them.

Director Leo McCarey, Ben Hecht and Charlie MacArthur, and several motion picture stars were present. I distinctly remember three separate fistfights after the party warmed up — I participated in one. Poor Dempsey had to take on the role of referee and bouncer.

Twelve steps led down to the long bar where Dr. Harry Martin, to one side sat stoned to the gills. He was losing a battle trying to rise from a booth to hit some fellow. Then the doctor's wife, movie columnist Louella Parsons — who possessed the gift of saying the right thing at exactly the wrong time — appeared at the head of the stairs. She spied Martin struggling from the booth, then falling on his bottom. His speech was slurry as he was helped to his feet. And along came that sterling moment when all stopped speaking and started gawking at the doctor. This was the moment Louella chose to cry out to her husband: "Now don't take too much to drink, 'Docky.' You know you have to operate in the morning!"

* * *

Knowing Fowler disliked traveling, Jack phoned Mother to tell her he would appreciate Gene's company on a trip he was going to take to San Francisco. "It's a grocer's convention," he said, "and I know if you ask Gene, he'll come along."

"I'm so immured to this nest I've set up down here for myself," Pop told me, "that a trip of any kind isn't too attractive. And I don't like the narrow beds and these luxurious soft pillows the hotels have. I can't sleep on the damned things, and usually you have to get a letter from your pastor, or have Congress pass an act to get you a hard pillow. I'm used to hard pillows. Like Jacob, I like to wrestle with angels."

They got to San Francisco by plane. There was to be a fight that night, and Fowler thought Jack was to see the fight in the course of his duties. "I was delighted when he said he wasn't."

Now Dempsey and Fowler sat in their rooms at the Fairmont Hotel. Nobody knew yet that Jack was in town, so they sat there with their coats and shoes off and relaxed.

Before they checked in at the Fairmont, however, Fowler had visited a bookshop. He came across a paperback copy of Shakespeare's tragedies and decided to play a harmless joke on Dempsey. Jack noticed the books under Fowler's arm and asked, "Can't you ever get away from bookstores?"

"I like bookstores," said Fowler, holding out the Shakespeare paperback. "I have a present for you. You see, I'd like to have you improve your mind. I am accustomed to associating with fine intellect. I don't mind being ruined socially with you, but I like someone who can talk with me in a high-toned way."

Dempsey began to burn. Fowler said he wanted Jack to make a speech the next day to these grocers, "and I'd like very much if you would memorize the second soliloquy of *Hamlet:* 'Oh, what a rogue and peasant slave am I.'"

Jack sniffed at Fowler to see if he had been drinking.

"And as an encore," my father continued, "after they see this great performance of yours and cry 'Bravo,' or 'Heave the bum out,' I wish you would memorize the Second Sonnet."

"The second *what?*" asked Dempsey.

"You see? That's the point. I've been going around with intelligent men, well, for instance, like Gene Tunney . . . "

By now, Dempsey was gritting his teeth.

Fowler thought that was that, but Jack's part Indian — Cherokee — and full of revenges. Quite often, if you played a trick on him, he'd get back at you two or three times over.

The following evening, they met with a group of conventioneering grocers, and when he had everyone's attention, Jack put Fowler to task, saying, "Say, Gene. About the Sputnik the Russians sent into outer space, how far away is the moon from earth?"

"Well, I don't really know," said Fowler as all waited for an answer.

"It revolves around us in an elliptical orbit," Jack studiously pointed out, "Which causes its mean distance of 239,000 miles from us to oscillate between 221,000 and 253,000 miles. How come you didn't know that?"

"Wait a minute," said Fowler, "I *did* know — once."

"I'm not asking if you *did* know. Do you know *now?*"

"No, I don't."

"Well, tell me, how many planets are there?"

"When I went to school, there were eight."

"You think?"

"It's been a long time."

"Then you don't *know.*"

Jack asked Fowler if he could name some of the planets, but he could come up with only five, ending with Mars.

"How far is Mars from us?" Jack pressed his attack.

"Well, I don't know, nor do I give a damn."

Jack was eager. "How long do you think it would take to travel to the moon?"

"Well, if you go by bus, I think it would take longer."

"Let's not kid about this," said Jack. "You must have some idea."

"I have no idea."

Jack asked Fowler about ten more questions relating to the universe, and he couldn't answer one. Jack stared at him dead-pan, and Fowler admitted that "we're *all* ignorant."

Jack had sneaked out to the bookstore early that morning, purchased an *Almanac*, and memorized a few pages.

Before they retired that night, Fowler asked Jack if he'd mind if they watched the news on television. Tuning in, they came upon a dramatic and meaningful thing: An old bison at some zoo had been king of the herd over some nine cows. He was being attacked by a younger bull. The fight had been going on for about a half hour before the television began transmitting it. They watched the tail end of the battle — the last round, you might call it. The young bull was in the background. He won the fight .and seemed proud. Now the magnificent old bison was attacked by the nine cows.

"I have a dim memory about reading about this kind of thing in nature books," said Fowler. "I suppose that the females do this sort of attacking feeble, or senile, or impotent husbands for the sake of developing a stronger breed."

The poor old bastard was standing there, his feet planted wob-bly and his great shaggy head slowly, slowly bowing while the zookeepers were prodding off the cows with pitchforks.

Dempsey and Fowler watched after the cows had been cleared away by several men who looked like Neptunes with tri-dents. They were silent.

Slowly, the head of the old bison lowered in a posture of mag-nificent dejection, and then in contrast to the slow lowering head, the body gave a quick whipover and the buffalo was knocked out. It died the following day.

Fowler looked at Dempsey. His face (Jack's) was set in an ex-pression of awareness, and a little sorrow came to his eyes which sometimes contained a look of repressed pain.

"Well, how about it, old boy?" Fowler asked.

"That's the way it goes," Jack answered. "We are all defeated at some time or another."

"Yes. In anything we do, we *do* have to meet defeat."

"And the dames, too," Jack quietly said. "They turn on you, don't they?"

"They do quite often. You should know," said Fowler. "I suppose that's nature."

* * *

On the way home in the plane, Fowler and Dempsey were being served dinner. Their attractive stewardess didn't recognize Dempsey, and this was unusual because almost everybody recognized the old Manassa Mauler.

Without Fowler knowing, Jack told the stewardess he was taking this dear old man to a sanitarium in Los Angeles but he didn't want to put handcuffs on him because he was of a wealthy family and didn't wish to bring them bad publicity. She should not be alarmed if he, Fowler, should become violent. He reassured the young lady who had become concerned.

When the stewardess returned for their drink order, Fowler said, "I'm on the wagon, honey." She nodded knowingly as Dempsey pretended to sleep in the chair next to him.

Later, the stewardess woke Dempsey to ask if he would like dinner. He declined, and pretended to go back to sleep. It was Friday, so Fowler ordered fish, then sneaked it into a waterproof sick bag, a gift for his cat. The stewardess caught this and was convinced she had a madman aboard.

As she turned away, Dempsey flashed his left hand and squeezed one of Fowler's balls.

Fowler rose in a scream of pain. The food was knocked all about. Even the co-pilot came out and, by the grace of God, recognized Dempsey, who watered down the whole thing.

Jack had gotten even two times over.

6

Uncle Claude

Following months of playing through varied miserable climates of winter, that magical day eventually emerges when rough grass — like a long-courted woman — unexpectedly yields; the breeze is refreshing and as clean as the sky; holes on the greens are all in the right places; you can't lose a Nassau bet as your final drive comes to rest on the verdant eighteenth fairway. You're sweet on your golf stick as thoughts drift to frosty drinks and the conviviality of the nineteenth hole. This is when I have my fondest memories of the actor I caddied for during the mid-1930s at a golf course along the shores of a lake then as blue as Loch Lomond in Southern California's arid San Fernando Valley. He was W.C. Fields, one of Fowler's lasting friends throughout the years he spent in Hollywood.

Malevolent and demoniacally intense in his professional moods, Fields was contrastingly amiable in his hours of leisure — especially on the golf course, where he dressed nattily in delicately tinted silk shirt and tightly knotted flower-designed necktie after the fashion of Walter Hagen. While "The Haig" ambled about the links with hair Vaselined flat, Fields promenaded, wearing a white cap to protect his Klaxon-horn nose from the sun's rays. When he addressed his ball on the first tee, Fields appeared as immaculate as a Beverly Hills surgeon about to make an expensive opening.

I was in my teens when my father and I visited Fields, who was living across Toluca Lake from the Lakeside Golf Club. Although he played around the course, and even paid for the construction of a large steam bath there, Fields, by his declaration, was never a member of the golf club.

The juggler hated his name, Claude, so inevitably his closest friends gave him the detested sobriquet, "Uncle Claude."

Fields had a favorite golfing crony in the husky, light-haired Italian motion picture director Gregory LaCava. Fields reveled when this man lost his temper while attempting to concentrate on a putt to decide in whose pocket $1,000 in cash might rest.

This day, I toted Uncle Claude's sack at Lakeside. Fowler decided not to walk, remaining at the house to enjoy the beauty of the small lake. LaCava lost heavily to Fields on the front nine holes. The director requested a handicap adjustment before entering the back nine. Fields refused any consideration. And, after a few holes more, LaCava found himself a disatrous five strokes behind. Following his drive on the seventeenth, LaCava's ball became wedged in a gopher hole abaft the midway marker.

LaCava's wrath was such that he turned viciously on his caddie. As the director saw it, the caddie could have at least disabled Fields' clubs or, even better, managed to sabotage the lie of the comedian's ball.

But Fields was much too nimble of both eye and limb to be victimized by anybody. As a matter of fact, Fields was a good shooter out of trouble. In rough, sand or on sandhill lies, his early experience as a juggler gave him unusual coordination of hand and foot.

Dallying close enough for his rasping voice to be overheard by the temperamental director, Fields would switch a toothpick from one side of his mouth to the other. He vaguely threw his monologue at me as I set his bag down. His words were foreign to the subject of golf, which irritated LaCava all the more as he vainly concentrated on rescuing his ball from the gopher's clutch without the penalty of a stroke.

"Did I ever tell you of the time I was in South Effingham? . . . No, it wasn't South Eff-ing-ham. . . . I guess it was Sioux Ci-ty. . . . Winter of nineteen-and-ought-six. I remember it well. Yes, indeed. . . . Bitter cold. Wind blowing two hundred knots and the citizens cowering in their snowed-under domiciles. . . . The Ohio River frozen solid . . . bank to bank. . . . I was madly in love

Gene Fowler and son Will (ten years old) at Floyd Bennett Field. This was in 1932, the early days of commercial aviation.

Author in Honolulu with Gene and Agnes Fowler. It was 1941, when there was still room on the beach. (Photo by Allan Campbell.)

Author with actress Colleen Townsend, featured in director
Michael Curtiz's movie *Janie*. She became a minister; he, a
reporter.

Author interviews Esther Williams at MGM—underwater, of course.

The "Gray Chrysanthemum" (Sadakichi Hartmann) at Bundy
Drive. Left to right: film editor Allen McNeill, the author,
artist John Decker, Hartmann, and Gene Fowler. About 1941.
Photo by Cliff Wesselman.

Author takes gin rummy lessons from Jack Dempsey, as Gene
Fowler looks on, about 1946. (Photo by George O'Day.)

Sketch of Gene Fowler, about 1933, when his romance with
Ann Harding flourished. (Sketch by Lew Schreiber.)

Westbrook Pegler with
Eleanor Roosevelt (in
happier days, before the
Pegler-Roosevelt schism).

Good companions. Left to right: W. C. Fields, Gene Fowler, John Barrymore, John Carradine, Jack LaRue, and John Decker.

John Decker's celebrated painting of W. C. Fields as Queen Victoria.

Artist John Decker, Gene Fowler and John Barrymore in
Decker's Bundy Drive studio, where the group used to gather.
About 1941.

Fields and Barrymore.

John Barrymore at height of his motion picture career in early
1930s. He is examining ancient manuscripts in his Tower Road
home.

Gene Fowler checking
comedy script with Richard
"Red" Skelton, about 1952.

Gene Fowler in Denver with
Arthur "Bugs" Baer in 1949.
(Photo by Fred Mazzulla.)

for a time. . . . Then it wore off. . . . Heard that her father was a crack shot. . . . The lady became a nuisance, but I got rid of her by a clever ruse: I pinned a note to my dressing room door at the theater. . . . It read: 'Gone for lunch.' . . . Or was it Klamath Falls? . . . "

By this time, LaCava had wrenched his golf ball from the gopher hole and hurled it at Fields, shouting, "It's a natural hazard, you miserable vaudevillian bastard! No penalty!"

"Godfrey Daniel," Fields cried as he dodged the director's grenade while holding on with both hands to the white cap that shaded his ripe beak. "That's *two* strokes penalty, you dago."

"Natural hazard, you three-a-day bum," LaCava reminded him as Fields switched his attention to a passing female twosome, then mused, "It was a woman who drove me to drink, and I forgot to send her a thank-you note."

*   *   *

Because his was a *dumb act* — not stupid, but an act wherein no words are spoken — Fields' juggling routine was in great demand overseas. Thus he began the first of his seven circumnavigations of the globe beginning in 1902. While filling an engagement in Johannesburg as the Boer War was nearing its end in South Africa, Fields was invited by an Englishman to play his first game of golf nearby that settlement in order to "erase some of that nighttime pallor with a bit of sun."

This was a period when the small wood golf driver was still referred to as a "cleek," and most golfers had not yet been initiated to the novel convenience of a bag in which to carry their several baffies, spoons, mashies and niblicks. Even the hard-cored guttapercha ball had not yet been replaced with the recently patented rubber-wound balls there.

Fields enjoyed the game and adapted easily to it, but modestly refused to divulge his score, terming it commonplace and pedestrian.

Never having toured a golf course before, Uncle Claude told me in later years, "I was oblivious to the fact that deep artillery wagon grooves on the fairways . . . and horses' hooves had been implanted on the greens . . . just to depreciate my chances of acquiring a par. . . . I gave up the game . . . for weeks . . . this problem being necessitated because I was aboard a ship at the time."

It was necessary one season that Fields depart South Africa for Paris, where he was to appear in the *Folies-Bergère*, billed above a fourteen-year-old comic named Charles Chaplin. Before he sailed north, Fields met two other Americans (a rarity in those environs) celebrating the war's end in a Johannesburg saloon. One was Will Rogers, an unemployed wrangler who had delivered a shipment of South American cattle to help feed British soldiers in the battle zone. The other was Tom Mix, a United States cavalryman who had seen Spanish-American War action in Cuba, and was on his way to participate militarily in the Philippine insurrection and China's Boxer Rebellion, consecutively.

*   *   *

During ensuing years, Fields found it difficult to locate golf courses on foreign soil, but he became the first juggler to make use of golf balls in his act. He was able to keep seven of them hovering in the air at one time while performing for Edward VII, King of England.

A star of international reputation in 1915, Fields was offered by cablegram an extremely high-paying contract by Florenz Ziegfeld, equally notorious for abhorring comics. On good authority, Fields had heard the producer of the *Ziegfeld Follies* had once remarked, "I like to put all the comics on stage at one time, and sit back and watch them try to devour one another."

Fields cabled back:

WILL NOT SAIL UNTIL SALARY IS DOUBLED WITH GUAR-
ANTEE OF FULL SEASON RUN. MY NAME MUST ALSO BE
BILLED ABOVE ALL OTHER PERFORMERS AND IN LET-
TERS TWICE AS LARGE. PLEASE ADVISE.

Fields' demands were met. He embarked for New York. As he sailed toward the United States, W.C. wrote the stage's first comedy golf routine, which he would premier in the *Ziegfeld Follies of 1915*. He had decided at long last to institute dialogue in his stage routines.

A poor judge of comedy material, Ziegfeld was taken aback by Fields' raspy voice. The Broadway impresario was unable to fathom the innovative golf routine. He threatened to cancel the act. Fields threatened to leave the show cold.

A compromise was made.

"I want a beautiful woman to walk on stage during the routine," Ziegfeld insisted.

"I can take care of that, too," Fields accommodatingly ventured.

At rehearsals, Fields showed Ziegfeld the cue he had written in his script for "Miss Morse . . . a smart-looking girl with greyhound dog at her side . . . upon stage entrance."

But Fields did not offer the producer his additional lines, wherein he would dismiss the lady from his demanding routine.

"Fine-looking camel you have there," he would say while viewing the dog.

*   *   *

By 1929, Americans were enjoying the game of golf over more than forty-five hundred courses throughout the country. During that year a musical comedy was produced with a golf background called *Follow Through*, starring Jack Haley, Zelma O'Neal and Jack Whiting. A golf movie in 1930, *Love in the Rough*, featured Robert Montgomery as its hero. Even Walter Hagen starred in a Mack Sennett comedy short, *Match Play*, with Andy Clyde. Fields repeated his links routine from the stage, but this time in its entirety, in a 1930 two-reeler sound film, *The Golf Specialist*. He also demonstrated his green trickery in *The Dentist* (1932), *The Big Broadcast of 1938* (which introduced Bob Hope to films), and *Never Give a Sucker an Even Break* (1941).

As an aside to *The Dentist*, ten-year-old Harry Watson was trying out for a part in the Sennett short, *The Barber Shop*. Fields was casting at his home with director Arthur Ripley. In seeking out a child actor, Fields was mainly interested in locating a boy who might bring him his drinks with dispatch.

Before handing him a page of dialogue, Fields carefully directed young Watson: "Now I want you to . . . very quietly . . .

rush over to the other side of the room . . . then turn on command . . . and return quickly."

Harry did this.

This time, Fields handed the boy a martini glass filled to the brim. "Now," said Fields, "I wish you to repeat the process . . . but this time . . . carrying a glass filled to the top . . . with thoracic lubrication."

Watson repeated the routine without spilling a drop. Fields was so pleased with the demonstration, he put his arm about young Watson — after retrieving his martini — then smiled at his director and said, "We could have looked a thousand years."

* * *

In 1931, the year following Bobby Jones' Grand Slam of Golf, the game's rarest film of all was produced. Warner Brothers paid the twenty-nine-year-old Jones $100,100 to make eighteen one-reel golf shorts in which the national hero offered lessons to top actors and actresses of that era — on film.

"All the stars were eager to take part," said director George Marshall. "They donated their time in order to have the chance of Bobby Jones working on their game." They included Jimmy Cagney, Edward G. Robinson, Loretta Young, Walter Huston, Joan Blondell, Douglas Fairbanks, Jr., Richard Arlen, Joe E. Brown and, of course, W.C. Fields.

All Jones would ever reveal on this matter, after playing a round with Uncle Claude, was, "Very interesting."

Fields starred with Jones in the first episode of the series dubbed *How I Play Golf*. W.C.'s was also the funniest of the segments.

Bunkered almost hopelessly, Fields upset the first take when his supposedly impossible sand shot popped right into the cup.

The only existing copy of the Jones series reported several years ago is the property of the Peachtree Golf Club in Atlanta, and it is believed to be in a reliquary of the Trust Company of Georgia.

* * *

"Fields dearly loved to rattle and distract Mr. LaCava on the tee," wrote my friend, eminent author, wit and long-time Fields observer, H. Allen Smith. In *Lost in the Horse Latitudes* (Doubleday Doran), he wrote, "As LaCava addressed the ball, Mr. Fields would take up a position immediately behind him, making just enough noise to let his presence there be known. Mr. LaCava would say, 'Listen, you son-of-a-bitch, get the hell out from behind me!'

"Mr. Fields would move a few feet, wait until Mr. LaCava started his backward swing preceding his drive, then timidly say, 'Is this all right?' "

If this did not disrupt LaCava, Fields would take a pliable lead-shafted driver and take a hefty swing, resulting in the club encircling his neck like a garter snake.

On one occasion, Fields and LaCava were playing for $50 a stroke. LaCava became so outraged at W.C.'s asides that he had his caddy leave the field, carrying his bag. "I don't need clubs to beat you. I can do better with my foot."

For the remaining fourteen holes, the director kicked his ball around the course. When the game was over, Fields informed LaCava that he owed him $1,000. But, with a sudden lapse of revenge, he generously said, "Look, Greg, I don't want your money. Let's say that this one's on the house."

This infuriated LaCava all the more. "Listen here," he shouted, "I can buy you ten times over! You'll never have as much money as me. You need it." Out came the checkbook and LaCava quickly scrawled on it, then threw it at Fields. "Here, you cheap bastard! I don't want to be beholden to *you*!"

"Nobody in the world could read the chicken tracks on that damned check . . . much less LaCava's bank teller," Fields chuckled while viewing a copy of the seminude Greek torso of the *Venus de Milo* in his garden. "Venus de Milo," he said. "I'll bet if they ever found her arms, they'd discover she was wearing boxing gloves."

*   *   *

It was a deadly game with Fields to work out how to undo a medical man in any manner devisable. He dragged several into courts of justice in disputes over what he considered were exorbitant fees — and occasionally beat them. And his guiding principle did not necessarily have to involve an amount of money.

In 1939, my father and I visited Uncle Claude, who had been hospitalized. He had broken his neck in an auto accident, and when taken to the emergency ward, refused to permit surgeons to place his neck in a plaster cast or in traction. He claimed he was capable of holding his neck in position until it knit.

"I am not going to suffer a stiff neck because of you croakers," he insisted to the doctors in attendance. "There are a lot of things I want to see in life yet, and don't want to have to turn my entire body each time I look."

After the medical residents vacated his private room, Uncle Claude remarked, "When doctors and undertakers pass one another, they always wink."

Two weeks later, when the cervical vertebrae were regarded as reasonably knit, Fields, repatriated to his home, called for a triple martini to celebrate his convalescence. The drink was brought to him and he rose to test his own powers of endurance. He was still holding his head high. This was not from pride, but from necessity. Consequently, he did not observe a chair in his path. As he began his march about the house, he tripped over the chair and crashed to the stairwell, tumbling to the floor below.

Uncle Claude had rebroken his neck, and also fractured his fundament.

"Anyway," Fields groaned as he was being carted off again to the hospital, "it was a complete job . . . . I've now been broken at *both* ends."

We followed Uncle Claude to the hospital, and when they trundled him off to his bed, Fowler asked, "How do you feel?"

"As sad as a street-walker's father," he moaned.

*   *   *

Months passed before Fields could wield a seven iron at the Lakeside practice tee alongside Toluca Lake. But to compound his pain, W.C.'s personal physician, whom the comedian held at arm's length, informed him that he must stop drinking — entirely — "or you won't live six more months."

"Exactly what a doctor in Berlin told me twenty years ago,"

Uncle Claude

Fields said. "Of course," he added, "he might have been going by an out-of-date Gothic calendar."

The doctor's Hippocratic sentence led Fields to a regimen of abstinence — for a single week. When the medic learned of the comedian's backsliding, he moved into Fields' home to watch over him — around the clock.

Again, Uncle Claude used his ingenuity and resourcefulness to stop the doctor from earning his heavy fee. But the healer tenaciously gained the whip hand, hauling down the tradesman's entrance sign. In addition, the doc located his numerous hiding places for varied spirits.

Bolder action was called for. Fields decided to meet the healer on his — Fields' — own grounds: the golf course.

Uncle Claude proposed that, after being imprisoned for such a time, the two needed fresh air.

In a gesture of peace, the comedian offered to teach his administrator the fundamentals of using a golf stick. He smiled like a choirboy.

The doctor agreed that this was a good idea.

Nattily attired in a pair of baggy tweeds, Fields instructed his newly found pupil that the principal point in golf was to "stare intently at the ball before swinging at it. . . . You can't stare at the ball too long," he continued. "Before you take a cut, count ten, slowly."

Fields, with the care of a still photographer, arranged his subject in a golfing stance, then stepped directly behind him. "Now . . . count."

"One . . . two . . . "

"Much slower," Fields insisted, swiftly extracting a miniature two-ounce bottle of bourbon from the folds of his knickers.

"One . . . two . . . " the healer repeated.

"Still slower," Fields urged, then polished off the bourbon.

"One . . . two . . . three . . . "

Fields tossed the dead soldier away. It rattled a nearby bush.

The doctor looked up from his ball. "What was that?"

"Snakes . . . noisy rodents . . . Don't take your eye off the ball."

They continued through a loop of four holes, by which time the comedian, whose nose that looked like what Jack Horner

Uncle Claude

pulled out of the pie, had depleted his cache of a dozen two-ounce bottles.

This ruse succeeded for a week. At the end of this period, with the doctor beginning to get the hang of swinging a golf club, the medic remarked, "Now you have been one whole week without a drink, and you're looking 100 percent better."

Fields' golf games were not always planned. Actually, they *never* were during his stay at Toluca Lake.

As the two of us sat in his backyard, sipping his favorite Bristol Cream Sherry from outsized wineglasses, we stared silently at the lake water lapping the grass's edge. Uncle Claude, in fact, was contemplating the arrival of his arch enemy — a large young male swan — which frequently used his lawn as an outhouse.

He slowly laid down his empty glass and leaned forward on the edge of his chair, chin resting on his favorite putter. His teeth were grinding and his nostrils flared. "I wonder how much he's got saved up this time," he snarled. "He does this to me on purpose." Uncle Claude seemed nearly paranoid in his hatred for the white swan.

As though traveling on a precise interurban timetable, the swan arrived at the shore's edge.

Fields' knuckles grew as white as the cob's sheen. He tightened his grip on the ancient putter.

The bird shook water from its plumage and started a slow waddle up the yard.

Fields grimaced. "Give me an axe, a heavy tomahawk, the Royal Mace of England."

The swan picked his spot and let loose his dump.

Like Stonewall Jackson, Uncle Claude charged the bird, waving his golf club in great arcs, shouting, *"Either shit green or get off the lawn!"*

The swan quick-stepped it until he reached his sanctuary in the water. A manservant appeared and disposed of the bird's droppings, allaying Fields' apoplectic rage.

Following a few emergency triple martinis, Fields managed to place the incident in the back of his mind. He suggested I row him to the other side of the small lake so he might play just one hole before the sun lost its daily arrangement with the night.

On the other side of the lake, I handed Uncle Claude his driver. He teed up his ball in the center of the fairway and resoundingly hit it toward a far-off green, which not only had nothing to do with the fairway he was in, but was alien to two other fairways he bisected.

As the ball came to rest on the faraway green, a player in an approaching foursome began to loudly harangue Fields with less than polite epithets. A club member guest in the group assaulting the hole on yet another fairway cautioned his irate partner, "You'd better watch yourself. W.C. Fields is out playing his special brand of golf again."

Rapturous over his long drive, Fields strode purposefully across the two fairways.

"What's the matter with you? You crazy or something?"

Fields blithely smiled at the perplexed athlete, then with his apothegmic form of speech, commented slowly from the corner of his mouth:

"What's the matter, indeed . . . my dear jolthead . . . my diaphanous ninny . . . and mooncalf . . . . Have you never seen the game of Lateral Golf played before?"

*   *   *

There is a kind of great laughter that becomes immortal. Rabelais had it. He handed it down in sublime bales. He was accounted lewd, lascivious, and utterly no-good by millions of critics who did not know that, beneath his laughter, there lay philosophy, learning and moral teachings. His laughter endured.

Voltaire's laughter was greatly feared because it contained a high mockery. Men fear mockery as they do ridicule. They would destroy at once the sources of a criticism higher than their own.

Twain possessed laughter that rang like handsome brass bells over the temple of his Truth. The same with H.L. Mencken.

W.C. Fields, who was truly born to play the role of Falstaff, also possessed this magic gift of giving laughter to the world. He did this first through the universal language of pantomime.

Then came his sparkling dialogue which he began to sandwich
into his juggling act. Then his classic motion pictures followed.
Many of them he wrote. And these were so deeply imbued with
his humor and wit that it might be necessary to watch one of his
pictures a second time to comprehend some hidden meaning
through his words. He is one comedian who I believe could survive in television today without the aid of an audience laugh
track.

* * *

Now, more than three decades have passed since Fields was visited by the Man in the Bright Nightgown, the comedian's fan-
cied phrase for life's ultimate curtain. And his final gesture —
the wink he offered the nurses at Las Encinas Sanitarium in Pasadena — seems to have happened only a few weeks ago. But it
was Christmas Day of 1946.

Douglas R. Dodge, the physician who had attended Fields at
Las Encinas during the actor's final months at this drying-out
spot, where the comedian vainly endeavored to cut down on his
intake of hard liquor, signed the death certificate and filled in
the immediate cause as cirrhosis of the liver, "duration five years
due to chronic alcoholism — duration unknown."

It could not be entered then that, of all Fields' diseases, his
most transient malady was loneliness. Only close friends, not
medical practioners, were aware of this.

There was no autopsy, and the body of our modern-day Gri-
maldi was removed to Forest Lawn Memorial Park in Glendale
where it would remain entombed for two years and six months
in a brown marble-faced receptacle identified only as number
10319. Located in the center of a seven-high tier of crypts in
Forest Lawn's Sanctuary of Ascension, Fields' façade appeared
as a blank-faced joker in a stack of Death's playing cards.

Now that all this time has passed, gaps and errors in his portrait have been corrected; rectified, updated and retouched so
that the picture has become more representative of this explica-
ble man of comedy. Most — with the exception of three blind
spots, e.g.:

1. His date and place of birth.

2. Where his "body" lies.

3. Was the saying, "No man who hates dogs and children can be all bad," another creation of Uncle Claude?

First, the Immigration Department in Washington, D.C., shows record that on November 13, 1854, John Dukinfield, a British combmaker, and his son, James L. Dukinfield (Fields' father), arrived in New York.

At the historical library in Philadelphia at Old St. George's Methodist Church, there are records of a no-longer-existing church at Eighth and Cumberland streets, which attests that there on Sunday, May 18, 1879, James L. Dukinfield married Kate Felton, Fields' mother. So far, no extant records show that the comedian was baptized. If standard biographer Robert Lewis Taylor's statement in *W.C. Fields, His Follies and Fortunes* (Doubleday) is correct, that Fields was born April 9, 1879, this would make the comedian a bastard.

The U.S. Census Department's records show that on June 5, 1880, a census taker canvassed houses on Woodland Avenue east of 64th Street, Philadelphia. In one of them lived a J.L. Dukinfield, 40, a "hotelkeeper," and his wife Katie, 25. Listed as the third occupant of the house was Claude William Dukinfield, not by name, but as "an infant four-twelfths of a year old." This had to be W.C. Fields. The building was described as being two stories between 6318 and 6322 Woodland Avenue. The heretofore unknown address where Fields was born was 6320 Woodland Avenue. This is on the west side of town; therefore, as Taylor had written that Fields was born in the Germantown district of Philadelphia, this had to be incorrect.

Family tradition has it that Fields was born in a "hotel in Darby." Fields also told Fowler and me that he was born in Darby.

A further search of the Woodland Avenue history turned up that it once had been named Darby Road, thus the legend of "hotelkeeper" and "Darby." The building at 6320 was torn down, along with a larger two-story building, in 1924, and in their place the Benn Theater was errected. When the Benn sign was placed in the ground, a picture was taken which includes the house where Fields was born.

The birthdate of Fields — January 29, 1880 — holds up. He was born in wedlock and therefore, indeed, was not a bastard.

Neither the Historical Society of Pennsylvania nor the Presbyterian Historical Society of Philadelphia have birth records of a Claude William Dukinfield, whose name was spelled by his father, "Dukenfield." The older British spelling of the name is Dukinfield.

* * *

Second, it depresses me when a purported W.C. Fields buff takes over a television talk show, his portfolio being a sheet of the comedian's personal stationery with a letter addressed to another person. After reciting several of Fields' sayings, he inevitably comes up with the overquoted homily, referring to the headstone of Fields' grave in the City of Brotherly Love: "All things considered, I'd rather be in Philadelphia." This indicates that the man is either misinformed, or a downright fraud.

The genesis of this aphorism was in 1937 when a representative of *Vanity Fair Magazine* inquired of several motion picture stars what they thought might be an appropriate inscription on their tombstones.

This is what happened to Fields' body:

Following about two and a half years of foot-dragging by all concerned, Uncle Claude was eventually allowed his wish to be cremated. It took a superior court decision to allow same. On November 19, 1948, his cremation was handed down by Los Angeles Superior Judge William R. McKay, so ordered by Superior Judge Harold B. Jeffery, and carried out by Fields' estate executrix and former secretary Mrs. Magda Michael. All this legal dallying might point out that it is often more difficult to get out of this world than it is to enter it.

Fields' body was taken from crypt 10319 on June 3, 1949, and Bud Pickett, in charge of these final expeditions of the flesh, transformed the body to ashes.

Permanent residence of Fields' remains are now in niche 20895, *Columbarium of Nativity, The Great Mausoleum, For-*

est Lawn Memorial Park, Glendale, California. I do not know
the zip code number.

Seven niches surround Uncle Claude's generous gold-breasted
pleasance. One to the south of his small temple is that of a Captain Lloyd A. Smith, lawyer. And most are aware of how much
the comedian abhorred attorneys. Now he adjoins one throughout eternity. Oddly enough, directly on the opposite side is a receptacle containing the ashes of a Charlotte Griffing, Charlotte
being a variant Spanish spelling of Carlotta, the same name as
Carlotta Monti, the beautiful young lady who gave so much of
her time and attention to make the final years of Uncle Claude's
illness bearble.

* * *

Last, where did the saying, "No man who hates dogs and children can be all bad," come from? At one time or another, famous comedians have been known to borrow irresistibly fine
lines from others. This was prime in the case of W.C. My
adopted uncle, H. Allen Smith, was responsible for tracking
down this quote to the bitter end:

In the late 1930s, Uncle Claude was given a testimonial dinner
at Dave Chasen's restaurant. The speeches began while the
guests were either drinking or having dessert. The talks were
several, and long. The guests' bladders began straining, but they
had to stick to the decorum of politeness and remain in their
seats. Next-to-the last speaker was Georgie Jessel. Smiles of the
invited became less evident. Now they were afraid to laugh. At
long last Leo Rosten was introduced. Guests let their belts out a
few notches, hoping to grit it through. Rosten said but one thing,'
"No man who hates dogs and children can be all bad," then sat
down. Listeners were so elated, they rose to their feet as one, offered Rosten a cheer, then scurried off to relieve themselves.

H. Allen, for several years, was under the impression that this
sterling utterance belonged to Rosten and let the world know
about it in *Lost in the Horse Latitudes.* But, sometime later,
Smith received a letter from Cedric Worth, a former New York
newspaperman who, as of 1976, lived in Claremont, California.
In it was attached an article from the November 1937 issue of

Harper's Magazine. The piece had to do with the reporting of a 1930 New York cocktail party where a man named Gastonbury "monopolized the conversation with an eloquent attack on dogs," Allen wrote. "When the party was ending, Mr. Worth found himself in the elevator with several other guests, including Mr. Byron Darnton of the *New York Times*. In that elevator this Mr. Byron Darnton uttered a remark which Mr. Worth promptly wrote down: 'No man who hates dogs and children can be all bad.' "

The author of *Low Man on a Totem Pole, Life in a Putty Knife Factory, Rhubarb, To Hell in a Handbasket, Waikiki Beachnik*, and thirty-three other books of humor, further pointed out that Darnton had made his electrifying observation "in the elevator at 30 Fifth Avenue (corner of Tenth), at approximately the sixth floor, in the summer of 1930."

Darnton was killed under air attack off the coast of New Guinea during World War II, and Smith wrote to Cedric Worth that he thought Darnton would be happy at finally having been given recognition for this lasting line.

* * *

Some time in the vicinity of the first half of the 1940s W.C. Fields fell into an agrument with the landlord of his DeMille Drive home. "The scoundrel wanted to up the ante on the rent," he complained, "but he wouldn't paint the premises." The comedian packed and took up residence in a small stuccoed bungalow at Las Encinas. There he waited for the coming of the Man in the Bright Nightgown.

A month before W.C. left us, while retail stores and advertisers were beginning their commercial attack on behalf of the holiday of Christmas, Pop and I visited him where he had openly established a bar. Uncle Claude's doctors were against this but considered that if he quit completely now, he would surely die immediately. "They could have saved their breath," Fields snorted. "It's like warning a madam to start knocking sex."

He asked if we would care for a "little token of my esteem" to which Fowler said, "I'd prefer a glass of milk if you don't mind — that is, if you have any in the house."

"Mind?" he snorted again. "Have you no sense of decency? Milk!"

"Tell me," Fowler asked, "when did you last have a drink of milk?"

"An hour before I left my dear mother," he answered.

There was no milk to be had in the bungalow, so Fowler settled for a glass of soda water, and Fields for some ginger ale. I selfishly mixed myself a bourbon highball. Uncle Claude stared longingly at the mixture. Incredible as it may sound, Fields had had nothing stronger to drink than ginger ale for the past month. There were bottles and decanters about the premises, however, and W.C. kept eyeing these necessities with the manner and mood of a vicious dog in the manger.

A nurse appeared, took Fields' temperature, pulse and respiration rate, then, departing, turned on the radio and there came floating over it a Noël chorale. "Turn it off! Cease!" shouted the man whose aversion to holidays was equal to his dislike of the film capital. "I'll smash the damned radio and its illegitimate fugue!" Then he added menacingly, "I'm changing my will. Nobody who observes Christmas will be mentioned in my last testament. Not a farthing for them, man or boy!"

An earlier Christmas, however, Uncle Claude had made a cartoon of himself dressed as Santa Claus and sent it to us as a postcard. I gave this to my actor friend Michael Cole. And the previous Christmas to that, W.C. had us delivered a large and very thick leather-bound book titled, *Places Where I Am Not Wanted*, by W.C. Fields. Upon opening it, we found it was the Los Angeles phone directory.

For a while this day, Uncle Claude chewed a toothpick, a technique he claimed was of help in curing him of the cigarette habit, then he said deliberately: "I used to believe in Christmas until I was eight years old. While carrying ice in Philadelphia, I had saved several pennies and nickels to purchase my dear mother a clothes boiler for Christmas . . . the kind with a copper bottom. I hid the coins in a mason jar in the basement. One black day I caught my father stealing my money. Beginning then, I have remembered nobody on Christmas, and I want nobody to remember me, either."

"Is that the real reason you hate Christmas?" Fowler asked. "You're always faking stories to cover yourself when someone hits on a sore spot."

Uncle Claude sat silent for a few moments, studying the two of us. With his spindly legs and portly dropped goiter stomach, he resembled a Micawber illustration from the page of *David Copperfield*. He waved his small, shapely hands. Perhaps he had the most graceful hands in the world. He had been that great juggler, but now an arthritic condition had hampered his swift fingers. "You're a nosy bastard," he said.

"I wouldn't discuss noses," said Fowler. "Not when yours is, shall we say, the beak of the century."

"Don't make fun of a man's affliction," said Uncle Claude," selecting another toothpick with the grace of a conductor about to summon his orchestra to attention. "All you newspapermen are nosy. A pack of poltroons who laugh at heartaches. A murder sends them cheering to the nearest saloon. Scandal makes them glow all over. And you, you supposedly tough Hearst reporter, and this whippersnapper son of yours. You all love Christmas." He ceremoniously placed the wooden stick in the center of his mouth.

"At least," Fields muttered, "they don't serve the tainted day here with snow. Sleigh bells give me double nausea."

He arose and retreated to the shade, carrying his wrought-iron garden chair. "All right," he said. "I suppose you'll go blatting to all the world about it, but I'm going to tell you why I eschew Christmas and other silly holidays. It's because those days point up a thing called loneliness. An actor on the road — as I was for so long — finds himself all alone on days when everyone else has friends and companionship. It's not so good to be in Australia, or in Scotland, or in South Africa, as I was on tour, all alone on a Christmas Day, and to see and hear a lot of happy strangers welcoming that two-faced merriment-monger Santa Claus, who passes you by.

"We're all lonely enough as it is. By God, I was *born* lonely."

Now Fields slowly started rocking on his stationary chair and reached into his white bathrobe pocket to check that he still had a few thousand dollars there. He called it his "Getaway money."

He had one eye on the gin bottle atop his portable bar constructed from a red, four-wheeled child's wagon.

"But Christmas and New Year's and Thanksgiving and all the rest," he went on, "make me even more lonely. So I observe only one day — April First. That's my day. It's Adam's birthday, too. If I remember correctly, the Holy Writ relates that Adam was created on April First. It explains a lot of things, especially politics and psychoanalysis."

Uncle Claude's gaze returned to the bottle of gin. "I've just reached a momentous decision," he announced. "I've either got to take a drink or shoot all the Santa Clauses infesting the boulevards." He made himself a triple martini. "It may interest you to know," he added, after a few sips, "that tomorrow I am removing both your names from my will. It was a hefty bequest, too. Oh, well, if you prefer mistletoe . . ."

The clouds had darkened, threatening rain. Following yet another refill of his glass, Fields began to feel mellow, then drowsy and smiling as the full-bellied sky began to relinquish a light rain. He started to tap the table where his empty glass rested. His swollen fingers made light staccato beats on the mahogany top. They tapped as though in concert with the pitter-patter of the raindrops beating on the roof. His eyes were slowly closing as he muttered, "If it's true everybody loves a winner, we ought to be crazy about Death." Then he fell off to sleep and Pop and I quitely departed.

Although we spoke several times with him on the telephone following the visit, this would be the last time we would ever see W.C. Fields.

* * *

The day after Uncle Claude's death, my father and I gathered with some of the comedian's confreres at Dave Chasen's restaurant. We sat near the portrait artist John Decker had painted of Fields in appropriate black mourning garb of Queen Victoria. I recall when Uncle Claude had viewed the painting for the first time. He shouted in protest, "Sabbotage! Decker has kicked history in the groin!" Then he hastily excused himself, saying he had to meet with a friend who had gotten into some trouble with a female. In his book, *Minutes of the Last Meeting* (Viking), Fowler quoted Fields as saying, "The impulsive chappie is too vain to wear glasses. Not long ago a lady in a bathing suit struck his fancy. He did not know that the little chickadee had just been paroled from a beauty clinic after a facelift and reducing job, and mistook her for eighteen." Fowler recalled his homily of that day. Fields had said, "Ah, how often we stick out our chins and get hit on the button. Our pal went to bed with Little Red Riding Hood and woke up with her grandmother. Silly boy."

At the wake, beside my father and myself, were Billy Grady, director Eddie Sutherland, Ben Hecht, Grantland Rice and Greg LaCava. Mistaking our laughter for disrespectful revelry, an elderly female tourist said, "How can you be so disrespectful of the dead?"

Fowler smiled at her and said, "Madam, your only concern is that you, too, have a not-too-distant appointment with the Black Master. Anyway," he added, "we here reserve our expressions of sorrow in the privacy of our own homes."

Fowler then went to the telephone where he called the *Hollywood Reporter* to take out a full-page ad:

> *The most prejudiced and honest and beloved figure of our so-called "colony" went away on a day that he pretended to abhor — Christmas. We loved him, and — peculiarly enough — he loved us. To the most authentic humorist since Mark Twain, to the greatest heart that has beaten since the middle ages — W.C. Fields, our friend.*

That Christmas Day Fields' obituary became my first front-page by-line in the *Los Angeles Examiner*.

On Sunday, December 29, Mrs. Harriet Veronica Fields, who had married W.C. Fields in San Francisco April 10, 1900,° and who had been separated from the comedian for about forty years, traveled to Forest Lawn Cemetery to participate in the morbid ritual of choosing a casket and planning private services.

°Marriage records had been destroyed in that city 's great earthquake and fire of 1906.

Uncle Claude

Driving Mrs. Fields to the cemetery was her only son, W. Claude Fields, Jr., who, until his death February 16, 1971, was an attorney.°

Mrs. Fields set the private services to be conducted Thursday, January 2, 1947, at Forest Lawn's Sanctuary of Ascension in the Great Mausoleum where the Presbyterian Reverend Ross Schaffer would officiate. It was a middle ground religious consideration because Hattie was a practicing Catholic, and Uncle Claude was an avowed athiest.

When the boy porched the newspaper the following morning, the story below a headline reading FIELDS ESTATE BATTLE LOOMS, hinted that relatives and friends were dividing camps, regrouping to launch separate court skirmishes over Fields' holdings. It also said that "a request of the bulbous-nosed wit asking that he be cremated will not be honored." Announcement to this effect came from attorney George A. Bisbee. Acting for Fields' widow and son, he said, "The services will be held Thursday, January 2, in the Church of the Recessional at 11:30 A.M." He added that "both Mr. Fields' widow and his son are opposed to cremation. In deference to them, the body will be placed in the mausoleum. Only intimate friends are requested to attend." Earlier that day, however, Fields' son had met with Fowler at the latter's home. My father warned him that there would be several of Uncle Claude's firends who would come to the services even if they were private. Therefore, young Fields adhered to Pop's suggestion and permitted services to be held in a location other than that of the private ceremonies.

The impending court battle over Fields' estate was expected to revolve around the fact that he was reported to have willed the bulk of it to founding an orphanage.

My father and I were the first to arrive at the Church of the Recessional on Thursday. I was not only attending the funeral of a friend, but was also covering it for the *Examiner*.

° It is curious to note that W.C. Fields, who averaged about two quarts of hard liquor a day during his prime toping epoch lived to be sixty-six years and eleven months, while his totally abstemious son lived only sixty-six years and seven months.

Then came Jack Dempsey, who had lived only a half block from the comedian with the Jekyll-Hyde personality. There were also Leo McCarey, John Decker, referee Abe Roth, Earl Carroll, Billy Grady and director Eddie Cline. Approximately fifty in all showed up for the first performance. Carlotta Monti was beside the comedian's flower-banked casket, sitting with her father, sister and two nieces.

The service commenced with an electric organ intoning Bach's *Jesu, Joy of Man's Desiring,* which lasted eight minutes, twice as long as the ceremony with its single speaker. He was ventriloquist Edgar Bergen, who eulogized the trouper. And for a man who demanded no funeral ceremony at all, W.C. Fields ended up with *three.*

At the first, Bergen said:

"He requested his friends not to weep in mourning for him. Of the five hundred religions in the world he had his own, and he hoped that his friends would understand his requests. It seems wrong not to pray for a man who gave such happiness to the world. But this was the way he wanted it. Bill knew life, and knew that laughter was the way to live it. We knew that happiness depended on disposition, not position. We simply say farewell."

The second service, the private one inside the Great Mausoleum, was attended only by widow Hattie, son W. Claude, and the comedian's brother and sister, Walter, and Mrs. Adel C. Smith, as the Reverend Ross Schaffer officiated.

Mrs. Fields had ordered that Carlotta Monti not be allowed in the Sanctuary of Ascension until Uncle Calude's sarcophagus had been slid into his crypt and the brown marble slab with two iron-headed bolts was cemented and sealed.

As she waited to enter the mausoleum, the captivating thirty-nine-year-old Carlotta, standing next to her Hollywood spiritualist friend Mae Taylor, talked with newsmen — myself included. "I am sorry for them. When they went in there my watch stopped," she said.

Then Carlotta said she had contacted Fields through the Reverend Mrs. Taylor. "Whoodie' told me last night to get a front seat at the three-ring circus. That is the reason I came."

"Whoodie" was her pet name for Fields.

Later, when the family emerged from this expensive hall of the dead, Carlotta said her watch had started working again. Since Fields' death a week earlier, Carlotta had mentioned that her watch, a present from the comedian, had behaved peculiarly.

After the Fields family had departed, Carlotta and her friends entered. The heart of white chrysanthemums and scarlet roses stood on an easel in front of Fields' unmarked hole in the wall. Carlotta had sent it. After spiritualist Taylor concluded her ceremony, Carlotta took three roses from the heart and exited, saying, "I'm going to keep on communicating with Whoodie."

As Carlotta and friends departed the cold marbled hall, they passed a hoary, unshaven gentleman bowed by the weight of time. His eyes were hollowed from seasons of disappointment. A newspaper stuck out of his frayed overcoat pocket. His collar and cuffs were scruffy. "Where is Mr. Fields' tomb?" he inquired of a custodian. "I knew him for thirty-five years in vaudeville first. Duffy and Sweeney . . . "

The attendant said he could not rightly say which crypt Fields' body was in, as it was unmarked.

The old man's eyes narrowed, seeming to fill with reminiscence. He turned to go. Talking to himself, a classic symptom of dotage, he mumbled, "Well, I guess it was all right that I just came here anyway."

* * *

In the long-gone mid-1930s, a discerning critic wrote of this man: "to believe that W.C. Fields was merely a funny man is to hold the opinion that *Huckleberry Finn* is a book for children."

7

Postmortem

Because it was the most controversial will, taking the longest time of a star in the entertainment world to probate, it is of historical interest for W.C. Fields' Last Testament to be registered here, one reason being that the document no longer exists. Also significant to record are brief notations of the probate highlights which have not heretofore been published.

In researching the Fields probate trial, it was necessary to study four huge volumes of court data. Lying on their sides, they reached about two feet in height and contained nearly one million words.

Added to the importance of touching on these highlights is that they might never again be examined. The explanation? When I returned at a later date to refer to these records, I was told the first two volumes were missing. They were the most important. The first contained the will. The second held the meat of the trial proceedings.

I issued a complaint regarding the missing files, but it didn't seem to disturb the attendant. He informed me that Rudolph Valentino's records had disappeared in the same manner. Luckily I had taped what I considered to be the most important papers and later transcribed them.

From the time Magda Michael filed the Fields will for probate on December 30, 1946, until she was discharged as executrix and made trustee to the estate on April 20, 1954, an extraordinary eight years, three months and twenty-two days had passed during which time the document was under deliberation.

Uncle Claude, who would have been one hundred years old in 1980, probably would have been amused at the confusion he had instigated.

With the exception of paragraph "FOURTH, b.," whose words seemed to leap from the document's bosom, the will appeared without loopholes, with its legal jargon covering all bases. FOURTH, b. read in part:

"Upon the death of my said brother Walter Dukenfield and my said sister, Adel C. Smith and the said Carlotta Monti (Montejo), I direct that my executors procure the organization of a membership or other approved corporation under the name of the W.C. FIELDS COLLEGE for orphan white boys and girls, where no religion of any sort is to be preached . . ."

Until his death, only two persons saw the will itself. They were Magda Michael and Gene Fowler. The two witnesses signing the miniment, Alanson William Edwards and Eldon Reed Frye of Kansas City, only saw the final page which they signed. This page did not contain any directives of the will itself.

Fields left the will unchanged for the final three years and eight months of his life, but gleefully continued to rearrange, take out and add names to a codicil in the form of a separate memorandum of instructions which was not presented in probate court until May 15, 1952, more than five years after W.C.'s demise. The reason for this was that legatees and those purported to be legatees lodged so many claims, it took this long to get to the codicil.

Following a period of pretending to be casual about paragraph FOURTH, b., Fowler made it a point to speak to Fields about the subject, which the author thought might eventually cast a gloom over the comedian's memory in years to come. One weekend early in 1943 I drove Pop and Gregory LaCava to Saboba Hot Springs, another Southern California spa where the aging juggler was taking one of his drying-out sabbaticals.

With an expression of perplexity ennobling his features Fields said, "I'd like to remember you good lads in my will with a chunk of dough, but you'd only give it away to your friends." Then he grimaced, as though from a twinge of the gout. "It's not your friends who destroy you, it's your friends' friends." He im-

ported a toothpick from the right to the left side of his mouth,
which served as a notice that he had something momentous to
say. "The necessity of keeping documents indicates we are a race
of liars and cheats." In *Minutes of the Last Meeting*, Fowler
quoted Fields:

> *"Why, if I knew the day and the hour the Man in the
> Bright Nightgown was coming to get me, I'd put all my
> dough into bills of large denominations, stand beside it
> on a balcony, and summon my dear relatives to watch
> me as I tore it into little pieces and strewed it like con-
> fetti to the winds."*

Fowler warned Fields that excluding all other races from his institution would be a mistake. "Such a narrow gesture will make
you misunderstood and much disliked."

"I've always been misunderstood," Fields rasped. "Besides,
did you ever hear of a corpse complaining of unpopularity?"

When the word "white" was discovered by reporters in the
will's paragraph FOURTH, b., Fowler explained the apparent
show of race prejudice in this manner:

> *If I were to apologize for W.C. Fields, or for any other
> member of our group for that matter, or attempt to jus-
> tify his or their wayward actions, their shades would cry
> out with indignation. False praise is the province of the
> epitaph-maker and is best done with a chisel on a stone
> seldom visited.*

Columnist James Smart of the *Philadelphia Evening Bulletin* is,
in my opinion, the authority on W.C. Fields' boyhood in that
city. Through the years he has ferreted out many unknown facts
about the comedian. Regarding the Fields College for white
boys and girls clause, Smart wrote to me:

> *The obvious afterthought in Fields' will about a W.C.
> Fields College for orphan white boys and girls, with no
> religion preached, must have been influenced by Girard
> College in Philadelphia. Stephen Girard, a wealthy mer-*

chant, established his college for poor, white orphan boys, and specified that no cleric might ever set foot inside the school. Girard College opened about thirty years before Fields' birth, and was one of the best-known institutions in the city when Fields was a boy. His neighborhood was the kind of working-class section from which many Girard College boys came. He may have known some of them. Was this odd bequest an attempt by Fields to establish himself as a proper Philadelphian after all those years of boozy exile? [In the past decade, Negro groups fought a long legal battle and succeeded in cracking the white-only aspect of the Girard will. The blacks are in, although the rich, the female and religious are still excluded.]

The will follows, along with bracketed information after each paragraph when necessary for clarification:

* * *

LAST WILL AND TESTAMENT OF
WILLIAM C. FIELDS

I, William C. Fields, also known as W.C. Fields, also known as BILL FIELDS, residing at 2015 DeMille Drive, Los Angeles, do hereby make, publish and declare this to be my Last Will and Testament, hereby revoking all prior Wills and Codicils heretofore made by me.

FIRST: I direct my executors hereinafter named to pay all my lawful debts and funeral expenses as soon after my death as is convenient.

SECOND: I direct my executors immediately upon the certificate of my death being signed to have my body placed in an inexpensive coffin and taken to a cemetery and cremated, and since I do not wish to cause my friends undue inconvenience or expense I direct my executors not to have any funeral or other ceremony or to permit anyone to view my remains, except as is necessary to furnish satisfactory proof of my death.

[Fields wanted an inexpensive coffin and as cheap a funeral as possible. He despised morticians as sedulously as he hated physicians, and he wanted them to make as little profit from his dissolution as possible.]

THIRD: I bequeth the following sums of money and property to the persons hereinafter named.

1. To Hattie Fields and W. Claude Fields, now residing at 123½ North Gale Drive, Beverly Hills, California, the sum of Twenty Thousand Dollars to be divided equally.

[When Fields offered his will for Fowler to read, he confided, "I'm worried about Hattie and W. Claude Fields. They'll give me trouble. I think if I leave twenty Gs between them, that'll be all right." He added, "I think Hattie raised young Fields to become an attorney just so they might take me one day."]

2. To Ann Ruth Fields now residing at 123½ North Gale Drive, Beverly Hills, California, Five Thousand Dollars.

[This was W. Claude Fields, Jr.'s wife.]

3. To Carlotta Montejo, known as Carlotta Monti and Ramona Rey, Twenty-Five Dollars per week until Twenty-Five Thousand Dollars has been paid. I ask the security First National Bank to set aside this amount. Should said Carlotta Monti (Montejo) die before the said Twenty-Five Thousand Dollars had been paid, the residue to revert to my estate.

[Carlotta was also to receive an additional twenty-five dollars weekly from paragraph FOURTH, a., as it was the plan, which would raise the amount to a fifty-dollar weekly payment.]

4. To my sister, Adel C. Smith (née Dukenfield) now residing in New Jersey, the sum of Five Thousand Dollars, said amount to be in addition to the provisions hereinafter made in the Fourth paragraph hereof.

[Unclde Claude liked Adel. "She never asked me for money" he told Fowler. "Because of this, I made it a point to send her some from time to time. We corresponded after and she and Walter looked after my interests in the East.]

5. To my brother, Walter Dukenfield, also known as Walter Fields, now residing at Waterford Works, New Jersey, the sum of Five Thousand Dollars, said amount to

be in addition to the provision hereinafter made in the Fourth paragraph hereof.

[In the comedian's early days as a stage juggler, Walter accompanied him as his manager. In later years, however, during the *Ziegfeld Follies* and *Earl Carroll's Vanities* days, Walter was replaced by Billy Grady. Grady was a more knowledgeable man regarding the stage and vaudeville and had far stronger theatrical connections.]

6. To Maud Fendick, now residing at 106 Brookside Place, New Rochelle, N.Y., the sum of Five Thousand Dollars.

[Maud had been an unpublicized lifelong friend.]

7. To Mabel Roach, a lifelong friend, now residing at 1931 Independence Avenue, Philadelphia, the sum of Two Thousand Dollars.

[Fields always took good financial care of his women friends.]

8. To Charles Beyer, my friend and manager, now residing at 6746 Wedgewood Place, Whitley Heights, Hollywood, California, the sum of Five Thousand Dollars.

[Beyer was Fields' last manager, replacing Billy Grady following a near knockdown-drag-out fight regarding $50,-000 Grady claimed the comedian owed him in commissions.]

9. To Adele Vallery Clines, my faithful housekeeper, now residing at 2227 West 26th Place, Los Angeles, the sum of Two Thousand Five Hundred Dollars.

[Fields had offered to give Mrs. Clines money to purchase a lot and build a home. She refused. He then made her a loan at a straight minimum of one percent interest over a comfortable period.]

10. To Magda Michael, my secretary and adviser, Two Thousand Five Hundred Dollars.

11. To Dick Howard, son of Neel Howard, One Thousand Dollars.

12. To Mabel Clapsadle of the Hollywood and Cahuenga Branch of the Security First National Bank of Los Angeles the sum of Two Thousand Dollars.

[Mabel Clapsadle was a name Fields fell in love with.]

13. To Herschel Crockett, now associated with Charles Beyer the sum of Five Hundred Dollars.

14. To my brother, LeRoy Russell Dukenfield, last known address, Philadelphia, Pennsylvania, the sum of Five Hundred Dollars.

15. To my sister, Elsie May, last known address, Penns Grove, New Jersey, the sum of Five Hundred Dollars.

16. To my executors hereinafter named in trust for delivery to the persons mentioned in a separate memorandum of instructions which will be found in my safe or safety deposit box, various articles of furniture and personal effects too numerous to describe herein.

FOURTH: All the rest, residue and remainder of my property, of every nature and description and wheresoever the same may be situated, whether acquired before or after the execution of this will, or any codicils thereto, I give, devise and bequeath to my executors, hereinafter named, in trust, to have and to hold the same during the lifetime of my brother, Walter Dukenfield, also known as Walter Fields, and to my sister, Adel C. Smith and Carlotta Monti, also known as Ramona Rey, to and for the uses and purposes following:
To collect and receive the rents, issues, income and profit of so much thereof as shall be real property, and to invest and keep invested, so much thereof as shall be personal property, with the power to call in and change the investment, or investments, thereof, from time-to-time, and to collect and receive the income and profits therefrom, and after paying therefrom all lawful debts and expenses pertaining thereto,

(a) To pay to my brother, WALTER DUKENFIELD, also known as WALTER FIELDS, during his natural life, the sum of Seventy Five Dollars Weekly, and to my sister, ADEL C. SMITH, during her natural life, the sum of Twenty Five Dollars, and to CARLOTTA MONTI, also known as RAMONA REY, during her natural life, the sum of Twenty Five Dollars weekly, said payments to commence as of the date of my death.

(b) Upon the death of my said brother, Walter Dukenfield and my said sister, Adel C. Smith and the said Carlotta Monti (Montejo), I direct that my executors procure the organization of a membership or other approved corporation under the name of the W.C. FIELDS COLLEGE for orphan white boys and girls, where no religion of any sort is to be preached. Harmony is the purpose of this thought. It is my desire the college will be built in California in Los Angeles County.

(c) I wish to disinherit anyone who in any way tries to confuse or break this will or who contributes in any way to break this will.

(d) I hereby nominate, constitute and appoint Magda Michael to be the executor of this, my last will and testament.

I also wish to bequeath to my friend, George Moran, formerly of Moran and Mack, the sum of One Thousand Dollars.

[As an afterthought, Fields tacked this paragraph on the end of his will because he had been informed that Moran, a member of vaudeville's team of the Two Black Crows, was ailing and nearly destitute.]

IN WITNESS WHEREOF, I have hereunto set my hand this *28th* [*holo*] day of *April* [*holo*], 1943.

Signature [holo]
William C. Fields
Testator

The following abbreviated highlights of the eight-year court probate proceedings should offer one an insight into the scope of its intricacies, deviousness, circuitous, delaying, tricky and dishonest ways as the plagued mind of a superior court administrator attempted to be as fair as Solomon with his justice.

Notices of filing and of hearing of the petition for determination of heirship number 264,050, through John W. Preston and John W. Preston, Jr., as attorneys for Walter Fields and Adel C. Smith were served to the following on January 28, 1949:

Charles Beyer, Dave Chasen, Adele Vallery Clines, Frank Clines, Mabel Clapsadle, Herschel Crockett, Elsie May Cunningham, Leroy Russell Dukenfield, Adel C. Smith and Walter Dukenfield, Ann Ruth Fields, Harriet V. Fields, W. Claude Fields, Jr., Maud Fendick, Gene Fowler, Dick Howard, Bob Howard, Gregory LaCava, Magda Michael, William R.F. Morris, Carlotta Montejo (Carlotta Monti and Ramona Rey), George Moran, Geraldine Bunnell, Mabel Roach, and Security First National Bank of Los Angeles, P.O. Box 2097, Terminal Annex, L.A.

After notice of filing was served to the aforementioned, and hearing for determination of heirship was set for March 16 under Sections 1080-2 Probate Code, the following occurred to set the proceedings back to May 2:

Widow Harriet sued for half a million dollars that she claimed the comedian had given away. She named names. New ones were Mildred L. Blackburn, Fay Adler and Grace George. . . . Fields' cremation was ordered on November 19, 1948. . . . A William Rexford Fields Morris filed a request claiming he was the illegitimate son of Fields (this was filed on January 25, 1949, followed on April 26 with letters purported to be in Fields' handwriting to Mrs. Rose Holden who claimed to have raised Morris). But a Bessie Chatterton Poole, who died during Prohibition days following a brawl in a New York speakeasy, Club Chez Florence, was claimed to be his mother. Cause of her death was attributed to alcoholism.

The hearings were to begin on the morning of May 2, but no open courts were found until about noon. This was the court of William R. McKay on the twelfth floor of the Hall of Records, an ancient, yellow-tiled building lacking air conditioning.

The case languished as an army of lawyers representing various litigants disappeared into several anterooms to confer with their clients.

Principals in the case would have been fine models for the caricaturist Daumier. They were studies of false remorse and impatience. Widow Harriet sat hiding her face from photographers with a folder. Carlotta showed little concern. She was overheard to say, "Spies," while the thirty-one-year-old Morris pretended to busy himself in a magazine. Magda Michael, who had suddenly loomed as Fields' executrix, politely stepped aside for photographers.

Following a recess for lunch, the first item on the agenda was for Judge McKay to hear a lengthy deposition by Mrs. Rose Holden, read by Morris' attorney, Louis Thomsen. In the deposition, Mrs. Holden claimed to have raised Morris from the time he was one month old, and that Fields and Bessie Pool Chatterton were Morris' parents. The deposition added that the infant was brought to Mrs. Holden to raise so the alleged parents might return on the road with the Ziegfeld Follies.

Before the case went to court, the Fields will was adjudged by experts to be valued at $800,000. This turned out to be an accurate estimate; the estate was finally valued at $771,428.°

Fields' sister Adel introduced in evidence on May 6, 1949, a letter he had written to her in 1941 while he was a patient in the Pasadena sanitarium when he feared he might be dying. It directed her to come at once to California "in case I should kick the [proverbial] bucket."

It continued:

> *If anyone asks you if you know Claude and Hattie, or if I was ever married, tell them you have heard of them, and you believe you have seen them once or twice, but you do not know of any marriage because I never mentioned it to you, which I didn't.*
>
> *Be smart and don't talk too much.*
>
> *The only reason they are out here is in case anything happens to me.*
>
> *When I was in the sanitarium, they were on my tail every minute, and ready to pounce on any money I might leave.*
>
> *They act like a couple of vultures, and the sanitarium would never let them in . . . .*

On the stand, fighting for her widow's share of the will (which in

---

° In these inflationary days, this amount would more likely represent $10 million.

California under the community property law is 50 percent), was Harriet. Having testified she had not lived with Fields as husband and wife since 1904 or 1905, she revealed she had been aware that W.C. was "romancing" with a chorus girl in his Broadway show while she was working as a waitress to support herself and their thirteen-year-old son, Claude. The chorus girl, said to be Bessie Poole, gave birth to young Morris in 1917. Letters from Hattie indicated that Fields was paying her $30 a week during those hard times.

In 1932, Fields answered one of Harriet's letters:

> *I note the derogatory rumors concerning my use of alcoholic stimulant and lavish living. It is the penalty of greatness . . . .*
>
> *I've made good as far as you are concerned as long as I have known you. I've never failed you with the bacon and all the money . . . .*

Another time, when Hattie wrote, "We've gone through a lifetime doing nothing for each other," Fields indignantly replied:

> *Sixty smackers a week for some forty years: $124,800 I've paid you. You consider it "nothing." Hi, he! Surprises never cease.*

* * *

Oddly, her letters were introduced by Fields' brother and sister to show that W.C. was making regular payments to his wife, and therefore she was not entitled to her widow's share.

During the court hearing on May 12, Carlotta Monti sprang up to insist that Judge McKay listen to a few things she wished to put on record regarding W.C.'s widow and son. Carlotta said mainly that she was upset about the funeral. "Mr. Fields was an important man, and he had his own ideas about a funeral. He wanted his friends, like Gene Fowler, Dave Chasen, and fellows he used to play golf with, to be his pallbearers.

"Instead of that, he had some cadaverous looking characters carry his coffin!"

She added that, because of her frugality, W.C.'s estate in-

creased considerably in worth. Carlotta ended her testimony by
assuring Judge McKay that she only wanted what Fields had
willed her, a fifty-dollar weekly income from trust.

In previous testimony an accountant, Thomas H. Morgan,
hired by Mrs. Fields, had challenged the amount Fields had had
in nine bank accounts previous to June 9, 1927. Executrix Michael had earlier listed a total of $356,107.47, which had been in
twenty-three bank accounts from 1903 until Fields' death in
1946. In the end, this put to rest the rumor that many of the comedian's bank accounts would never be found. He was fastidious
about his bookkeeping.°

Following a brief period, Magda Michael was on the stand to
identify the little black book in which Fields kept his accounts.
Judge McKay declared a recess until July 7.

The trial had hardly been adjourned when Fields' widow's at-
torny Ernest Tolin handed Carlotta a summons demanding an
accounting of $100,000 suppposedly given her by Fields and
claimed by the widow as community property.

The purpose of the recess was to allow attorneys to prepare
and file briefs on the essential points at issue:

1. when Fields took up legal California residence, bear-
   ing on the widow's right to half the estate's community
   property;

2. if Fields had made a formal financial support agree-
   ment with Hattie;

3. whether Morris was the illegitimate son of W.C., enti-
   tling him to one third of the comedian's estate.

When the court reconvened on July 7, Judge McKay ruled
that Fields had been a legal California resident since 1927,† that
Mrs. Fields was entitled to a community property settlement

°On one occasion, Fields claimed he had $10,000 in the Bank of Berlin,
"just in case that son-of-a-bitch Hitler *wins!*"

† Established by the date on his California auto club membership.

precluding all of his earnings prior to 1927, and that Morris was not the comedian's illegitimate son.

This sounded cut-and-dried, the end of all the legal arguments. But it wasn't, not by a truckload of milestones. Carlotta said she wanted parital distribution of the estate so she might start receiving the $25 a week W.C. had willed her. Widow Harriet wanted the $100,000 allegedly given Carlotta. Executrix Michael asked that $17,500 be paid her from the will for "extraordinary fees." She added that she had learned a new claim might be filed against the estate by a blind Chicago woman, Mrs. Edith Williams, who was saying she had been Fields' wife.

On November 16, McKay ordered that Hattie be paid half the monies kept in banks outside California. The full amount totaled $128,000. On September 28, McKay had ordered that Carlotta receive $3,400 in partial payment.

Coming into the Christmas season, on December 14, McKay also killed the will's plan for setting up a W.C. Fields College for white boys and girls, stating that "Mr. Fields in his lifetime could have discriminated against other races, but he can not in death . . ."

McKay ruled that three persons would be paid an income for the remainder of their lives. They were brother Walter ($75 a week), sister Adel ($60 a week) and Carlotta ($25 a week). By this time, the estate's value was drastically diminishing now estimated to be worth about a half-million dollars.

And, speaking of milestones, one had finally been reached on May 23, despite objections made by counsel representing executrix Magda Michael. McKay had directed that Hattie receive a $100,000 payment. He also ordered Mrs. Michael to pay Carlotta $3,850 on account of her bequests. Another $11,550 was ordered paid to Walter, and $9,240 to Adel.

Mrs. Michael's attorney, Leo L. Schaumer, declared that the court had not taken into account the share of taxes which the heirs should pay in proportion to their shares of the estate. He added that the estate, mostly in cash and negotiable securities, had further dwindled to $464,501.

McKay, on June 20, also ordered that a group of legatees be awarded one half of the sums bequested to them. They were:

W. Claude Fields, Jr., $5,000, and his wife, Ruth, $2,500

Maude Fendick, friend, $2,500

Mrs. Magda Michael, secretary, $1,250

Mabel Roach, friend, $1,000

Charles Beyer, manager and agent, $2,500

Adele Vallery Clines, housekeeper, $1,250

Dick Howard, friend, $500

Mabel Clapsadle, bank worker, $1,000

Herschel Crockett, agent, $250

LeRoy and Elsie May Dukenfield, brother and sister, $250 each

George Moran, friend who had died during this litigation, $500, to be distributed to his heirs

*   *   *

On June 21, Morris, who was a Texas commercial airlines employee, filed an appeal for one-third of the estate claiming that he was Fields' illegitimate son.

Following four years of bitter strife among claimants, compromises were announced on December 12 by Judge McKay. There were two surprises in the claimant agreements. One was that Willaim Rexford Fields Morris was given a share in the property, although the amount was not disclosed. The other was that heirs and claimants agreed that the controversial clause FOURTH, b., which would provide that a W.C. Fields College be established exclusively for white boys and girls should be reinstated limiting maximum funding to $25,000. At first this would seem confusing, but I realized that by the time funds were exhausted this issue would never have come to fruition. I also considered that this move was made mainly because it would go against a possible breaking of the will's demands, which would have placed monies coming to the legatees in jeopardy.

Regarding the proposed Morris settlment, it was disclosed that $15,000 would be paid him through the monies received by

Fields' widow; therefore, as it was announced on the last day of the year, Hattie's attorney, George A. Bisbee, told the court, "We arrived at the settlement in the belief that the expenses which would be incurred in fighting the claim made by Mr. Morris in the long run would be greater than the $15,000 we agreed to pay him."

On January 20, 1951, a pathetic little old blind lady from Chicago said she was going to file claim to the Fields estate. This statement was made by a Mrs. Williams in the offices of her attorney Sydney Tannen of Beverly Hills. She claimed she was married to the comedian in New York City, June 24, 1893, when she was only thirteen. She said Fields had given his age as thirty-two, adding that she bore six children by him. Finally, she said that W.C. had deserted her in Chicago in 1910 after promising to give her some money for the support of her children. Her claim was filed on January 25.

At the outset, this was obviously a weak claim as in 1893, Fields himself was only thirteen years old and could scarcely pass off his age as thirty-two. Further, in 1910, Fields was not even in the United States on the date Mrs. Williams said he was. He was touring the world.

During the time Mrs. Williams' claim was under consideration, Judge McKay awarded Hattie another $10,000. A day later, on September 24, the court turned down Mrs. Williams' claim.

On August 12, 1952, Judge McKay finally distributed Fields' personal belongings, described in the will's Exhibit A, to fifteen relatives and friends. His booze supply at his death numbered seventeen cases of various kinds. It was split three ways among his brother Walter, director Gregory LaCava and manager Charles Beyer. Carlotta Monti received the much-publicized sixteen-cylinder 1938 Cadillac equipped with a bar in the back.

Fields also left Walter his billiard and pingpong tables plus little things such as a "General Electric portable radio, traveling clock, one-half remaining trunks in basement, one-third neckties (first choice) . . ." Dave Chasen and Bob Murphy shared Fields' paintings created by John Decker, which were mostly pornographic. Under the impression that my father would eventually write his biography, Fields bequeathed Gene Fowler a leather

trunk and its contents including W.C.'s few hundred early-in-
the-century handwritten stage skits, along with motion picture
scripts and numerous papers which might be important to an author writing such a book. Fowler gave me this material in the
mid-1950s.

Identifying all of the exhibit's property from the witness
stand, executrix Magda Michael spoke of the liquor disburse-
ment, testifying that "almost every time I called on him [Fields]
at the sanitarium, he would request that I bring him some of his
liquor. Sometimes I would take as much as a case of gin, half a
case of vermouth, and a case of beer about every week."

Finally, on March 4, 1954, after more than eight years of con-
troversy over the $771,428 estate left by W.C. Fields, Judge Wil-
liam R. McKay ordered distribution of the remaining $84,401.

Widow Hattie had entered litigation at the age of sixty-six.
She was now seventy-five. In establishing her community property interest, she had won $65,000 in settlements of Fields giving
away large sums of money without her consent. Also she had
been awarded approximately $55,000 from the estate. But it had
been necessary for her to pay her attorney fees, reported as $80,-
000, along with the $15,000 won by William Morris. and her ex-
penses during these many years of litigation were extremely
high, not to mention exorbitant inheritance taxes levied by the
state. In all, the inconveniences and frustrations she must have
suffered during this long period were probably not worth it.

The curtain of the final act had been lowered. Carlotta, who
had stayed in the background during the comedian's lifetime,
ended up the star of the marathon legal circus. This was by virtue of her dazzling Latin beauty matched with an outspoken attitude which included a sailor's vocabulary. Now she could drive
away in the black 1938 Cadillac which had been gathering dust
while impounded by the court for the past 1,564 days.

At the end of these proceedings, several critics said that the
trial had tarnished the comedian's image, and that his name
would shortly travel into limbo. But they have been proven
wrong. Through his motion pictures, his gifts of comedy have
been captured alive and marveled at by successive generations as

Postmortem

though they had discovered, each time, the Eighth Wonder of
the World.

Or, all things considered, do you think he would still rather be
in Philadelphia?

8

What Ever Happened
to What's His Name?

"There are two easy ways to become unpopular," my father once told me. "One of them is to forget a man's name, and the other is to expect him to remember yours. All my life I have been plagued by an inability to remember names. Almost everyone, other than former Postmaster General James A. Farley (I believe that is his name), slips up at times when introductions are going around.

"But I not only black out whenever someone pops up with 'I bet you don't remember my name,' I actually go out of my way to earn a new enemy."

When Fowler first met Helen Hayes, he remembered seeing this remarkable actress as early as 1919 when she appeared as a child with William Gillette in *Dear Brutus*. Now, in 1928, she had grown up, become quite famous and was married to Charles MacArthur.

Charlie persuaded Helen that her education was not complete unless she met Fowler, "a most peculiar fellow," as he put it.

At the time Fowler was managing editor of the *New York Morning Telegraph*, a newspaper largely concerned with two pleasant necessities for well-being: racehorses and actresses.

The day when MacArthur and his collaborator, Ben Hecht, escorted Miss Hayes to Fowler's office, my father had been admiring a photograph of one of the young actress' competitors in the theater, Miss Helen Menken. When MacArthur introduced Fowler to his wife, what did he do?

He stammered, "Won't you sit down, Miss Menken?"

Although the two were to become fast friends, Miss Hayes avoided Fowler for at least a year.

Fowler felt better when other men showed a tendency to forget names, as did two great athletes of his time, James J. Corbett and Babe Ruth.

Mr. Corbett got around his trouble by calling everyone "Doc" or "Kid." Ruth made no effort at all to remember names. Ruth, however, did a very courteous thing: whenever he met anyone, he would say right off the bat, "My name's Babe Ruth." His face of course was known to millions of Americans, and there was little need of his introducing himself. Even Fowler could remember Ruth's name. "But it would be a wonderful circumstance if everyone followed the Babe's example of identifying himself on sight," said Fowler.

Back in the 1940s when I was a reporter, I interviewed then California Governor Earl Warren, later Chief Justice of the United States Supreme Court. When we met, he held his hand out to me and said, "Hello, I'm Earl Warren." Until that moment, I had been nervous about getting the interview.

*   *   *

It was not until he was in his sixties that Fowler chanced upon a real solution to his problem of forgetting names. "If only I can get up the nerve to do what is needed," he said, "then my troubles will have vanished."

We were sitting with the daddy of the *one-liners,* columnist Arthur "Bugs" Baer. The setting was Toots Shor's Manhattan restaurant where renowned sports figures gathered. The year was 1954 when a self-assured fellow galloped over to our table to call out:

"Hello, Bugs, old buddy! I bet you don't remember *me!*"

Baer replied matter of factly, "Why should I?"

Ranked one of the ten funniest men in the world while in his mid-fifties, Baer came out of Philadelphia. Seventh of fourteen children, he had his professional start at fourteen as a lace designer. He attended art school at night. His salary was two dollars a week when he became an office boy for the *Philadelphia Ledger.*

Bugs' twenty-first birthday in 1915 found him writing fillers
for the editorial pages of the *Washington Times*. One of these
made him famous overnight during a time when war atrocity
stories were rife. He had noticed a cat struggling with a bottle of
milk on a doorstep one night. The next day, he wrote, "The lady
who thinks the atrocities of the War are just too terrible for anything will soon go away for summer and leave the cat with a can
of condensed milk and no can opener."

After a hitch in the army, during the Great War, Bugs joined
the *New York American* (later the *Journal-American*), where he
would stay until he retired. His column reached millions through
the Hearst Syndicate. He became extremely wealthy though
some complained that he wrote over the head of the average
man. To this, he responded, "I don't think anybody is smarter
than the average man. It's to him I write. If I'm writing over his
head, then this is an indictment against the grammar school system of Philadelphia."

This American journalist gave birth to one-liners which would
become clichés during his lifetime. Among them: "The guy was
born with two strikes on him," "Hotter than a two-dollar pistol," "He's so dumb, they had to tear down the schoolhouse to
get him out of the second grade."

Walter Winchell was one of Baer's devoted fans. He said Bugs
had a horrible toothache but didn't know of a dentist to visit.
Winchell gave him the name of Dr. John Jaffin, whose offices
were on the thirty-fourth floor of the newly completed (1932)
Empire State Building. Baer shot a night letter to him:

"Dear Doc, I have more things the matter with my mouth
than a political speaker can find in a rival administration. Every
time I walk fast, one of my teeth falls out and by next week I will
be able to supply all the Elks in the world with vest ornaments. I
will drop in tomorrow and if you do me any good, you will be
more welcome than a rainmaker in Hades. I am a very busy man
but I also need teeth because I cannot go through life biting on
cream puffs and soft-boiled eggs. The last time I was to a dentist
was before I joined the Army in 1918, so you can guess that by
now my teeth look like a hobo's pocket comb."

Baer ran deep with his minuscule sayings such as, "Rumor has no more roots than a penciled eyebrow." My favorite Baerism is, "Paris is a city where they name a street after you one day, then chase you down it the next."

His columns bounced about the pages of the *Jounal-American* like a nervous pickpocket. One day he would be found in the sports section, on another, his by-line was on the first page. But he was usually in a special niche in the first section.

Each year, Bugs would attempt to write the authoratative Christmas message in a newspaper column. On his fortieth year, he chaired himself down to knock off "a terrific Christmas article that would become as famous as 'Yes, Virginia, there is a Santa Claus.' "

He said the nearest he had ever come to it was when writing about a lady *named* Virginia who had run up the remarkable score of twelve husbands and twelve divorces. He slugged the story, "Yes, Santa Claus, there is a Virginia."

Baer's brimming talent scored Bugs as being newspaperdom's prime ribald memo writer. On one occasion he received a letter forwarded to him through the advertising department asking the columnist to give some free publicity to a new ad client, *The Creative Box Company*. He could not overlook this double entendre. He referred the letter to Fowler, then the managing editor of the *American*, with the following remarks:

> *Have diagnosed evidence submitted in above case and can find nothing impugning the ability of the writer. The discovery of that slogan "Happiness in every box" was not responsible for the attack by the contented cow on the eugenic father. There is so much similarity between Cutex, Kodak and Kotex that the recital might make a man lose his self-possession and forget that he had pinned his money in the middle of the bed where he could keep his eye on it.*
>
> *I am sure that Fowler knows more of this subject than I do as I hear that it required force to keep him out of the lady's lap when she sat in the electric chair.*
>
> *Yours, for the products of this company without the metal edges . . .*

Forever falling in love with characters, Baer was attracted to Fowler, whom Ring Lardner dubbed "The Last of the Bison." Fowler was the inspiration for several of Baer's columns about the boys in Rufftown. I wrote to Baer many years ago, asking if he might fill me in further about his fable. He responded:

> *Both boys were born in the wide open spaces between law and disorder. Whenever they met in the* New York American *office, they stopped all visible means of support and argued about their home towns. Runyon was from Pueblo, and claimed it was the toughest town in America.*
>
> *So all that was where the idea for Rufftown came from. Gink Fowler was naturally none other than Gene Fowler. Now continue with the story.*
>
> *The idea behind the Rufftown champ was the fundamental one of every man's inherent suspicion that he comes from either the best or worst town on earth.*
>
> *Before losing his championship to Bozo Ruff and The Glutt, the Rufftown champ got very popular and then died colder than a turkey in the refrigerator.*
>
> *Here are some of the characteristics of Rufftown from a hasty grab at our memory:*
>
> *The Rufftown railroad was so rough that the Pullman chef could serve nothing but scrambled eggs.*
>
> *The Rufftown kids were so tough they played tiddly-winks with manhole covers.*
>
> *The entire community was so tough that even the canary birds sang bass.*
>
> *Gink Fowler was never defeated in an unfair fight.*
>
> *Whenever he stepped through the ropes, there were two hundred pounds of courage and gooseflesh in the ring.*
>
> *Gink Fowler may never go down in printed record as the champion, but we are glad of this opportunity offered by the* Boxing Record *to say a word in favor of the greatest fighter who ever nozzled the resin.*

During periods of frustration created by the censors, Bugs would dash off a column which only circulated through newspaper city

What Ever Happened to What's His Name?

rooms on Park Row. Mild today, this racy column biting at the State of New Jersey never made the newspaper's composing room in the 1920s:

> *The State of New Jersey is named after the Isle of Jersey, famous for its blonde, fat cows, the most prominent being Lillie Langtry.*
>
> *Lillie was known as the Jersey Lily in spite of the fact that she was oftener found in the watercress.*
>
> *But we are not there to tickle history. For instance, Pharaoh's daughter, Minnie, claimed to have found Moses in the Bulrushes. That was her story and she stuck to it.*
>
> *Moses turned out to be a wild man in after life. He never once referred to the incident with Minnie in the Bulrushes.*
>
> *They are not so considerate in Jersey where the motto is, "Get married and see the great outdoors."*
>
> *The Romans buried their bodies in catacombs, the Persians burned their bodies atop funeral pyres, but the Jerseyites lay their bodies out at night.*
>
> *The popular version of the old minstrel wow is now: "Who was that lady I saw you on last night?"*
>
> *Married bliss in Jersey is exemplified by the example of hordes of hard peckered Jerseyites rushing out with their divining rods to locate hidden treasures. It is a long lane that has no turning. But there is plenty of turning over in De Russey's lane.*
>
> *We don't know where May's Landing is. But she must have landed on her prat. The clear tinkle of running brooks in Jersey has a new significance, for where there is running water there must be towels.*
>
> *A man walking through Jersey at night was the originator of the Highland Fling. He had to walk that way to keep from stepping on his paired neighbors.*
>
> *The shortest story in the world sprung from the loins of our misguided but happy state. An elephant, escaping from a circus, roamed around at night and stepped on a man's back.*
>
> *A woman's voice said, "Thank you."*

What Ever Happened to What's His Name?

The governor of the State of Jersey will move his offices to Bush Terminal.

An in conclusion we wish to recite the joyful poem by Riley Fields Chapman, "Out where the beds are a little closer, out where the gals are a little doser, out where the wife's beneath the grocer. That's where the East begins!"

When he reached seventy-one, Bugs informed me that his vices were less expensive and easier for him to finance than of yore. He had been operated upon for warts of the bladder, which he called "the chambered Nautilus." He said that the doctor chalked his cue with cocaine and that he, Bugs, possessed the only male organ that was a narcotic addict. He wrote me after the operation to say that every time he urinated there was a rainbow over the bedpan.

9

The Inscrutable Lardner

The tall, very tall, dark-eyed Ring Lardner was one of the most respected newspapermen to notch fame as the 1920s were ushered in. It was 1885 when he was born in Niles, Michigan. He had four sons, two of whom (John and Ring, Jr.) became superior writers. Ring got into his reporting starting blocks in 1905 on the *South Bend Times* before traveling to Chicago's *Examiner* and *Tribune*. He possessed an avid love for sports which led him to the editorship of St. Louis' *Sporting News* at the age of twenty-five.

Becoming famous at an early age is not unique today. But until the ushering in of the 1920s (in the United States), confidence was usually invested in big business presidents, bankers, politicans, publishers and those in high positions of responsibility and art, who were aged and bewhiskered.

But so often it happens that when a man's talents bloom early, he also dies young. Take Keats and Shelley, Edgar Allan Poe, Joyce Kilmer, Mozart, Stephen Crane, Robert Burns, Lord Byron and Raphael. Lardner lived only forty-eight years.

Lardner was an inscrutable man. The only dependable facet of his nature was that he was an eternal prude, both in manner and in writing habits. He even influenced Fowler in his profession. However, when he shed his robe of respectability while drinking, Fowler could become publicly shocking. This always distressed Lardner, but it did not threaten their bond of friendship.

Although Ring was not publicly outspoken while in his cups,

he did take part in several bizarre incidents. While dancing with a lady even taller than he, his partner said, "Mr. Lardner, won't you please say something clever?"

He peered at her with his protruding black eyes and said, "This is the first time in my life I have ever looked into a lady's nostrils."

This is as daring as Ring would get. And, as a matter of fact, he would go out of his way to keep Fowler on the "straight and narrow" with his books. Upon publication, Fowler sent his first biography, *The Great Mouthpiece*, to Lardner. It traced the life of New York criminal defense attorney William Fallon. Some weeks later, Lardner took the icing off Fowler's literary endeavor with his usual discreet cautions:

> *I always try to answer a letter within three weeks or a year of receiving it.*
>
> *You know how it is when a guy comes to interview you, particularly when you aren't feeling so hot. [Lardner had less than two years to live at this writing.] You say whatever comes to your head, and lots of things that really don't.*
>
> *I, who am nauseated by the very thought of a fifty-word night letter, have a fine license to criticise anyone who has patience enough to write a whole book. But I was sincere in wishing you would keep the dirt out.** *Hecht, Dos Passos, etc., need it. You don't. . . . I like books and stories that I can recommend to my children and very few lady friends without a qualm. Where sex and its by-products are necessary, as in Zola or Dostoevsky, use them.*
>
> *Otherwise, I like your stuff and hope there will be more of it soon. It might interest you to know that during the three months I supported the Doctor's Hospital, the Fallon biography was the only thing I could read.*

---

*Lardner seemed to be so obsessed with an abhorrence of anything vaguely touching on anything scatological or obscene, that this author wonders if he might have been shocked in his childhood by witnessing a physical action of this nature, something he was not mentally prepared for.

The Inscrutable Lardner

Most biographers in treating Lardner had not adequately exploited the then living sources — for instance, John Wheeler of the Bell Syndicate, and Grantland Rice. Lardner worked with both men.

But it would have been difficult for Rice to go too deeply into Lardner's character. Rice was only able to seek out the goodness of a man. In effect, Rice was aware that Lardner was a sorely troubled person, but he harbored a sympathy for all men, even those whose actions he despised. We are all troubled, but some of us do not display our sores.

Lardner was reserved and had impeccable, almost courtly manners; he minded his own business, and expected strangers to mind theirs. If, as occasionally happened, something offended Ring's sensibilities, he would open the gates of his wrath. A Lardner reprimand seemed to stun the person who had invited it. It was as though a statue of Pharaoh Ramses II suddenly spoke out in a deep bass voice.

So it was at the World Series game when Ring's expert knowledge of baseball, as well as his trained ear for dialogue, were offended by the loud babblings of a newcomer to the press box.

The name of the offender was Graham McNamee. He was engaged in a somewhat historic performance, the first radio broadcast of a baseball World Series game.

In that faroff day the broadcaster had no lordly place of his own, out of earshot of the elite of the working press. Mr. McNamee's debut was marred by the fact that he did not seem to know the difference between a fielder's choice and a poem lovely as a tree. Mr. McNamee had been a baritone vocalist in churches and on the concert stage, and once gave his lungs a workout at Aeolian Hall. He was a likeable, enthusiastic chap, but emphasized the wrong thing about the wrong participant in the wrong situation, and on the air could make a foul tip take on the importance of a home run with the bases full. However, he became a favorite with the radio audiences. It was their sacred right to measure the worth of a sports event in terms of the big noise and ballyhoo. Did you ever hear a prizefight radio report less exciting than the Battle of Hastings?

It was halfway through the game. Arthur Robinson of the

The Inscrutable Lardner

New York American sports department said it was the last of the sixth inning — when Mr. McNamee had Babe Ruth batting right-handed instead of left. Lardner could stand no more. Getting to his feet, he announced to his fellow journalists: "For the last hour, I've been looking at one game and listening to another. I refuse to be present at two games played simultaneously!" With these words, Lardner departed the press box.

As he weaved his way toward the exit, Lardner was given a big "hello" by cowboy actor Tom Mix. Lardner was in no mood to appreciate the glory of the cowboy or the grandeur of his fancy attire. He wore a purple neckpiece hammocked over his chest and shoulders; a puce-tinged, frogged buckskin tunic which was red and vociferously enhanced with yellow sleeve fringes: and many other contributions to an ensemble which once caused a nearsighted tourist in Rome to ask a guide what the Cathedral of St. Basil was doing so far away from Moscow.

"I said 'hello' to you, Ring," Mix again called out.

Lardner leered at him for a moment, then broke into a smile. "Oh," he said, "I see you are in mourning."

* * *

Lardner's works were often misjudged by pristine critics of the time. Ring, however, did not look upon himself — if we are to believe it — primarily as a humorist. Rather, he regarded himself as a reporter. He endeavored to set down what he heard.

Back in the late 1940s, Ernest Hemingway wrote an article in *Esquire* magazine about Lardner. Fowler said he did not recall much about it except that he thought it a bit disparaging, and detected in it a "slight bit of envy." Hemingway has been acclaimed the most masterful fellow at handling dialogue. "His clipped sentences have placed his devotees in a condition of incurable ecstasy," said Fowler.

"Now, Mr. Hemingway undoubtedly is one of our foremost writers," he went on, "but I find many of his same sentences, in effect, in the third grade readers of my own boyhood. When we read these very wonderful things in school, we understood them, and thought they were all right, but I do not recall any of my comrades having swooned with delight upon reading the same."

The Inscrutable Lardner

Hemingway will eventually — as he has already — enjoy a more considerable fame than Lardner. But when we speak of the dialogue of athletes, particularly of ball players and fighters, Lardner was unsurpassed. His unbiased ear impounded not only the dialogue, but made it apply to the actions and innermost feelings of his protagonists. Jim Murray° possesses that talent. Murray, whose friendship stems from our days as cub reporters, is today's craftsman; he has taken over in popularity from Lardner and Rice. But, unlike Murray, Lardner was aloof, a man of few spoken words.

"Ring did not believe it was necessary for an author to indulge in the kind of writing that one may find in James Jones' *From Here to Eternity,* or James Joyce's *Ulysses,*" Fowler said. "He was as well aware as anyone that everybody goes to the bathroom and the toilet. But he felt, as do I, that one need not incessantly remind the reader of these sodden functions which are paraded on television in the guise of physics, deodorants, and other things that are for sale at the pharmacists'. Certainly the masters of the past have been realistic without constantly pounding the fact that we sweat, evacuate, and are, in effect, walking septic tanks. Man seeks to be lifted above and beyond the sewage levels, which are entirely important to health, but not conducive to the contemplation of a Grecian urn or the gleam in a loved person's eye! If a man has to shit, let him do it, not describe it. The toilet seat makes democrats of us all, but not geniuses."

* * *

Lardner's greatest ambition was to write lyrics. When he did this for *June Moon,* a play with music, he did not drink for seven or eight months. He told Fowler he was so occupied with trying to write the songs, and so interested in the theatrical work, that he found no need for the bottle.

Ring was not a polished lyric writer, but that was his ambition, just as it was Lord Byron's to be an athlete, and Sir Walter Scott's desire to be a military expert. Authors seem to be built along

°Syndicated by the *Los Angeles Times,* Jim Murray has won the National Association of Sportscasters and Sportswriters Award thirteen out of fourteen years.

these lines: that is, they would like to do something other than the thing at which they are experts. Authors and other artists are rarely satisfied with what they are best at.

Fowler said that he did not believe Lardner disliked mankind, as it was privately believed, in the broad sense of the word. Nor would my father call him a cynic: but he didn't think that Ring was a do-gooder, or that he accepted people with ease. Nor did Pop think that Lardner would go out of his way to make friends. When he drank, he remained dignified: indeed, he looked like a wooden Indian whenever he was potted. At the Friars Club, where New York actors gathered to trade lies, Ring once sat for forty-eight hours in a dinner jacket without getting so much as a fleck of dust on himself, or acquiring a wrinkle. He rose to go to the bathroom occasionally, but he was the most immaculate man of drink Fowler had ever seen. When he departed the club following his forty-eight-hour sit-in, actor Jack Hazard looked in the following morning and shouted, "The statue is gone!"

* * *

Lardner's stories were accepted by the public as rollicking humor, but Fowler did not believe that the underlying grimness and reality of his character types became apparent to a majority of the reading public until after the 1920s.

Fowler said he remembered Grantland Rice telling him that Lardner's model for his character "Alibi Ike" was a blustering young hillbilly who joined the New York Giants baseball team before the turn of the century. This powerful young man got on the Giants training squad, annoyed everyone with his boasts, but made good. For instance, Hank Gowdy, the ancient catcher, was the best pool player on the Giants club, and this rookie brashly boasted he could beat anyone at pool, was taken up on his claim, and Gowdy was appointed to give him a lesson. The young man, however, proceeded to display great powers and ran off forty balls in succession.

Rice said that this fellow astounded manager John McGraw with his native ability.

Mr. McGraw coached this hayseed on the finer points of baseball, and in an exhibition game, the young man made a sensational appearance at the bat, in the field and running the bases. Toward the end of the game, however, after stealing three bases, the kid broke his leg while sliding home. It was a compound fracture which crippled him for life. He retired, one of the finest prospects in Giants history.

* * *

There was one period in his life when Lardner was not only without a job, but much in need of money. At the time, Fowler was editing the *Morning Telegraph.* A front-page statement preceded Lardner's joining the paper.

> *We are pleased to announce that Ring Lardner, a great writer who never went literary, has agreed to write for the* Morning Telegraph, *beginning next Tuesday. He is supposed to be writing around and about the news of the day, but he probably will write about anything. Sometimes he will write about nothing. We can imagine only one general topic more entertaining than Ring Lardner on anything: that is Ring Lardner on nothing.*
>
> *We do not expect that he will have our readers going around in hysterics every day. Our new fellow has a great change of pace. He wrote* The Romance of Esther Fester, *you may remember, but he also wrote* Golden Wedding, *which was quite another story.*
>
> *But we are not trying to introduce him to his own public.*
>
> *We only mean to announce that he will be with us.*
>
> *Company is coming for a long visit, and we are all of a flutter.*
>
> *Mr. Lardner will conduct his column under the title of "Ring's Side."*

This announcement was written by Westbrook Pegler, then working for the *Chicago Tribune Syndicate.* He had no New York outlet at the time. It was then that Fowler gained permission from Colonel Patterson of the *New York Daily News,* who was not using Pegler's stuff in that city, to allow Fowler to use Peg's material in Gotham. Fowler was the first to publish Pegler in New York — for better or for worse.

The Inscrutable Lardner

As Fowler continued to run ads about having acquired Lardner, he even enticed James Montgomery Flagg to do a red-penciled rendering of the colunist for the *Telegraph*.

On the morning of December 4, 1928, after much preparation, Fowler changed the format of the newspaper, introducing a new typeface, and removing many of the old ads placed by touts and racetracks at a considerable loss of revenue to the paper.

Lardner's first article concerned the phenomenon of going back to work again. He mentioned that he would explain this "in a few well-rounded gutterals." He claimed, "After all, a newspaper should have some news. Hire an old-fashioned go-getter, the kind that ain't too blasé, to register a 'scoop,' the kind that takes pride in scoring a beat. Tell him money is no object."

In the column, he placed an asterisk following the word "scoop," and two asterisks after the word, "beat." At the foot of the story, he defined the word "scoop" as a utensil for bailing boats. In explanation of the word "beat," he wrote that it was "a biennial plant producing a root much used for food, and also for making sugar."

One of the few stories Fowler assigned Lardner to concerned a fight between two palookas. My father had also assigned several other prominent writers, each to cover one round of the fight. The bout came to a sudden end in the fifth round, just as Lardner's turn was coming up. This did not cause Ring to falter. Rather, he wrote in detail about the sixth round that he envisioned.°

On another occasion, Ring wrote a one-paragraph story about a preliminary in which a white man fought a black man:

> *Last night at Madison Square Garden a white boy met a colored boy, and as they shook hands in the middle of the ring, the white boy said, "I'd like to tell you a story.*

°Other writers signed to write one round each were Ben Hecht, Charles MacArthur, Bugs Baer, Damon Runyon and Westbrook Pegler.

There was a white boy and a colored boy, and if you've heard this one, stop me." He did.

It was an agonizing process for this man to produce stories that read so smoothly. In an article on poisoned liquor, he ended it with, "Note to Santa: Please bring this little Lardner boy a wastebasket and don't attach a card saying you hope he will make use of it."

*   *   *

A writer named H. C. Witwer wrote stories similar to those of Ring, but they lacked the Lardner quality. Witwer published an essay, *The Leather Pushers,* and felt crushed when readers accused him of imitating Lardner. He wrote Ring a letter saying he had not intended to imitate him, and that it was a literary accident; he hoped that Lardner would not resent the fact that some of his stories may have had a "Lardner touch."

Lardner replied, "Don't worry. I have a wastebasket with lots of stuff in it, and you are welcome to it."

On his tape, Fowler said, "I will give you this much of an example which comes to mind where Lardner wrote under his label of *Ring's Side,* a sub-heading, 'Wanted: One Hardboiled Shirt in Good Repair: Must Stand Sponging During Heavyweight Nuptials at Mr. Rickard's Laundry: No Dealers.' "

At the head of this story, Ring had written, "The office where I worked (Cries of 'Office Where Who Does What?') is just across beautiful Eighth Avenue from Madison Square Garden, so handy to same that it looks as if I would almost be compelled to rent a dress shirt and accept whatever seats Mr. Rickard offers me for New York's share of the heavyweight eliminations."

*   *   *

One of the final stories Lardner wrote for the *Telegraph* had to do with an upcoming heavyweight fight between Jack Sharkey and a fellow named K.O. Christner of Akron who was "breaking into the game at the age of thirty-three." At the conclusion of this yarn, Lardner wrote, "The winter should provide plenty of entertainment for we morons, but most of us are impatient for the Fourth of July."

The Inscrutable Lardner

Lardner was a strong man until his many illnesses set upon him. He was not a good businessman. It is curious that such a much-read writer should be represented by a lifework of slender proportions. Part of this was caused by his illnesses, and part because he was a perfectionist. He did not just "dash out" his copy. When he was writing for the late Ray Long, editor of *Cosmopolitan Magazine*, one of his stories miscarried. Fowler recalled that Ring afterward reconstructed the story, but was never satisfied with it.

Lardner had such a low regard for his work that he considered keeping a carbon copy of same a waste of time.

10

Damon the Demon

When Al Santoro, then sports editor of the *Los Angeles Examiner*, phoned my father to tell him on December 10, 1946, that Damon Runyon had died — the victim of throat cancer, cirrhosis of the liver and a bad gall bladder — the slight Italian editor asked Fowler if he would write something about "The Demon."

Fowler said, "There is nothing to write." But, realizing Santoro needed something personal about Runyon, he went on to say that Damon was a "patron for a lot of us guys now growing older." He likened Damon to a baseball scout, always scouring the tall uncut. "He attracted many superior newspapermen to the attention of editors, and probably the only black mark is Fowler. He brought me to New York."

Fowler added that Runyon never wrote a bad story, "and I'd hate to write a bad one about him now." He and Damon were friends for thirty-seven years, going back to the time when Fowler was reporting for Denver's *Rocky Mountain News*.

Fowler told Santoro, "You know, I don't think Runyon's characters talked like Runyon wrote about them. I believe the characters tried to talk like Runyon wrote. But he did write with simplicity."

Runyon's search for fame was tedious but Manhattan seemed to be his destiny. (He was born in Manhattan, Kansas, October 4, 1884.) Most believe he was whelped in Pueblo, Colorado, but he moved there as a child when his father was widowed. Following his apprenticeship as a reporter with small Colorado papers,

Damon the Demon

Damon went to work for the *San Francisco Post* in 1900. In 1911, he signed with William Randolph Hearst on the *New York American*. He reported General John J. "Blackjack" Pershing's punitive expedition in Mexico in 1916, then traveled to Europe in 1918 to become Hearst's World War I correspondent. This was when Damon sent for my father, then a reporter in the sports department of the *Denver Post* under Otto Floto.

Runyon used to say that great men, like the teeth of a hippopotamus, come few and far between. He himself was the most powerful newspaperman around, prior to Walter Winchell.

In Denver, Runyon had regard for a *great* man named Jim Wong, the night steward of that city's Press Club. The Oriental used to loan trusted members money at no interest.

Runyon needed $500 to travel to New York, where Fame had lately been blowing kisses his way. This amount also meant that Damon would be allowed to marry pretty Ellen Eagen, young society editor of the *Rocky Mountain News*.

Jim Wong loaned Runyon the money, but Ellen had other ideas. Damon was a heavy drinker and she bargained that he was to precede her to the Big City: if he quit drinking "completely," she would follow and marry him. This came to pass: Runyon gave up the hooch for the remainder of his life. In later years, Damon told Fowler that the desire to have a drink never left him. Those who claimed to be intimates of Runyon "when he used to sit up all night getting drunk in Manhattan" were overstuffed with *merde*. When he departed Denver, Damon also left the booze.

Runyon was deadpan and undemonstrative, and a listener. He was considered aloof, and several Runyon biographers maintained that "no one knew Runyon," and "no one ever got close to him." This is also untrue, because a few knew him well, as did Arthur "Bugs" Baer. Damon was not a taffy saint, except to the Broadway legend makers.

Fowler also knew Runyon well, and took offense when, in a burst of mysticism, Bill Corum worte that "nobody knew Damon." Following Runyon's death, Baer and Fowler had discussed this man's character in depth. "I obviously had to keep Damon well within my ken when writing about him," Fowler told Baer. "When I never took his advice on anything, including going to work for $60 a week, he would get sore at me. I think he liked me after a fashion, and I certainly liked him and admired his great talent." At the time of this discussion, Fowler was preparing to include Runyon in his (Fowler's) tome, *Skyline* (Viking). "Robbie° who is genuinely loving and loveable, did some checking on the two-hundred pages I have written, and rather scared me by saying I was giving a bit of the 'minus side' of the Demon. But I am damned tired of pulling ALL my punches. And I don't think it takes away one bit from Damon's real character or his importance to set down a few behind the scenes matters, which, in my estimation, show some of his foibles."

Bugs told Fowler that he did not agree with the ethereal side of Damon either. But he did not discount Robbie's inalienable right to count the Haunted Houses.

Baer had lived and traveled with Runyon. "I used to spend a couple of weeks at his house in Saratoga when his wife [Ellen] was living there with Damon, Jr., and daughter Mary," Bugs said. "He would never have married his second wife if the first one hadn't died."

The creator of the one-liners said that he was "bridesmaid" at Runyon's marriage to Patricia. "They were married by the right-reverend Jimmy Walker who tried to talk Runyon out of the trap. When his efforts failed, Jimmy pronounced them man and wife and then fell flat on his intoxicated face. *Veritas Vino Veritas Boppo.*"

Baer said he was with Damon when he rode up to the middle of Florida and stashed his son in a military academy. "The kid never lived in the Hibiscus Island Mansion. He never got further than the combination tool, hen and guest house at the gate."

Baer said that Damon never forgave the kid for rum-potting his teens, exactly what Damon did when he was a lad.

Referring to Runyon's second marriage, Bugs said that the romance was as one-sided as an Amazon's chest. "Patricia took

°Arthur "Robbie" Robinson was a sportswriter on the *American* in the twenties.

all the gravy, signed all his movie contracts and the kids got the smell of stone-soup.

"There wasn't a time when Runyon wouldn't throw a drowning man both ends of the rope. Yet, he was a soft touch, and as I wrote about Jack Kearns,° he would cry at card tricks.

"Runyon had the mind of a druggist's scales that weighs poison and its antidote with the same clinical impartiality. He scored heavily with his short story collections and rightly so. But success came so late in life the Demon didn't share in the harvest."

Baer was aware that he could not stop Fowler from writing about the past through rose-colored eyeballs. "You always were a sentimentalist," he said, "who packages sunsets and eavesdropped the bird-song in a creaky door."

Damon Runyon was perhaps the dapperest dresser along The Great White Way. In this case, legend was based upon truth. He never wore a necktie more than once, a suit rarely more than three times. Sartorially, he was compared to Jimmy Walker, Grover Whalen and Richard Harding Davis.

Ellen and my mother were fast friends and when Ellen discovered that Damon had taken up with another woman, the Victorian Mrs. Fowler wrote Mr. Runyon off her list. This unfortunate circumstance of Damon's wandering was said to have caused Ellen to die of a broken heart.

In the early New York days, the Runyons and the Fowlers lived on Amsterdam Avenue. As Damon's fame grew, he had less time for his wife. My mother consoled Ellen in regard to the other woman, but to no avail. Ellen took to the bottle.

The single puncture in Runyon's friendship with Fowler came when he accused my father of informing Ellen that he had taken up with Patricia. Fowler was never a malicious defamer or gossip and this was not the case, but the unforgiving Runyon stuck to the fantasy that Fowler had blown the whistle on him.

Never conspicuous for writing to women, Runyon *did* correspond with my mother after he had married Patricia, following Ellen's death:

°Kearns managed many of the champion fighters in those days.

Damon the Demon

We leave tomorrow for Miami. Damon [Jr.] got home yesterday from Riverside Military Academy at Gainesville, Georgia. . . . You tell Gene I think Timberline is the outstanding American effort of that kind. . . . If you folks should happen to come to Miami, we have a house on Hibiscus Island, and the latchstring is always out. And if you don't come to Miami, let's get together when we return. I want you to meet Mrs. Runyon.

Mother did not answer the letter, nor did she ever meet his second wife.

* * *

Runyon held title to a sense of humor during his youth. During a state-wide labor strike, he perpetrated a hoax which became known as *The Finger Incident.*

At the time of this episode, martial law was declared with the governor calling out the National Guard to keep the peace. Commander of the state troops was Adjutant General Sherman Bell, the most hot-headed man since Henry VIII.

General Bell grew especially furious one day when his paymaster disappeared from view with a valise which held $3,000. This money had been drawn to pay the general's officers and men. It seemed a foul embezzlement. Military sleuths and the civilian police force were making a house-to-house search for the villain.

Runyon was then a police reporter on the nightwatch for the *Post.* His city editor was Josiah M. Ward, a veteran journalist, who had a marvelous nose for news.

The morning after General Bell's paymaster disappeared, police reporters were playing hearts in their narrow quarters in the basement of City Hall. It came Runyon's turn to visit the police desk just outside the reporters' room to see if anything newsworthy had been entered on the blotter. While making his routine inquiry, Runyon chanced to see the police surgeon at work on a citizen who somehow had caught a forefinger in the bathroom door of a nearby saloon.

The surgeon amputated the man's finger, laid it aside, and sutured the stump. Runyon picked up the finger, placed it in his pocket, saying nothing about it, then returned to the reporters' room where he sat down at his typewriter to compose an anonymous letter.

He addressed this letter to Adjutant General Bell, whose military headquarters were at the Statehouse on Capitol Hill. The letter informed General Bell that the absconding paymaster of the National Guard had been kidnapped by union sympathizers. And unless the General's Cossacks were summarily withdrawn from the scene within the next forty-eight hours, his paymaster would be dismembered, bit by bit. As a guarantee of this grim eventuality, the General could see the paymaster's finger, enclosed in the envelope. Next day he would receive a big toe, then an ear, and so on.

Having mailed the unsigned letter, and finger, Runyon estimated the hour of its probably arrival on General Bell's desk. Then he telephoned City Editor Ward, saying that a "mysterious tip" had come to the police reporter, something about "a finger," and that a strange voice over the telephone had advised Runyon to "ask General Bell about the finger." That was all.

Mr. Ward, a man who always "looked into everything," said he would instruct statehouse reporter James R. Noland to ask General Bell about "the finger."

Meanwhile, Runyon confided in his fellow reporters at City Hall. Damon and his merry group were at the Statehouse when the dignified Mr. Noland entered General Bell's office. Jimmy must have asked about "the finger" or called the General a foul name, because the lurking reporters heard the loudest commotion since the Battle of the Little Big Horn. Runyon opened the door a crack to see the screaming red-faced General, hands gripped upon Noland's throat. He was demanding the "source" of Noland's information.

The day after this tumult, the paymaster was discovered in the home of a woman friend, too drunk to explain his disappearance, but the valise full of money was found intact. The guardsmen were paid. The prank of "the finger" was charged against Runyon, but he did not admit it until many years afterward.

* * *

When he arrived in New York, besides doing his column, Runyon was principally a short story writer. Each of his works was a gem. But he was a man so much in his shell that few were able to enter his private labyrinth.

Runyon did come out of his conch one autumn afternoon at a World Series baseball game between the New York Giants and Yankees. One of concessionaire Harry Stevens' rookie vendors entered the press box to distribute some snacks, free of charge, to the sports reporters. He asked Runyon to "please pass this here hotdog to that big guy with the necktie on crooked in the end seat up front." He was referring to Heywood Broun.

Receiving not the slightest response, the vendor wished to know if Runyon had gotten sand in his ears.

Annoyed, Damon left off writing to fend off the sandwich, which was dripping mustard. "I do not happen to be a busboy," he said. "And if Mr. Broun can't crowd the wrinkle at home, then let him tote a lunch bucket."

* * *

Arthur Brisbane, Hearst's highly paid editorialist, often offered the verdict that Runyon was the greatest reporter who ever lived. However, though Damon was perhaps one of the best writing reporters of his time, facts bothered him. He would select one idea or happening and build into it an interesting story. His genius for style, his ability to capture atmosphere and depict character, so far overshadowed the conventional facts of the story as to make his work preeminent. I believe two things prevented Runyon from becoming as great a columnist as then *Scripps-Howard Newspapers'* Heywood Broun: his reluctance to criticize anyone or anything, and his imitation of Brisbane.

Directly following Runyon's death, Fowler wrote to their mutual friend in Denver, Lee Casey, editor of the *Rocky Mountain News:*

> *We all expected Runyon to die a year before he did. In all the eulogies about him, there was hardly a hint as to the really great personal tragedy that soured his glory. He was a lonely, frustrated man, but he met his problems with vast courage.*

Damon the Demon

When Captain Eddie Rickenbacker strewed Runyon's ashes from an airplane over mid-Manhattan, one gallant man was doing a last service for another man of his own kind.

In summation, Fowler said, "I prefer to remember Alfred Damon Runyon as a great human being rather than as a candy angel, aloof of mind and remote of heart."

11

The Acid Typewriter

I will never mix brandy and bourbon again. . . . I will never mix brandy and bourbon again. . . . I will never mix brandy and bourbon again. . . . I will never mix brandy and bourbon again. . . . I will never mix brandy and bour-bon again. . . . I will never mix brandy and bourbon again. . . .

*　*　*

And so it repeated itself, taking up the eight hundred words that King Features Syndicate allotted him. Considering his hangover, this was a most provocative column for Westbrook Pegler to write.

Peg had written this after he had become a cosmic columnist, joining Roy Howard on the *New York Telegram,* later the *World-Telegram.*

Fair Enough was its title, and this particular column was written the day following a visit with W.C. Fields, artist John Decker, Fowler and myself. The night on the town started at the Beverly Hills Hotel where Peg most often lodged when he hit the West Coast. We moved on to Dave Chasen's restaurant and ended up at Fields' home on DeMille Drive in Hollywood.

It was about three o'clock in the morning in Uncle Claude's upstairs office where stood his legendary rolltop desk. The large room was also equipped with his four-wheeled wagon bar, a steam cabinet and a rubbing table where the comedian's trainer, Bob Howard, kneaded the kinks.

Fields was nursing martinis and the rest of us were drinking Napoleon brandy and chasing it down with chilled Mumm's Cordon Rouge champagne. The effects of this concoction caused us to feel as though we were walking in slow motion about one foot above the thick carpeting.

"There is some good in the worst of us," Fowler was saying in answer to a fusillade of epithets directed at the incumbent President's wife.

"But I hate that FDR and the whole goddamned Roosevelt clan," Fields whined in a voice that Alva Johnson described as sounding like "a Stradivarius violin being bowed with a rat tail file."

Ignoring Pegler and Decker as they left the office to view one of the latter's recent pornographic works, Fields said, "I know how much Pegler dislikes the Roosevelts. But not as much as me! He has a column . . . with which to vent his spleen. . . . No one hears *me*. . . . Not even you, Fowler. . . . You're not listening!"

"I was just recalling a time when I telephoned Pegler at his Tucson ranch," said Fowler. "He was moaning through the entire conversation. I finally asked him what was bothering him, and he told me it was his great right toe that was throbbing."

"What happened to it?" Uncle Claude asked. "Use it as a cork . . . or a bung starter?"

"He just said he broke the damned thing."

"Probably busted it kicking at the door of the White House," said Fields.

Fowler told of another time Peg was writing a piece attacking Mrs. Roosevelt, a poem that was too strong to be published. He heard a noise at his window, turned to see a cow leaning in, chewing its cud. And after he had driven the cow off, a buzzard flew in, and Pegler said it looked like it was picking its teeth with its claw.

As Decker and Pegler returned, Fields said, "The cow didn't like what he was writing."

As Uncle Claude continued degrading the Roosevelts, the columnist with the acid typewriter decided to play it straight, as though he had repented and changed his mind about his feelings. "No man is altogether bad, Bill," said Pegler. "After all, FDR is a good son. He loves his wife. . . ."

"He cheats on her," Fields interrupted.

"He loves his children."

"All spoiled rotten. Never did a day's work in their lives."

"Now you take . . ."

"What *is* this?" Fields cried in wonderment. "Have we a Benedict Arnold in our midst? Godfrey Daniel . . . a turncoat if ever I saw one. . . . Remove this knave, this scoundrel . . . and miscreant from earshot . . . else I shall have him dragged to the Tower . . . to have him drawn and quartered."

"I'm sorry, Bill," Pegler objected. "I've been thinking it over and have finally decided that Franklin Roosevelt after all is a great man, from a fine stock."

"A fine stock!" Fields exploded after quaffing a freshly poured martini. "His grandfather was an opium ped——ler!"

"Calm yourself," Fowler warned, "your anger is turning your nose into something that looks like a taillight."

With an attempt at composure, Fields frowned. "Do not make fun of a man's affliction."

"I think Mr. Pegler was making a good point there," Decker put in.

"*Et tu, Brute?*" Fields snarled. "Why you son-of-a-bitch, Decker. It was you who suggested . . . you execute an oil painting . . . of Eleanor — *à la* Goya's *Naked Maja* — for me. . . . And now, you rogue . . . you turned on me!"

"But I asked nothing for it," said Decker.

"Until I offered you a check for a thousand," the man with the thousand-watt nose insisted.

"Good God," said Pegler. "How did I miss this one, Decker?"

"See it?" cried the actor-political partisan of incendiary zeal. "The goddamned FBI came here and absconded with it. . . . I'll wager J. Edgar Hoover . . . has it hidden away in his home . . . waiting for the next . . . Republican administration to take office . . . so he can unload it for a neat profit. . . . Profit, hell! He paid nothing for it . . . to begin with."

"Well, how the hell did the FBI discover you owned such a

painting in the first place?" Pegler inquired. "There had to be a snitch somewhere."

"Snitch, indeed," Fields smirked. "One of my acquaintances is a poltroon and a coward."

"That's hardly an explanation," said Fowler.

"I hung the painting in the dining room downstairs . . . next to my barber's chair° . . . with a narrow shade on a roller which came down to conceal it. For a month, I charged my so-called friends five dollars a look. . . . Naturally, I forwarded all the proceeds to the Republican party . . . for its future convention."

"And one of them . . . " Pegler interrupted.

"They *all* squealed," Fields interrupted back. "Drat! The FBI's gone communistic!"

* * *

Shortly after Viking Press published Fowler's biography of Jimmy Walker, *Beau James*, in 1949, Pegler wrote a column pointing out that Fowler had skirted mentioning all the black marks the ex-Mayor of New York had scored against himself and others. It was so scathing, even mentioning that Fowler was a weep-easy reporter, that scores of other newsmen took arms against Pegler, backing up Fowler in print.

Most important among them, circulation-wise, was Jim Murray, who was writing for *Time* on the West Coast.

"Did you read Peg's column about Pop's book yet?" Jim asked me over the phone.

"I did," I answered.

"What do you think about it?"

"How far can a friendship go?"

"Do you know how I can get in touch with Gene to get a statement?" Murray asked.

"You won't believe it," I said, "but at this moment Pop's in Tucscon with my brother Gene, having lunch with Peg."

Murray contacted Fowler to receive the following statement:

°An insomniac, Fields used to sleep in a barber's chair. It was the best way he knew to get a few winks.

The Acid Typewriter

Westbrook Pegler is an extremely honest and able reporter. His article on me in no way affects our personal friendship. If we are to have free speech and free expression as we so widely announce everywhere, I think this should apply to Pegler as well as any other citizen including myself.

I am having lunch with Mr. Pegler, but am eating nothing except cocoanuts and the inside of French bread which was not baked on the premises.

I sometimes think that Mr. Pegler goes too far when he throws rocks at ghosts but in this instance, so far as I am concerned, I am still alive and faintly kicking. As for Jimmy Walker, I did not try to excuse him in my book. Rather I endeavored to explain him in relation to the time that produced him. There is a fine but definite distinction to be made here.

Nor am I a moralist loaded down with profund truths and messages. Before I could become one, provided I chose to set myself up as an arbiter, I would first have to improve my own way of living.

I believe in Biblical teachings although I do not practice all the precepts contained in Holy Writ. One of the things I always have tried to do is live up to the admonition of the Scriptures and I quote, "Judge not, that ye be not judged."

Pegler was later unable to fathom Fowler's attitude toward him regarding the Walker book.

* * *

Peg hit Hollywood one day while Fowler was away somewhere. He asked if I might take dinner with him at Chasen's. It was in January of 1960 when I was television news director at KTTV. It was a late dinner and most of the Hollywood characters had departed with their girlfriends or wives. It was quiet and only a few tables were occupied as Chasen came to sit with us.

Pegler was talking about how bad Fowler was with remembering names. "I tried him out one time by just making up any name. I think it was George Clarke. I said to Gene, 'Remember old George Clarke, the reporter on the *Herald Tribune?*' And

Fowler said, 'Oh, yes, good old George. How is he now? Have you seen him lately? What's he doing?' Gene was filled with enthusiasm. Then I said, 'Why, you old son-of-a-bitch, there is no such person as George Clarke!' Your father thought a second, then said. 'Well, if there ever *was* a George Clarke, I'll bet he would have been a wonderful man.' You just couldn't ever fault that damned Fowler."

*   *   *

The trouble with Pegler was that he was unaware how far too far was to go in print, and he was unable to take what he had dished out to others.

12

The Dean and the Georgia Peach

I first met Grantland Rice, the dean of sportswriters, during the Ember days of the New York Yankees' Babe Ruth. I was a kid, but my memory was sharp when introduced to Yankee Stadium. My father had been away from the newspaper business for two years. We were Granny's guests. In those days, the press box was still on ground level near the players' bullpen and sometimes, while they were waiting their turn at bat, players would stop by the press box, lean on the rail and strike up a conversation with reporters covering the game.

This day, Ruth visited the press box to say hello to Fowler. The two hadn't seen one another for some time. The Bambino clutched a hot dog in one hand and a bottle of Coca Cola in the other. This was his diet between each inning. And if the game went into extra innings, the Babe's stomach would rumble as he rounded the bases.

When Rice had introduced Ruth to President Calvin Coolidge, the Babe said, "Hi, Pres. I'd like you to meet some members of the team." With his inability to remember names, he said, "This here's Carrot Nose, an' Fat Ass, an' Big Chaw, an' Pivot Tooth," and so it went.

* * *

When Rice was producing his motion picture short subjects, *Sportslights,* he was coaching Ruth what to say about a World Series game the Yankees had won. "An important line I want you to get across," said Granny, "is, 'As the Duke of Wellington

said, "The Battle of Waterloo was won on the field of Eton." ' "
Either the budget was low in those days when there was seldom
a filmed retake, or else what Ruth said was so hilarious that the
producers decided to leave it in.

During the filming, Ruth's speech came out this way: "As
Duke Ellington said, the Battle of Waterloo was won on a field in
Elkton, Maryland."

When Rice asked, "How in hell could you get something so
screwed up like that?" the Babe said, "Well, you know I don't
know the Duke, but I have some very good friends of mine livin'
in Elkton."

*   *   *

Rice liked to tell this about himself when asked to recall his days
as a newspaperman

"When Don Marquis and I were young reporters down south,
we were on an out-of-town assignment, had played poker, and
lost our expense money, with the exception of seventy-five cents.
This had to do us both for a week. Marquis asked me what we
might do to survive with this stipend. 'Just do as I say and you'll
be all right,' I said. 'We'll solve the food situation and have
money left over.' "

In the hotel, Rice sent down for a mince pie, which cost ten
cents.

"A mince pie for breakfast?" asked Marquis.

"Just do as I say," said Granny.

After the pie arrived, Rice cut it in half, and each ate his fill.

Along toward noon, Marquis complained of a severe stomach
ache and indigestion and said, "We shouldn't have eaten that
pie."

Rice said, "Do you want some lunch?"

"Christ, no!" moaned Marquis. "I couldn't eat another thing
today. Doesn't your belly ache?"

"Sure it does," said Rice. "It has a big lump in it, and I don't
want to eat either. That's the idea. You eat a mince pie every
morning for breakfast and you're not only not able to eat, but are
lucky if you don't die before nightfall."

Some years later, Fowler was Rice's guest in another press box. It was the 1937 New Year's Day Rose Bowl football game in Pasadena between the universities of Pittsburgh and Washington. By this time younger sportswriters were addressing Granny as "Mr. Rice." He had gained that much renown and respect.

Following the game, which Pitt won, 21-0 the two were heading toward the exit when Granny noticed this nineteen-year-old sweating over his typewriter. He had no lead. He had not even put one word down on paper. Other sportswriters had already wrapped up. "Are you having any trouble son?" Rice asked the young man.

"Yes, Mr. Rice," he said. "I'm a student sports editor . . . for the University of Washington, and the *Seattle Star* gave me this assignment to cover the game . . . and I'm so shocked we lost, I just don't know where to start."

"What do you think was the turning point in the game?" Rice asked.

"I think, Mr. Rice," said the teenager, "it was when Bill Daddio of Pitt made the interception in the first quarter and ran sixty-seven yards for a touchdown."

"You know," said Rice, "I think you're absolutely right. You should open your story that way with some kind of a line like, 'It was a rainy day today for the Washington Huskies . . .' and then just sort of recap the game from the interception."

Forty years later, that young reporter went on to become a successful book and magazine writer — and my friend. He is Al Stump.

* * *

There is much in Grantland Rice's background of which few are aware. He was proud of being a sportswriter, but his other credentials were also impressive. This graduate of Vanderbilt University — Phi Beta Kappa — had authored several books, mostly poetry. Amond his hard-cover publications were *Songs of the Stalwart, Songs of the Open, Only the Brave* and *The Final Answer.* He was also a master at creating a rhyme on the spot, just as he was renowned for offering *nom de guerres* such as *The*

Four Horsemen° and *The Seven Mules*. Also, *The Galloping Ghost*, Illinois' ball carrier, Red Grange. And the New York Yankees' *Murderer's Row*.

Rice was also filled with fascinating stories and recounted them as a gifted toastmaster. His favorite story on these occasions was *How to Tell Bad News:*

"A bookmaker named Brown died at the horse racetrack after a long shot came home and financially broke him. His fellow touts chose one of their comrades, a man known as 'Tactful Timothy,' to approach Brown's house to gently break the news to Mrs. Brown.

"Timothy knocked at the Brown door, and when Mrs. Brown appeared, Tim took off his hat and said, 'Am I addressing the widow Brown?'

" 'I'm Mrs. Brown,' the lady insisted, 'but I'm certainly not a widow.'

" 'No?' said Tim. 'Well if you think you ain't the widow Brown, five will get you ten you're wrong.' "

*   *   *

In January of 1941 Jimmy Demaret beat out Willie Goggin in match play on the fifteenth hole in San Francisco. Baseball's Ty Cobb had invited Rice and Fowler up to view the final day of the golf match. I tagged along. We had traveled up on a train named *The Lark*. Fowler dubbed it *The Lurch* because it made so many sudden milk stops. Because of his erratic manipulations at the throttle, we talked about the possibility of the engineer being a sex deviate.

Rice and his entourage filled three drawing rooms. Among our traveling companions were Babe Ruth, Walter Hagen, actors Richard Arlen and Guy Kibbee, humorist and columnist Henry McLemore, my father and myself.

Following the tournament, Cobb offered to drive the bulk of us in his station wagon to his home for a squab dinner. On the way, we were passing an airport as a small plane was taking off.

°The Notre Dame Four Horsemen were backfield members named Harry Stuhlderer, Elmer Laden, Don Miller and Ed Crowler. Their average weight was only 168 pounds.

It was very low and Cobb avoided a near air-to-ground collision. Fowler shouted, "Jesus! This is the first time I've ever been in a car that almost knocked a plane out of the sky!"

To Tyrus Raymond Cobb, this was not amusing. He lacked a sense of humor as long as anyone could remember, and that went back to when he broke into the minor leagues in Anniston, Alabama, at the age of sixteen.

Continuing toward his Spanish villa at Atherton — which was surrounded with high-voltage electric wires — Rice told of how in 1904, Cobb used to send him postcards from Anniston, which read: "Watch the 'Georgia Peach.'" After receiving so many of these cards, Rice said he decided to look this kid over. "He turned out to be the finest young ball player I'd ever seen. I contacted a Detroit Tiger executive who came down to watch the youngster play."

I noticed a frown from Cobb when Rice mentioned the word, "youngster."

"The rest is history," Rice said. "The next year, Ty went up to Detroit and the major leagues. He was only eighteen."

"What the hell's my age got to do with it?" Cobb asked. "Most important is I played outfield for the Tigers for twenty-three years and managed them six."

When Cobb retired from baseball at the age of forty-two, he had played in more games (3,033), scored more runs (2,244), and finished with a higher lifetime batting average (.367), than any other major leaguer. He had led the American League in batting twelve times — nine in a row. Three times he had hit .400 or better, and he hit .300 or more for twenty-three years in a row. In the first election to the Baseball Hall of Fame at Cooperstown, New York, in 1936, Cobb received the most votes.

Arriving at his Atherton home on the San Francisco peninsula, Cobb had a manservant turn off the gate's electric power so we might drive in.

The mansion was impressively large, and the dinner was sumptuous. As we were served Napoleon brandy and the finest Havana cigars, all sat around the large dining room table, recalling — much to his pleasure — Cobb's days in baseball. My father had warned me earlier not to bring up anything like Babe

Ruth's home run record or any other baseball records which might affect Cobb's vanity, "or else he might just fly into a rage and crack a bottle over your skull." I was unaware that Cobb harbored such a temper, but felt that I was in physical danger and had to be alert at all times.

I did respectfully put a question to the veteran. "Night baseball's six years old now, Mr. Cobb, and a lot of players complain that it affects their batting average. If you were playing today, what do you think your average would be?"

"I guess I'd be hitting in the low three hundreds," Cobb said. "But you must take into consideration that I'm fifty-five years old now."

After we repaired to the living room, Cobb excused himself and returned to the dining room, where I noticed him pouring the unfinished brandy back into its original bottle. The expression "tightwad" came to my mind, but after he had shown me a gash on his back (which looked like a surgical incision) and a pair of the most deeply scarred legs I had ever seen, I thought it wise not to make any smart remarks about his frugality.

If Ty Cobb ever liked anyone in his later years, it had to be Al Stump, who spent a trying year with this unpredictable man, taking down his biography, *My Life in Baseball — the True Record* (Doubleday). Cobb, a heavy-drinking gambler, was then a diabetic, dying of cancer.

Some years after Cobb's death in 1961, Stump and I were hoisting a few at the Los Angeles Press Club when I brought up the question of the athlete's wealth, his frugality and the stories I had heard from my father about his wildness.

"As far as Cobb's wealth went," said Stump, "I figured when he died he was worth about $12 million. He was known as 'Mr. Coca Cola.' He held more than twenty-five thousand shares which were worth $85 a share at the time. So with his vast General Motors stock holdings and the million dollars worth of negotiable government bonds he used to carry around, stuffed into an old brown bag — well, you figure it out."

"What about this million he used to carry around?" I asked. "That's interesting. When I used to write for Red Skelton in the early 1950s, he had the same hangup. Maybe he didn't trust the banks, or anyone else. My father and I caught up with Red at the Los Angeles Airport. He was trying to skip town carrying a small suitcase with $400,000 cash in it."

"Cob was such a mean son-of-a-bitch," said Stump, "I think he was just daring someone to steal it from him. He always carried that damned automatic pistol with him everywhere he went."

"I never heard about the pistol," I said.

"Cobb said he pistol-whipped a man to death in Detroit. Three hoodlums jumped him in the street early one morning in Detroit. One of them stabbed him in the back, and Cobb took out his automatic. It wouldn't fire, so he started beating on the guy who'd knifed him. I was taking notes like hell and asked Ty, 'Just where in the back?'

" 'Well, damn it all to hell, if you don't believe me,' Cobb roared, 'take a look!' He threw a half-full whiskey glass at me. And, not wishing to be killed, I took a look.

" 'Satisfied?' he said.

" 'With the odds three-to-one,' I said to Cobb, 'that must have been a relief when the hoodlums fled.'

" 'Relief?' Cobb continued shouting. 'Do you think they could pull that on me? I *went after them!*' "

Stump told me that Cobb chased one of the mugs into a dead-end alley where he hit him for about ten minutes with his gun, "until he had no face left. Left him there, not breathing, in his own rotten blood."

Stump asked Cobb what the situation was when this happened.

"To catch a train to a ball game."

"You saw the doctor, instead?" Stump asked.

"I did nothing of the sort, damn it!" Cobb swore. "I played the next day and got two hits in three times at bat."

Then Stump said, "Records I later inspected bore out every word of it: On June 3, 1912, in a blood-soaked, makeshift bandage, Ty Cobb hit a double and a triple for Detroit, and only then was he treated for the knife wound." Then Stump added, "He *was* a demon. That's how he set all those records that nobody has come close to since 1928."

"What about Cobb being a tightwad?" I asked.

"He was the world's champion pinchpenny," Al laughed.

"Some one hundred fifty fan letters reached him each month, requesting his autograph. Many enclosed return-mail stamps. Cobb used the stamps for his own outgoing mail. The fan letters he burned. 'Saves on firewood,' he would mutter."

Before Stump took on the Cobb "autobiography," he was warned by one of the baseball champion's former teammates to "back out of this book deal. You'll never finish it and you might get hurt." The man said that "Nobody can live with Ty. Nobody ever has. That includes two wives who left him, butlers, housekeepers, chauffeurs, nurses and a few mistresses. He drove off all his friends long ago. Yeastcake heir Max Fleischmann was a pal of Ty's until the night a Fleischmann house guest made a remark about Cobb spiking other players when he ran the bases. The man only asked if it was true. Cobb knocked the guy into a fish pond. After that Max never spoke to him again. Another time, a member of Cobb's family crossed him — a woman, mind you. He broke her nose with a ball bat.

"Do you know about the butcher incident?" Cobb's ex-teammate rumbled on to Stump. "Ty didn't like some meat he bought. In the fight he broke up the butcher shop. Had to settle for $1,500 on the butcher out of court."

"But I'm dealing with Cobb strictly on business," Stump reminded him.

"So was the butcher," the man replied.

* * *

Stump was trying to get his book started while the two were alone in Cobb's luxurious hunting lodge on the crest of Lake Tahoe. Cobb went on a gambling spree in Reno. It came to an end following some fistfights, gunplay on Cobb's part, and just too damn much drinking coupled with no insulin medication for his diabetes.

After Cobb was thrown out of the hospital, where he camouflaged a tumbler of straight bourbon whiskey by depositing his false teeth in it, Stump had another surprise awaiting him.

Cobb had decided the two would repair to his eighteen-room

Atherton mansion to work on the book. When they arrived at the Spanish-California villa at 48 Spencer Lane, Al found there were no lights, no heat, no hot water. The seventy-three-year-old Cobb explained, "I'm suing the Pacific Gas & Electric Company for overcharging me on the service. Those rinky-dinks tacked an extra $16 to my bill. Bunch of crooks. When I wouldn't pay, they cut off my utilities. Okay — I'll see them in court."

The following morning, Al told me he arranged with the gardener to turn on the lawn sprinklers so he might take a shower. "From then on, the backyard became my regular washroom."

Al was no Handel. He wouldn't take writing by candlelight, so he made arrangements with a neighbor to string a two-hundred foot electric cord across the yards, through the hedges and into Cobb's study, "where a single naked bulb hung over the chandelier providing illumination. The flickering shadows cast by the light made the vast old house seem haunted," Stump said. "No 'ghost writer' ever had more ironical surroundings.

*   *   *

The end was nearing, and Al invited Cobb to be his house guest by the Pacific in Santa Barbara. Two doctors examined Ty at the beachouse and confirmed Al's suspicions. Cancer had invaded the bones of his skull and he had but a few months to live. During this time of intensive work on the book, Cobb took Stump by surprise. "I've decided that you and I are born pals — meant for each other — and we're gonna complete a baseball book beating anything ever published." Cobb, who had refused opiates for his severe pain, spoke with a clear head, and Stump believes he meant it.

The last time Stump saw the Georgia Peach was in Atherton. "What about it? Do you think they'll remember me?" Cobb asked him, as though it was an offhand remark.

"They'll always remember you," said Stump.

Stump reported to me, some time after Cobb's death, that his last words were: "People are no damned good."

13

The Specter, Winchell

Winchell . . . . Walter Winchell was a self-appointed Nebuchadnezzar conqueror of Broadway, and he never let anyone forget it. After he left his profession as a hoofer, he began to gather show business tidbit news items and sell them to various newspapers. He had an insatiable desire to write. And with his new clipped style of putting words on paper, he viciously fought his way to the top. At the pinnacle of his success with the King Features Syndicate, Winchell's column appeared in more than eight hundred papers. He also had millions of families, ardent listeners to his Sunday evening radio broadcasts, each opening with his familiar "Good evening Mr. and Mrs. North and South America and all the ships at sea . . . let's go to press!"

During the Depression, even movie houses, desperate for customers to fill their empty seats, shut down their projection machines to patch in the Winchell broadcast through their loudspeakers.

Winchell's power became so great that at one time he demanded to be obeyed — offstage, as it were — by actors on their way up, and by press agents, many of whom were exclusively hired just to feed items to him while he was having his daily evening shave at New York's Taft Hotel barbershop before repairing to his exclusive table number fifty at Sherman Billingsley's Stork Club. This columnist treated the flaks, hoping for a puff in his paper, like cattle.

Oddly enough, Winchell rarely checked the authenticity of an item passed on to him. And if he had not been factual with an item — which might make him look bad — the press agent who fed same to him was automatically placed on Winchell's Drop Dead List. Sometimes if the flaks were fortunate enough by offering Walter an item he could not resist, the press agent was removed from condemnation. But Winchell would never apologize in print for a false item . . . unless he could shape it into a cute remark starting with an "Oops . . ."

In his revealing book, *Winchell* (Doubleday), my friend Bob Thomas wrote that just before Franklin Delano Roosevelt decided to run for his third term, the columnist was secretly invited to the White House. While weighing the third-term decision — if there was one — Roosevelt would first welcome Winchell into the Oval Office, asking him about any new stories he might have heard along Broadway. In return, the President would trade gossip about certain senators and representatives. This was dynamite for Walter's column. If they were too hot to handle, W.W. would place them in the form of a question, such as, "What certain Western Senator is about to get the heave-ho from his wife because he was caught in a compromising position with a Capitol secretary?"

During this world-changing period, an attorney, Ernest Cuneo, closely associated with the Roosevelt administration, approached Walter with an item: "Roosevelt is considering running for a third term. Put it in your column and break it on your *Blue Network* show." Walter was elated, but when the fourth time around he was aksed not to repeat the news story — and the official announcement had not yet been made — Winchell cried that it was beginning to sound like a repeat performance. But it finally paid off the fourth time. The President made the announcement the following day. From then on, no one was allowed to utter anything derogatory about FDR in Walter's presence unless they dared to be placed on his Drop Dead List.

*   *   *

Winchell was Jewish, but curiously he neither admitted nor denied it. His grandfather, Chaim Winechel, was both a cantor and a rabbi, a heritage of which to be proud.

With the exception of a chronic sinus condition, the chain-smoking head of the Damon Runyon Cancer Fund was a healthy man. Until he became one of the most powerful voices in this country. He was considered a good family man to a faithful wife, June. As his children, Gloria, Walda and Walter, Jr., grew up, he found it impossible to communicate with them. Walda changed her name twice, and Walter, Jr., shortened his first to "Walt." He became a recluse, but sporadically emerged from the bushes to fall in love with one girl after another.

*   *   *

I was about fourteen when I first met Winchell. It was during a summer's weekend when my father and I rode in a Los Angeles City Police unmarked prowl car with a Lieutenant Joe Filkas. An insomniac, Walter enjoyed playing cop, and took advantage of carrying a pistol . . . sometimes *two*. In New York, the police department gave him a siren for his car in order to get to some fast-breaking story more swiftly. In one of his columns, he mentioned that when he passed his home on one of these mercurial missions, he would turn off his siren so he wouldn't awaken his baby daughter. What about the other kids?

But he liked riding in the police kiddie kar at night. During one of these tours through the red-light districts of south Los Angeles, Winchell was telling Fowler about his latest young female conquest. He was personally planning to lead her to stardom. He admitted that he was physically attracted to the buxom lass. "I refuse to hide in back alleys if I want to see a dame," he said. "If I'm gonna go out with a dame, I'm gonna go out with a dame."

"But you're a public image," Fowler reminded him. "What will your fans think about you?"

"They're my fans," Winchell came back. "They'll just have to take it. What the hell," he reminded Fowler, "you a hypocrite or something? You like the dames yourself. What about that time your wife Agnes caught you with a young gal in a Gower Street apartment?

Winchell was referring to when my father had rented an apartment across the street from RKO Studios, where he was turning out scripts. Above his front doorbell was printed, "J. C. Witherspoon, eccentric juggler." It was noontime when Mother parked her Pierce Arrow and went upstairs to discover a young lady answering the bell. The only thing she was wearing was a blush. Then Pop appeared in the nude. When he saw Mother, he was at a loss for words. He even forgot to get some piece of clothing to cover himself as he followed Mother downstairs to her car. Passing several gawking pedestrians, he placed one of his feet on her running board as she prepared to drive away. The only thing he could think to say was, "But, Mama, this is Hollywood!"

I had three friends whose wives had caught them in the very same dilemma, but they had been undiplomatic enough to be playing Adam and Eve, catch-as-catch-can, bedroom polo, or whatever you wish to call it in the confines of their own homes.

The first friend, a television star (still alive), locked his bedroom door before pursuing his Riviera posturepedic romp. Arriving home unexpectedly, his wife knocked loudly on the door, objecting to its being locked. "Let me in!" she cried.

"I can't," my actor friend whined. "I'm in the *nude!*"

My late friend Brian Foy, motion picture producer and eldest of vaudeville's headliner Eddie Foy's "Seven Little Foys," also had a physical attraction for the lovely ladies. When in trouble, especially when caught dallying by his wife, he tended to become dictatorial. On one occasion, when discovered on the rise, Brian turned to stare at his wife. In a moment of clarity, buttressed with gemoetric psychology, he theorized, "Are you going to believe what you see, or are you going to believe what I tell you?"

My third acquaintance, an American Airlines salesman, was crushed and filled with utter panic all at one time when his conjugal partner discovered him in the sack with a cooperative, comely wench. Sobering immediately, the only thing he could think of to say was "This . . . is . . . not . . . *me!*"

* * *

In his early days as a newspaper columnist, Bernard MacFadden's *New York Graphic* had employed Winchell, who eventually became impatient about the weekly $300 he was being paid by MacFadden in 1928. Fowler was still editor of the *Telegraph*, housed in a former barn for horses that pulled trolleys. After putting an edition to bed, Fowler would often lean back on his swivel chair, put his feet up on the desk, clasp his hands behind his neck, and cry, "Can you smell that horse shit? What a great place to put out a horse paper!"

Amibitous to make more money, Winchell approached Fowler to learn if he might ghost write a column for the *Telegraph* while sitting out his contract with MacFadden. "I have enough Broadway news to fill three columns," he said.

"It's all right with me," said Fowler, "if you don't think it will get you in any trouble. Naturally, we can't use your name."

Winchell agreed and Fowler created the column head, *Beau Broadway*. After it started circulating, the *Telegraph* was accused of copying Winchell's style in the *Graphic*.

* * *

As the years passed, the letters Walter had written to Fowler, asking professional advice, dwindled. While his success accelerated, Walter's wife felt neglected by her husband. She took to heavy drinking as she waited for him to come home to Scottsdale, Arizona. He finally did arrive, but this was during the last year of her life.

June would briefly leave Scottsdale to visit my mother in Los Angeles. She told my mother that she could not resign herself to being forgotten. "I will not give up my man for some young slut who'll take him for everything he has."

"One thing I can say about Gene," said Agnes, "is that he always comes home."

During the conversation, June asked Agnes, "Did Gene ever have anything to do with Dorothy Parker? You know what I mean."

"Good Lord, no," my mother said. "Dorothy was a witty writer, but she wasn't prone to that sort of thing." She deliberated a moment. Then, "June? Do you know what Dorothy once said about your husband?"

"What?" she asked.

"Dorothy said, 'Poor Walter. He's afraid he'll wake up some morning and discover he's not Walter Winchell.'"

Young Walt was reaching out for acceptance and love, something his father had failed to offer. He possessed the problem of many progeny of the famous. Not wishing to be identified with their parents, preferring to make it on their own merits professionally, and not because they are "the son of ———."

Underage, Walt joined the U.S. Marines. He loved guns. Following his discharge, he developed a yearning to visit East Africa. He wanted either to be alone with his woman of the moment, or to travel among the wild animals of the jungle. He also knew that there, no one had ever heard of or cared about a Walter Winchell.

Walt adapted easily. Never a bartender, he became a good one in Arusha, on the northern border of Tanganyika, adjoining Kenya. Never a white hunter, he became a good one.

Along the way, Walt discovered Gene Fowler, a man who would understand him and answer his letters and exchange ideas.

The younger Winchell also had a talent for writing. He possessed a basic imagination and was capable of expressing his feelings. In one of his letters to Fowler, Walt wrote:

> *Have seen one particular lion in the Serengeti Reserve that I am sure is a reincarnation of Barrymore. . . . Same profile, sort of mane and roar. . . . I've heard John Barrymore's voice on records and the resemblance is astounding. This lion always has a pride of comely females with him to heighten the illusion.*

As with so many great men, he created his own undoing. Up until FDR died, Winchell, I believe, thought of himself as Achilles minus the vulnerable heel. But all this changed when Harry Truman took over the Presidency. Truman agreed with history in that his office, and not the man, should be respected.

Playing under the FDR game rules, Winchell visited President Truman, and was upset not only at not being granted an audience, but at being told that in future he must make an appointment to see the President. In old Harry's words: Whenever I have anything to announce, or to be announced, you no longer have precedent over any other members of your profession."

It was then that Winchell began taking pot shots at the President's daughter Margaret's "inability to sing." Defied on his homegrounds, Truman felt mortified and vented his anger at Winchell.

To compound his sudden decrease in popularity, Winchell made the mistake of switching from the Democratic to the Republican party. This was a matter of vanity over political belief. Anyway, a person who "changes sides" is often doubted by many, and for many reasons.

When his popularity reached drydock in 1957, Walt made an attempt to return to the company of his father. Although this effort might have been casually expressed, Walt wrote Fowler:

> *Talked with Dad yesterday. He's in the city and hasn't been out to the old fort in months. He's off for California in July to film a TV series with Desilu. Seems very bored with New York lately. Wants to get back on the air and hates the idea of being sixty. Have tried to get him to go fishing with me for years, or play golf with some of his friends, but the only interest he's ever had is the typewriter and I don't press it anymore.*

Ten years later young Walt, a married man now, took a gun and blew out his brains on Thanksgiving Day.

* * *

The last time Walter and I met was in 1966 at the Del Mar Race Track in north San Diego County. My wife and I were there to see Del Mar's celebration of the Lake San Marcos Handicap. We were guests of Beverly's cousins, Gordon, Donald and Robert Frazar, who had developed the nearby Lake San Marcos, building houses for those in a comfortable income bracket.

Passing through the Turf Club area, Winchell, sitting with two of his latest protégées, called me to his table. He began extolling my father to the young ladies. Walter seemed in a jovial mood when I asked if he might pose with the Frazar brothers and the winner of the Handicap.

The Specter, Winchell

A sudden coolness interrupted our friendly talk. Walter acted strange, almost paranoid, when he whispered as he peered about, "I can't do that, Will. Ever since I turned Republican, the CIA has been after me. . . . A sniper could knock me off while I was posing with your winner."

I let the subject lie and politiely bid them all a hasty goodbye.

* * *

Now Walter Winchell, incapable of sustaining a love for his wife while being blinded by false hero worship, was finally alone in Scottsdale. His son, who could find no place in the world to fit comfortably, was dead. His wife, who had died an alcoholic while waiting for her husband to come home, was gone, too. The hurrahs had faded from the mouths of a fickle public.

One of the most powerful men in the United States who, during his public omnipotence, held the ear of millions and could demolish a professional career with a few paragraphs, was finally laid to rest next to his wife and his neglected son.

Only two persons attended his funeral in Scottsdale: his daughters Gloria and Walda.

14

Sadakichi and the Baron of Bundy Drive

John Decker's English country-style home on Bundy Drive rests sideways on a small lot with a fifty-foot frontage. It is mainly living room with cathedral ceiling. Its bay window faces the street to the east. The sun has not shone through it for years because tall pine trees block its rays. There is but one bedroom, one bath, a small kitchen and a modest dining alcove. On the thin wooden front door which leads directly into the living room, Decker created his own coat of arms in oil with the words, "Poor, Insignificant Artist."

In those days the place was not even hooked up to the public sewer, and above the cesspool grew a prolific avocado tree. In the kitchen, Decker painted a fat chef holding a frying pan on the wall near the stove. The ceiling was speckled with a number of yellow splotches. This was oven-heated urine the artist forgot to remove from his diabetes test tubes. The result? An explosion.

The lack of sunshine from the bay window bothered Decker not in the least. He always painted by electric light. "That's the way people view my paintings."

The upstairs to the house consisted of a loft with a balcony which years later was transformed into a bedroom. A toilet and sink were also plumbed in.

In the backyard were penned several chickens and a lonely duck which, by necessity, had his sex habits altered. It took this misguided Chanticleer some time to balance with agility atop these surprised hens. I wondered, if he had not used them for breakfast, what would have come from the eggs if they were allowed to hatch . . . Chucks or Dickens?

Fowler described Decker's Bundy Drive retreat in *Minutes of the Last Meeting* (Viking) as a meeting place for still-lively survivors of bohemian times, "an artist's Alamo, where political bores never intruded and where breast-beating hypocrites could find no listeners. The men seen most often at the Bundy Drive studio had been persons of mark, yet never long-haired nor precious nor hoodwinked by false prophets. These men lived intensely, as do children and poets and cheetahs."

Of the many who frequented Bundy Drive, only four are left: Anthony Quinn, Vincent Price, John Carradine and myself. Among the others who escaped to Bundy Drive were, of course, John Barrymore and W.C. Fields. Then there were actors Thomas Mitchell, Norman Kerry, Roland Young, Alan Mowbray and Errol Flynn. There were also goldsmith Philip Paval and Pulitzer Prize-winning poet Robert Hillyer and author Ben Hecht.

The unique character by far was a man named Sadakichi Hartmann. Sadakichi was half-German and half-Japanese, living on an American Indian reservation near Banning, California, *during World War II!*

Hartmann was referred to by all, except W.C. Fields (who hated him), as The Gray Chrysanthemum. Fields would refer to Sadakichi as "Itchy-Britches," "Hoochie-Koochie," "Itchy-Scratchy" or "Catch-a-Crotchie." If W.C. showed up at Decker's place and Sadakichi was present, he would make an immediate about-face and leave.

To his face, Fields had accused the Eurasian of affixing himself like a frayed barnacle to the hull of the nearest reputation. The comedian was aggravated that Fowler was actually going to write about this gargoyle. "Sadakichi," said Fields — using his name correctly for once — "belongs in print only among the pages of Steckel or Krafft-Ebing. He has been a peeping tom, a cap-and-bell interloper at all the art shrines."

* * *

But Jack Barrymore was in love with the skinny, prancing, cynical, yet beauty-loving wraith. He appeared a forgotten bamboo stalk, that is, with the exception of the area of his crotch. There, existed a huge bulge, as though he were the heaviest of hung studs to come along the pike. But the lump was not a marvelous exhibition; it was a problem. Sadakichi had a gross scrotal hernia which he supported with a homemade hammock. And, supplied with enough booze and/or barbiturates, with an echo of youth entering his being, Sadakichi would leap to his feet and shout from his toothless mouth: "Everything is forty-five degrees!" Then he would pose, his long feet at an angle of forty-five degrees. Before going into a dance solo which contained a bit of East Indian, Balinese and Japanese gestures, he would cry out some anomaly such as, "The only imperfect thing in nature is the human race." Then he would do his routine wearing a gummy smile, and demanding all about to pay strict attention to his acrobatics as his truss swayed side to side.

* * *

Fowler first met Sadakichi while working on a motion picture with director Leo McCarey. For some reason, Decker felt forced to take this skinny wild man to meet Gene Fowler. At first, they had little luck at the studio gate, but Hartmann began to demonstrate his expertise in Kendo with his cane. Following a swift whipping of the gate cop, a phone call gained them entrance to the studio Sadakichi entered Fowler's and McCarey's office while McCarey was giving a piano rendition of his latest song, *Tear Bucket Jim.*

Fowler related that Sadakichi rose from his praying-mantis position, and began a slow dance. "As we all sat and watched him, the walking straw moved his hands and legs with rhythmic exactitude, grotesquely, but in arresting patterns of mobility."

"I am able to answer any query or express any sentiment by my gestures," Sadakichi remarked as he swayed with his music.

"I prefer to dance in the desert. One day I shall landscape it, command waters to flow into it again, as in ancient times, and cause trees to grow. And then I shall have a stage that barely match my genius in size and meaning and beauty. Thank you very much. Hah! Hello!"*

In a letter to Jack Barrymore, my father quoted Hartmann:

> *Gene Fowler sleeps most of his time on earth. I do not quite see how you can claim to know him. Whenever he comes to Decker's studio the bed is occupied. Even Decker with his funny little moustachio has no chance to cope with Fowler's flophouse tendencies. It takes a lot of leisure to write half-way beautifully! Einstein denies "Time." Fowler actually has no time. He has to jot down whatever comes to him as soon as he awakens. Hello!*

Barrymore and I were together one day when Pop entered to witness another of Sadakichi's demonstrations. At its conclusion, Jack said to Fowler, "You are a connoisseur of human oddities. Here is your chance to chronicle a living freak presumably sired by Mephistopheles out of Madame Butterfly."

This was a tempting proposition and Fowler seriously considered the project for a year. He even started taking notes on the Gray Chrysanthemum, but when Sadakichi became aware of the project, letters began to bombard Fowler. "I want more morphine" (and Fowler acquired it until his physician demurred). "Send some more brandy to my modest home in Banning. It is cold up here and my heart grows weak." Then, "Purchase me a casket, immediately.

"Sarah Bernhardt used to sleep in one, and I, the great Sadakichi Hartmann, shall be marked down in history more indelibly than *that* shrieking female. Thank you. Hah!"

There were also continuous demands for drafts of money in order to keep Hartmann in bus or taxi transit. Fowler finally withdrew assistance other than sending him enough money for food (which he rarely ate) and transportation to anywhere but Bundy Drive.

---

*"Thank you" and "Hah!" when spoken by Sadakichi meant he had just completed a historical statement. Two other verbal oddities were that when he said, "Goodbye," he meant "Hello," and when he said, "*Hello*," he meant "Goodbye."

* * *

Hartmann was born in 1867 in Japan. His German father was Oskar Hartmann and his mother, Japanese, was named Osada. After serving as artist Whistler's secretary, Sadakichi began lecturing about art throughout the world. He also became an authoritative writer and art critic. According to Harry W. Lawton and George Knox in their landmark book on early photography, *The Valiant Knights of Daguerre* (University of California Press, 1978), Sadakichi allied himself with our early foremost American artist photographer Alfred Stieglitz in 1898. From then on, Hartmann became so obsessed with the subject of photography that he wrote many impressive essays on the art form.

* * *

Up until World War I, Sadakichi proclaimed himself the King of Bohemia in New York's Greenwich Village. Author of several important books of the time, such as *The History of American Art, The Last Thirty Days of Christ,* and several portfolios of poetry and essays on art and photography, the Gray Chrysanthemum (named so by John Barrymore) became the icon of the Professional Photographer's Society of New York at the turn of the century.

Hartmann should also be given credit for artistically showcasing such photographic experts as Stieglitz, Henry Havelock Pierce, Lewis Godlove, William Crooke, M.N. Sale, Fred J. Feldman, Frank A. Rinehart, H. Walter Barnett, Frank Scott Clark, A.J. Fox, E.E. Doty, E. Swarzwald and Albert Edward Steiner.

Harry Lawton told me that Sadakichi's well of writing dried up in the early 1920s, and after a lifetime study of this supreme egotist, I must agree because there is nothing of consequence that I have read by Sadakichi since his play, *Confucius,* in 1923.

* * *

Barrymore had given Decker the Rudolph Valentino chair and the actor, who would go for days without sleep, caught catnaps in this uncomfortable straightback. While purloining a half hour, Jack was awakened by the perfume of one of his favorite dishes. Chef Decker was feeding his hens and the horny duck in the backyard. Jack headed toward the kitchen where he discovered an omelet just prepared. He devoured it in two minutes, and returned to doze off again in the Valentino chair.

Stepping into the kitchen to place his omelet in a warmer, Decker became enraged to find it missing. He stormed to the dining alcove, where Barrymore was sporadically snorting in his sleep. Unable to arouse him, Decker returned to prepare another omelet. This time he took the opportunity to sneak from the house to purchase a cheap bottle of scotch. His reasoning was that as long as Barrymore's belly was full, he would sleep for a time. Decker nipped along the way home, then remembered his omelet on the stove. ". . . and I'm all out of eggs," he thought. Arriving home, he was relieved to find Barrymore still asleep. He went into the kitchen. There was still time; no odor of burning.

Now he discovered the second omelet had disappeared. "Thief!" he cried. "I have Fowler coming down for a meal and you, you son-of-a-bitch, have eaten up not one, but *two*, omelets!"

"What omelets, m'dear boy?" Jack asked.

"You know damned well what omelets."

"Don't remember a thing, m'lad," said Jack.

"Don't try to fool me. You ate both my omelets. I can see part of the last one on your moustache."

"If it be true, O Shylock," Barrymore eloquently said, "then take your pound of flesh from me, but not one egg."

* * *

Decker hated the pursuit of his work. When he had enough to live on, his brushes became hard and dry. He hid his money behind his bed at Bundy Drive. It took only a few dollars to make him happy, as long as it kept him in food and whiskey. The drawback, however, was that when he had enough booze in the house, Sadakichi could always be found within sipping distance.

Among other things, Hartmann had a problem controlling his voiding, which was encouraged by the pressure of his water-

W. C. Fields holding a halo over his head and symbolically
pushing away liquor during one short period when he gave up
drinking.

John Decker's portrait of
Fields in his Poppy costume.
Inscribed to the author,
May 1940.

Fields poses by a portable
bar of his own design
between games of tennis.

Portrait of John Barrymore, 1939.

Gene Fowler clowns with composer Dave Rose and Red Skelton at 1952 barbecue.

Author Ben Hecht poses besides his portrait painted by John Decker, about 1945.

Thomas Mitchell with Gene Fowler at 20th Century-Fox Studios. They hold a document declaring them the only two members of the 1960 Beverly Hills Great Grandfather's Club.

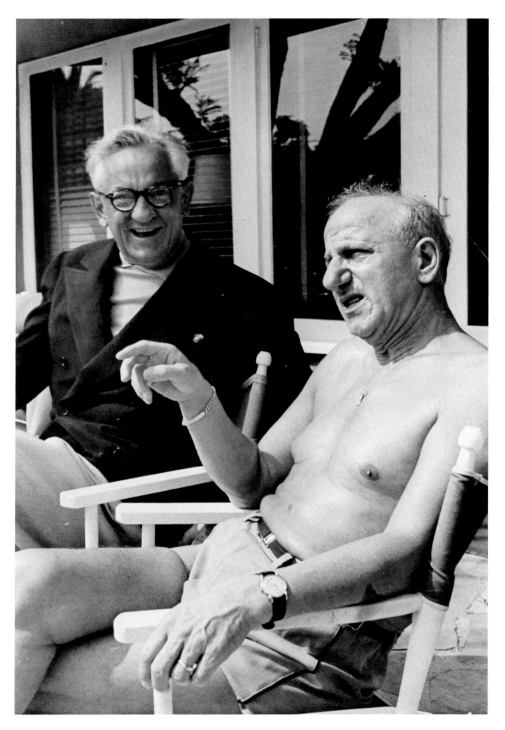

Gene Fowler demonstrating one of his explosive laughs while
listening to Jimmy Durante at the comedian's Beverly Hills
home. It was in 1950, when Fowler was writing the Durante
biography, *Schnozzola*.

Fowler sits with Westbrook Pegler at the columnist's Tucson home in 1949, on the same day Pegler published a scathing article about the author's recently published biography of Mayor Jimmie Walker, *Beau James.*

Closeup of Dempsey and Fowler in the boxer's Broadway restaurant. The 1952 photo is inscribed, "To Will: We wuz robbed" and signed "Jack and Pop."

The author with film
director Irwin Allen, 1975.

Gene Fowler, Honorary
Director of Social Security
and President Emeritus of
the Free Loading Sons of
America, is shown here
accepting new awards
bestowed on him for his
invention of the stream-
lined celluloid cuff in 1959.
The Oscars were donated
by a pawnbroker who was
retiring from business.

The last formal portrait of Gene Fowler (late 1959) taken in his
Brentwood home by Frank Q. Brown.

melon-sized scrotal hernia. He often shouted out to Decker, "Where's the bathroom?"

"You know damned well where it is," Decker would usually answer from the kitchen while cooking or testing his urine.

"*Bring it to me*," Hartmann would insist.

"If you piss on my sofa," Decker threatened, "I'll throw you out just like that millionaire friend of yours did."

The artist was referring to the time Sadakichi was the houseguest of a wealthy midwestern man some years earlier. Five days was all the gentleman could handle Sadakichi. He had him thrown from his mansion. And as Hartmann was being turkeywalked through the front reception hall toward the door, the Oriental bellowed, "When the world learns that Sadakichi Hartmann slept here, this building shall become an edifice to his name! . . . Looms there no isle for my peace of mind . . . where I may be appreciated? Hah! Thank you very much. . . . Hello!"

A year later, Sadakichi had forgotten that he had given his millionaire acquaintance a hard time, and that he had been thrown from his home. So it was not odd that he wrote the gentleman to ask if he might be his guest this coming winter.

The reply was a resolute "No!" with an addendum that the house would be "boarded up while we spend the season in Europe."

This was all the information our derelict needed. He waited a week following the first snap of winter and took a bus to the midwestern town where our millionaire's home stood prominently like a Victorian castle atop a brooding hill. The place was boarded up, but Sadakichi tenaciously pried open a window and entered. There, he set up light housekeeping beside the library fireplace. He was annoyed because the house was not heated. Therefore, to start a fire and keep it going, Hartmann dismembered antique wooden furniture to use as cord wood. He even managed to wreck the grand staircase railing and render it, piece by piece, to the outsized fireplace.

When Hartmann decided it was time to move on, the house looked a shambles. But before he decamped, Sadakichi drew every shade in the manor house, then lit each electric bulb in the place. That he had torn several rooms and the grand staircase to

shreds bothered him not in the least. As a gesture before his
adieu, Hartmann left a note:
  "Let there be light!"

*   *   *

The Bundy Drive house was not a bus station of activity. But the
characters who visited there always seemed to do things that
would be remembered. This was especially true when Sadakichi
was present, cursing whomsoever he might find handy — even
the duck in the backyard.

During a quieter day Hartmann was holed up in his Banning
shack. Barrymore, having escaped his male nurse, was temporar-
ily at peace. By habit, he delivered an aside to Decker, asking if
he might have a bit of nectar in the house, " a drop of ambrosia."

The artist apologized for the lack of alcohol on the premises,
but said he would go pick some up at the neighborhood liquor
store. He repaired to the small tin box hidden in the crawl hole
behind his bed to make a withdrawal. He descended. Then, like
a slow moonrise, appeared again. There was a combined look of
dismay and grief on his face. "It's all gone," he whispered to
himself. "The money's all gone."

I answered my phone, and Decker explained his plight. I told
him I knew where a bottle of scotch was hidden. I stole it and
rushed to the artist's house within five minutes.

When Jack noticed the bottle cradled in my arm, he poured
blessings on me. After fixing three highballs, we sat on the couch
at the rear of the living room. Decker brooded across the way,
wondering how he was going to raise enough money to support
his needs.

It had begun to cloud up and Barrymore peered out at raindrops beginning to form on a nearby window. He was silent for a
time, then said, "Ah, this place would have been a refuge for my
old departed pal John Gilbert. There were so many times when
he wished so to get away from everything." Then, thinking back,
he said, "You know, Will, Gilbert was one of the finest actors of
his day on the screen. And that horseshit about his voice being
high . . . Christ, it was as normal as hell. . . . I know for a fact that
that pissant L.B. Mayer was trying to break John's contract at

MGM, and that's why Mayer had his press agents put out the rumors that his voice was too high for the talkies. God, Gilbert often had a greater box office draw than I did." He snorted, "And that's a lot for one actor to admit about another."

I wrote to Gilbert's daughter, Leatrice Joy Gilbert (now Mrs. Leatrice Fountain), to inquire about the authenticity of what Barrymore had told me years earlier. An author herself (*Love to the Irish* [Doubleday]), she kindly answered my inquiry. Although she is presently working on an extended biography of her father, Leatrice was generous enough to pass on the following:

> *MGM disseminated such crap after his [Gilbert's] fall when they were trying to break his contract. They said he was stupid, overly theatrical, even a bad actor. They have all forgotten that Robert E. Sherwood, the playwright and film critic for the old* Life Magazine, *called him "one of the finest actors I have ever seen on the screen."*

She noted that her father had won the *Photoplay Medal of Honor* for best actor in 1925, before the days of the Academy Awards. She also wrote that he was voted *King of the Movies* by the *New York Daily News*. This was in 1927.

Leatrice agreed with what Barrymore had told me: that film historian Kevin Brownlow called Gilbert "the first modern actor to appear in the movies."*.

"He set the model for the great stars who came after him," she continued. "Gary Cooper, Robert Montgomery and Clark Gable."

"And why had Greta Garbo stuck so steadfastly to Gilbert all these years?" I had asked Barrymore on this rainy day so many years ago.

"For God sake," Jack said, "he was most instrumental in helping make her a star, teaching all those nuances, those little gestures. Sure, Garbo had to have talent to start with. But Gilbert honed it."

In her letter, Leatrice corroborated this:

The Parade's Gone By.

Sadakichi and the Baron of Bundy Drive

Clarence Brown, who directed my father and Garbo in
Flesh and the Devil, *told me personally that it was Jack*
[Gilbert] *who taught Garbo her film technique and* not
Mauritz Stiller, as is generally supposed. He said, "Com-
pare her performances before Flesh and the Devil, *and*
after."

Leatrice ended her letter with, "Like your father, Will, he was a
hellion, an upstart. He was intelligent and self-destructive."

"Yes," sighed Barrymore back in Bundy Drive, "this would
have been an interesting atmosphere for Gilbert. I miss him. All
of my little playmates seem to be deserting me."

At this, Decker downed the last dram of his scotch and said,
"That's it. I'm going to have to lock myself in." What he meant
was that he would cease all drinking and go into seclusion to
think upon a theme for a new exhibition. Then, in about four
weeks, he would emerge with about fifty paintings representing
this theme. Next, he would arrange a one-man show at the Francis Taylor Galleries in the Beverly Hills Hotel. A host of friends
would be invited. They would drink his booze, get into a few
scuffles, marvel at the beauty of Taylor's child, actress Elizabeth,
then purchase the paintings. Decker would be solvent again, and
there would be nothing to worry about until the little tin box behind his bed was once again empty. Until that time, the artist's
paintbrushes would dry up once again.

*   *   *

Decker was never fully appreciated by the hierarchy of art critics — although there were a few who recognized his potential,
such as S. McDonald Wright, Roland McKinney and Arthur Mil-
lier. These men began to notice him following a one-man show
at Vincent Price's Little Gallery on Santa Monica Boulevard in
Beverly Hills prior to World War II. Among Beverly Hills
cognoscenti visiting the show were Sergei Rachmaninoff, Igor
Stravinski, Ernst Toch and Dr. Arnold Schönberg.

Following Price's show, Hecht wrote of Decker's works: "Mas-
terly, impish, and as bristling with talent as a Sultana, John
Decker is California's one-man Renaissance."

Unfortunately, John lost some of his glitter when he hit upon a

painting which sold well. He would copy the painting, sometimes four times, and sell it as the original. This was disastrous.
As a prime example: Fowler commissioned Decker to paint a
portrait of W.C. Fields dressed as Queen Victoria, executing it
with a nineteenth-century technique. It turned out so well that
when restaurateur Dave Chasen saw it, he said, "God, John, I've
just got to have one of these." It was as though he were purchas-
ing something in a department store. But, smelling the easy
money, Decker immediately went to his studio, duplicated the
painting and delivered it to Chasen the following day.

Then Sir Cedric Hardwicke (whom we dubbed "Sir Seldom
Hard Prick" when I was a publicity man at Paramount Studios)
wanted one.

When people visited Fowler's house to view the original, they
would say, "Oh, that's a copy of Dave Chasen's painting," or,
"That's a copy of so-and-so's painting." Annoyed by this, Fowler
had the original packed up and delivered to Uncle Claude for a
Christmas present.

There was other devilment deep in Decker's soul for turning a
much needed buck. One evening he was having dinner with actress Paulette Goddard. She was decrying the lack of painters
capable of capturing the Venetian scene. "They're all so much
the same," she told him.

"I agree," Decker smiled over his brandy snifter. "They're all
the same."

Then Miss Goddard went on to explain in detail what kind of
Venetian painting she would consider buying if she ever found
one.

"I know just the painting you're talking about," Decker said.
"May I bring it over to your house tomorrow and show it to
you?"

Miss Goddard agreed, and Decker was off to his studio to
paint half the night, then age his Venetian work in order to show
it. When she studied the oil the next day, she bought it on the
spot.

* * *

Years ago, Decker came across a gilded frame about six feet by three. He had this insane idea that he would paint a still life of two buildings with a railroad track running diagonally across the work. To do this, the painting would be executed horizontally. But when he had completed the work, he was dissatisfied. "How the hell am I going to sell a monstrosity like this? Nobody will buy it. It's too wide and not tall enough."

I suggested he saw it in half.

It took Decker no time to realize the possibilities. Ten minutes later, I was busy in his garage with a carpenter's finishing saw parting the painting from itself in order to fit two other vacant frames he had hanging there. He realized a good price on both paintings. (More often, he painted on wood.)

* * *

An ancient member of the Bundy Drive group, Thomas Mitchell, was a thoughtful collector of paintings. His tastes went mainly to the modern. But he did wish before he died to own a Rembrandt. Even in these days of the early 1940s, the cost of owning a Rembrandt was prohibitive. However, Decker had the answer. "I can get you a very small one, but it's an example of his early works."

"How much do you think it will cost me?" Mitchell asked.

The thought of $2,000 came to Decker's mind. It was a reasonable price and, too, the little tin box was getting empty.

Mitchell jubilantly cried, "Get it!"

The problem confronting Decker now was to come up with a Rembrandt. "It'll take me about six weeks or more to deliver it."

"I don't care if it takes six months," said Mitchell. "I want that painting."

"Wood," said Decker that evening. "Wood's what we need. Do you have an old slab of wood?" he asked me.

"Not on me," I said. "But why don't we go to one of those outdoor places that sell antique furniture? I'm sure they'll have something to fit your needs."

The following morning we drove down Ventura Boulevard in the San Fernando Valley. The offroads west of Sepulveda were still mostly dirt. We found one of these outdoor antique places and noticed a dresser with one drawer missing. We asked the proprietor the price.

"Well, there's only one drawer," he pointed out.

"I can see that," said Decker. "How much?"

"One dollar."

"Sold."

The dealer was mystified because we took only the drawer and left the rest of the dresser behind.

Back at the studio, Decker said, "How large should it be?"

"How small, you mean," I said. "How do they measure paintings in Europe?"

"By the centimeter," he said.

I was unable to figure how to mark off centimeters on an American T-square, so I penciled off eight-by-ten inches, the popular size of a movie star's photo.

Decker locked himself up and began work to create a Rembrandt. (For obvious reasons, I do not care to disclose the painting's subject.)

The next step was to have the painting authenticated by a Flemish expert. Decker had one. He was W.R. Valentiner, then director of the Los Angeles Museum of Art. He authenticated the work as being that of Rembrandt — an early effort. Decker paid Valentiner $600 for his services.

Next John fractured the wood's obverse side, then had it transferred to Holland where experts cradled (reinforced and straightened) it. When the painting was returned to Decker, it was registered with the Netherlands government for export, thus adding authenticity to the painting.

Now Decker presented the "Rembrandt" to an overjoyed Mitchell.

Several years following Mitchell's death, the newspapers carried a story that the same painting had been sold for in the vincinity of $100,000.

*   *   *

Although most of his paintings were applauded as typically American, John Decker was a German baron. This, as was Sadakichi's nationality, remained a secret with a few close friends.

Nonetheless, the artist was apprehensive about his heritage during World War II. For two years during World War I, the artist had been a political prisoner on the Isle of Man, subsisting only on bread and water. He considered that a repeat would be a personal disaster, even though the food quality might be upgraded.

John was Baron Leopold von der Decken, born in Germany to Count von der Decken and his opera-singing wife in 1895.

When John and his wife Phyllis moved into the Hollywood studio Errol Flynn had secured for them, he celebrated his new warren by giving a one-man show. His own paintings, naturally. Among them was a work he titled *Pigs in Clover*. He painted it from his studio window, which looked out on the rear of the Mocambo nightclub on the then swanky Sunset Strip. Junk — including garbage cans, an old fence and an ice wagon — was carelessly strewn about. In the upper center background of this nighttime scene was a row of lighted windows behind which the suckers sat, dining and drinking.

Decker showed the painting to Mocambo owner Charlie Morrison, who promptly had the rear of his nightclub put in order. As a gesture of friendship, Morrison allowed Decker to have drinks on the house any time he visited the Mocambo. The artist took polite advantage of this, but always gallantly laid a heavy tip on the waiter.

Unflaggingly, there was much to drink at a Decker exhibition. This night held to form. A fight started. Soon it seemed that everyone was in on it as I calmly took refuge with my glass behind the bar. Diana Barrymore, Errol Flynn, Jack LaRue, Alan Mowbray, Anthony Quinn, Lawrence Tierney and Ida Lupino were all in there punching and throwing bottles.

When the police arrived, everybody offered different versions of the scuffle. They were informed as to who was giving the party, then approached Decker in the upper gallery. The artist was picking up pieces of a nude statue he had named Mona. He told the officers that he didn't know how the fight had started, but that he was mad because "some son-of-a-bitch broke my Mona." The police were tolerant and asked John if there had been any drinking. The artist became indignant. "Certainly there was drinking. What the hell kind of parties do you think I give?"

No one was arrested but Jack LaRue was taken to a Hollywood emergency hospital to have stitches for his head wound.

The next day, the *Herald and Express* carried the headline:

ACTOR IN HOSPITAL
AFTER HOLLYWOOD BRAWL

A photo displayed Decker with a broom and dustpan in hand sweeping up Mona's remains.

Decker decided his next exhibition would be more austere. Guests were carefully hand-picked. This night Decker's gallery seemed to exhibit more important paintings than the Los Angeles Museum of Art displayed. Among the twenty-five paintings, twenty of the world's greatest artists were represented, including Rembrandt, Whistler, Van Gogh, Gauguin, Lautrec, Matisse, Picasso, Braque and Modigliani.

Shortly after this impressive show, Tallulah Bankhead, in town making a picture, *Lifeboat*, at Fox, invited John to escort her to a dinner party. It turned out to be a political rally. The dinner was free, but soon the speeches began. A free soul, Decker not only knew nothing about politics, but despised them.

Blank checks were distributed to the guests, who represented the crème of the movie industry. After the checks were filled out and collected, the master of ceremonies began to read aloud the donation amounts and the contributors' names. "Here we have a check from that great producer William Perlberg for $1,000." Names continued to be read and amounts given. Applause followed each announcement. The Screen Actors Guild donated two thousand. Now came Tallulah's check, and this was followed by ". . . and here we have a check from, ahh, uhh, uhh . . ." For a moment the emcee looked helpless, then he regained his composure and continued to the next. The check he put aside with the ahh, uhh, uhh, was from Decker. On it was written, "Two-dollars-and-fifty-cents for the dinner, which was lousy. I should have made it out for a dollar, but I didn't want to appear cheap about it."

After driving Tallulah home from the party, Decker was stopped by a motorcycle officer. Tallulah had given John a few fortified nightcaps for the road and he was unable to pass the street sobriety test. He was hauled in to the Santa Monica jail where a doctor was called to give him further tests. The medic was about five feet one inch tall and had an annoying, squeaky voice. "What do you do for a living?" he asked as he examined Decker.

"I'm an artist," John smirked.

"What kind of an artist?" came the squeaky voice.

"A painter. I paint portraits." Another smirk.

"Do you think you could paint my portrait right now?" Another squeak.

Decker stared up at the ceiling. "No. I don't paint miniatures."

* * *

During a sober week, John began to prepare for an exhibition of his works to be held in San Francisco. When he was ready, he boarded the train for the city of Saint Francis, along with such cronies as Thomas Mitchell, Errol Flynn, Artie Shaw and a sprinkling of woodwind and string virtuosos.

That evening, Decker was occupying a room in Flynn's suite at the St. Francis Hotel. Indeed, he was lying in state on one of the beds when the porter arrived carrying, not the ordinary luggage of the world traveler, but a lady who was hanging head-down on his back. She was screaming in a muffled sort of way because her petticoats were hanging over her face. All manner of scandal was stirred up and blamed on the innocent, wined-up Decker. The lady, it seems, was an admirer of Mr. Flynn, although he did not know of this until he heard that his friend Decker was being accused of bribing the hotel porter to serve him flesh hot off the griddle. Mr. Flynn, whose reputation for gallantry exceeded that of D'Artagnan, blithely permitted his friend Decker to bear the onus of this madcap occurrence. Ergo, Mr. Decker was roused from his bacchanalian stupor and given the bums' rush from the hotel. With his long locks hanging over his hatchet face, he screamed at the injustice of it all and added several epithets having to do with sexual intercourse as applied by a man to his own person, and he looked exactly like a maniacal Uncas.

* * *

Next adventure on the agenda was a sea cruise down Mexico way on Flynn's sumptuous sailing yacht, the *Zaca*. The junket was a combination pleasure and science trip. Flynn wanted to escape the reach of Jack Warner, for whom he was working at the time. As a smokescreen, Errol brought along his father, Dr. Theodore Thomson-Flynn, a zoologist and dean of the School of Science at Queens College in Belfast, Ireland. Other guests were Professor Carl L. Hubbs of the Scripps Institute of Oceanography at La Jolla, Swiss composer and erstwhile nightclub operator in Mexico City, Ted Stauffer, professional archer Howard Hill and Flynn's wife, Nora Eddington Flynn. Counting Decker and the crew, there were seventeen in all.

The *Zaca* had been at sea nearly a month when the schooner anchored at Acapulco, where, after the guests hit the beach, it was obvious there had been a clash of personalities aboard. Referring to Nora, Decker said that "women, men and yachts don't mix."

He said that after Nora got her sealegs she took over command of the ship "like a Captain Bligh of the ship *Bounty*. "I thought I knew her before we started out on this damned trip, but I discovered now that I didn't. She just took over and started shoving everybody around. I guess she resented Flynn always being with the men. The talks we had with Flynn were man talks, and she couldn't enter into them.

"It's too bad this little mosquito has come between us. I can't really lay my finger on anything important she did. It was a constant pin-pricking process calculated to drive me nuts."

Everything came to a head when the *Zaca* hove to in a lagoon at Cedros Island off the coast of Lower California. Decker told me he emerged on deck shouting, "The woman has locked up my insulin in the icebox! What the hell's going to happen if I go into shock?" After some harsh words, Decker said Nora had recanted and returned this vital medication to him.

During a rare quiet moment, a seaman named Beery dived into the lagoon waters, taking a lethal spring harpoon gun in order to spear a shark. Instead, he harpooned his own ankle. Berry was hauled out of the water and it was necessary for Dr. Thomson-Flynn and Professor Hubbs to operate on the leg in order to remove the weapon. "Over Nora's protests," said Decker, "Flynn was persuaded to head for Acapulco one thousand miles away because there was a fear of infection, and a more competent medical man would be able to tend to the wounded seafarer. Nora accused Flynn of going to Acapulco because he wanted a drink," said John.

When they arrived, Decker marched off the ship with two of the guests carrying the wounded Beery. None of them would return aboard. Flynn's sidekick Jim Fleming had missed the Los Angeles departure, but rendezvoused with his pal in Acapulco. After listening about the goings on aboard the mutinous ship, he boarded her only to remove his effects.

Nora was mainly disturbed because she expected Flynn's friends to work as seamen. Decker said she thought this was unsatisfactory, adding that she objected to the artist using four-letter words.

"Did you?" I asked.

"Sure I used four-letter words. But I told her I could also use two-and three-syllable words, which is more than I can say about some people."

In spite of it all, John emerged with his one-man show held at his Hollywood studio. In all, with Mexico and the *Zaca* as his theme, Decker had painted twenty-four canvases for the exhibit in two weeks, which turned out to be most successful.

Too much success, however, killed him. His art output lessened as he began drinking against his doctor's orders, and he was spending too much time out on the town. Finally, he hemorrhaged from the stomach and was rushed to the hospital. He was placed in a deluxe suite there, a circumstance that no one would have denied him, except that the charges were just a little bit foolish, amounting to $2,500. (This was thirty-three years ago.) He had three nurses whom he abused roundly, and there were frequent resignations on the part of the shocked Florence Nightingales. Numerous suggestions made to them by the dying man as to where they could place the bedpans and what they could do to themselves in general (and in particular) caused complaints such as to rouse the faculty to threats of expulsion.

He died in June of 1947 following a second trip to surgery, where they found it impossible to stop the hemorrhaging of his stomach, which was like a sponge in its varicosity.

I arranged for the funeral a few days later at John's Hollywood studio. He had once told Phyllis he wished his body to be laid out on his bar, but she wisely decreed that it be displayed among the easels. He wanted the deathbed picture of Jack Barrymore propped upon the casket beside the dutch-door lid of the receptacle, the upper half of which was raised.

The boys at the funeral parlor wanted $4,000 for the obsequies, thinking that our John had died as rich as he had lived. But John always spent everything he made faster than he could paint. I descended upon the morticians with the wrath associated with the journalists of my day. I hammered down the body-snatchers from four grand to $500, and proceeded to raise the money among his friends.

The ceremonies at the studio included a phonograph recording of Decker's voice reciting the "No Thank You" soliloquy from Rostand's *Cyrano de Bergerac*. A spray of red roses hung from the Barrymore deathbed sketch.

At the very moment the minister said, "Let us pray," the spray of flowers came down with a plop onto the unopened half of the casket lid. Ben Hecht, who was there, told me that if anyone could come back from the Great Beyond, Barrymore could do it. Perhaps this was some kind of a benediction, or its antithesis.

Decker had dark auburn hair. His moustache grew out red, a color he disliked because it reminded him of sunsets and his mother — both of which he also hated. So, before the funeral and in the presence of several of us, Phyllis took one of John's sable brushes, and some dye, and painted his moustache.

A week later I was out circulating among friends, trying to induce thirty of them to give the hospital a pint each of blood in payment in kind for the thirty transfusions given to John. He had practically bankrupted the Cedars of Lebanon blood bank of the type of blood that he needed. Only Tony Quinn seemed to have the kind that matched his type and this generous fellow, who once before had supplied a quart of his blood to John in an earlier illness, seemed to regard the matter with haggard apprehension. The vast total of thirty pints staggered his imagination and made him appear furtive.

Quinn had met Decker when the former was twenty years old. At the time, the two were trying out for a part opposite Mae West in George S. George's Hollywood production of *Clean Beds* at the John Golden Theater. But, acting as producer, America's perennial sex symbol had dismissed him as too young.

A few hours later, Tony strayed into the theater proper where several young men, imitating John Barrymore, were trying out for the part. He asked a nearby stranger why all the actors were aping his idol. "Mr. George wrote *Clean Beds* with Barrymore in mind, but he's busy with his new wife and told the writer to go fuck himself," was the answer. "Also, the play predicts that Barrymore will wind up a drunk in a flophouse."

Chancing to catch Quinn while reading the part of a sixty-five-year-old man, Miss West had second thoughts about his talent and persuaded her director to hire him.

On opening night, dissatisfied with his makeup, Tony made an emergency phone call for his friend, the son of Russian basso Feodor Chaliapin. Feodor, Jr., presently arrived with Akim Tamiroff in tow. Tamiroff was as good a makeup artist as he was an actor. He credibly transformed Quinn's Aztec-Irish features into those of an aged man with a puttied Barrymore nose to accompany the "camel walk."

The great Hamlet was in the audience that night and later introduced himself to Tony backstage. Extremely complimentary to Quinn about his acting ability, Jack invited the young man to visit him at his Tower Road home.

Following a dilatory bus ride and a walk up the steep hills that brood above Beverly Hills some time later, Tony was turned away by Jack's Japanese caretaker-gardener, Nishi, who notified him in his strained English accent that Mr. Barrymore saw no one. Disappointed, Quinn started down the lonely road, when he heard a ribald shout crack the quiet hillside with, "Hey, *shithead*! Where have you been?" (Jack reserved this epithet for those he dearly loved, such as W.C. Fields and Sadakichi Hartmann.) The two struck up an alliance which lasted until Barrymore's death in 1942.

Some time after Tony had gravitated into the Bundy Drive group, he asked me, as did my father, what I thought was Jack's outstanding characteristic. I said, "He was so young. He never seemed old, never at any time, and that was a wonderful thing."

A year following Decker's cremation, a letter came to Phyllis claiming that the rent was due on the artist's ashes. Phyllis said that this was untrue, that the rent had been paid. When she told me about this, I thought John would have greatly enjoyed being behind on a bill, even after death.

15

Faulkner and Hecht in Hollywood

Anybody can win any reasonable thing. The world is not against you. If you break a leg while climbing a ladder, it is not the ladder's fault but your own. Either you forgot to place the device so that it would not slip, or failed to see to it that the apparatus was solid, or were thinking of your girl when missing the next rung.

In the 1930s, Hollywood columnists, among other savants, too often depicted an author's success in the motion picture producing city as something gained overnight with an effortless, jackpot magic possessed only by breathtaking women or lucky cads. But the writers more than paid their dues long before they arrived in Hollywood.

The vitality of the Hollywood columnist's legend caused great unhappiness among thousands of young persons innocent of the fact that almost every success in the arts is founded upon preparation, perseverance and practice. The yearners for glory meant to leap immediately onto the scented thrones of Hollywood, there to receive acclaim neither earned nor merited. Then, embittered and rooked, the thwarted Kings and Queens for a Day left town to wail against Fate.

It would have been an excellent procedure for each columnist daily to delete from his essay on nightclub society the names of four or five addle-pated playboys and substitute for them a line or two to indicate that the successful ones prepared intelligently for their careers.

Of course, any advice given to an ambitious person is as unwelcome as a cockroach at Dave Chasen's restaurant. I recall a time when my father was visiting a small New Zealand village near the Franz Josef Glacier. During a moment of amnesia, he had revealed that his resisdence was Hollywood. That confounded label brought a charming lady to his hotel with the earth-shaking news that her daughter was another Shirley Temple. Fowler endeavored to persuade his visitor that life in the motion pictures was extremely precarious; that thousands of Shirley Temples arrived annually in Hollywood only to be informed, none too kindly, that they were untalented brats. Furthermore, Fowler sought to convince the lady that even the infant Shirley Temple had been denied a valid girlhood; that she had to play on her expensive swing under the eyes of chaperones and policemen, and was attended by doting and asinine studio personnel who directed her every movement. Had the child fallen, word of the catastrophe would have devastated some producer's brittle arteries.

The lady looked at Fowler with a kind of cold, belligerent horror. For days she refused even to speak to him, and persuaded her neighbors that he was a vile cynic who had inflicted on her an immoral injury comparable to the indignity of rape.

Notwithstanding the Iron Curtain rung down on common sense whenever minds are set upon sudden and miraculous success, preparation is the secret of accomplishment. Men have found oil or gold in the backyard, just the other side of the pigpen, but almost always one must have experienced the drudgeries of purposeful study. There are certain talents born within all human beings — other than the army of imbeciles who turn out the majority of television scripts and prance about, announcing to anyone who will listen, that they are "writers." And when a man applies industry to his talent, he has a guarantee of success.

In the boxing business Gene Tunney became world's champion because he set his mind upon it and developed himself. Actor Efrem Zimbalist, Jr., refused to take up the violin because he was overwhelmed at the hours of practice his father put in on that instrument. Paderewski once told Fowler that for him to neglect practice on his piano even for one day meant that he would perform poorly at the next concert. If he missed two days, his manager would ask questions. If he missed three, the critics would be offended. If he missed four, even the public would think him off the beam. If he missed five days of preparation, posterity would damn him.

Perhaps no one in the theatrical circle works with such prodigious constancy as our delightful little friend Helen Hayes. Since childhood this lady has striven as hard as a stroke oar to perfect the rhythms of an art that makes her seem so natural when upon the stage or on the motion picture or television screens. In private life she makes no effort to seem glamorous or handsome. Still, the moment she apears professionally, she assumes great beauty and an aura of youth which has long passed her by. She becomes an electric presence. These qualities are part of her inner self, but she had to work hard and long to bring them, full blown, to the audience. The same was true of John Barrymore and Feodor Chaliapin, Sarah Bernhardt, and — don't laugh — W.C. Fields, and his successor, Red Skelton. Among the writers, Eugene O'Neill worked night and day, and Ben Hecht knew as much about being a galley slave as Cervantes did.

Painters, poets and successful columnists, such as Jim Murray, *work*. Walter Winchell, like him or not, used to treat himself like a convict in Folsom. Since I can remember, beginning in the mid-1930s of Hollywood, the gospel of regimentation and its false prophets preach "Share the wealth" without sharing the risks and rigors of achievement. The Buddhas of Bunk would make it seem that everybody becomes automatically a genius or a captain of the Ship of State the moment he draws the first breath in some obstetrical room. The old saw that poets are born and not made should be revised to read: "Poets are born and *then* made."

Yes, in the 1930s, it was mainly the proven writers, who had done their homework, who were called to Hollywood to lead the way in the production of finer motion pictures. But many departed, talking to themselves because unmeaningful and less intelligent producers were strangling their art at its source.

*   *   *

On weekdays my father's tall, attractive secretary, Agnes Bane, would walk north from the bus stop on Sunset Boulevard toward the house on Barrington. If Pop was working on a book, he would be going to bed about this time. While writing his habit was to rise about three o'clock and work for about five hours. While he was sleeping, Agnes would transcribe his latest pages and have them ready for his editing by about noon.

One morning, walking to the house, Agnes was joined by a man who appeared to be in his early fifties. His hair was salt-and-pepper gray and he wore a fairly generous moustache. He was clad in an old pair of tweed trousers and the top of his head came only to her nose.

"One thing I'll never forget," Agnes told me, "was that he smelled terribly of whiskey. I presumed by his appearance that this little fellow was either a gardener or neighborhood handyman. He was polite, though, when he asked if I minded if he joined me."

To Miss Bane's discomfort, this continued for a few weeks. "He spoke very little, just mentioning that his name was 'William,'" she said, "but when he did, there was always that foul smell of stale liquor on his breath. I began to loathe what used to be my refreshing morning walks and wished he would report to his gardening, or whatever job it was, before I arrived."

Then, one morning, the small walking distillery did not appear to greet Agnes. She sighed with relief and a quickness came back to her step as she headed toward the house.

When she entered, Agnes looked down the long corridor past the dining room and into the open breakfast room. "There, sitting with Mr. Fowler having tea," she said, "was this awful little man. I couldn't believe my eyes. Mr. Fowler had heard me close the front door and called out for me to come into the breakfast room. I really didn't want to go."

When she entered, both men rose and Mr. Fowler said, "Agnes, I'd like you to meet William Faulkner. He's out here writing a movie and just dropped in to autograph some of his books for me."

I met Faulkner later that morning and began to strike up a quiet friendship. Several times we went to dinner at one of his favorite restaurants in Hollywood, the Har Omar, where we ate lamb and rice wrapped in grape leaves. When we had dinner alone together, he did not drink. He seemed interested in my thoughts of society and the world through the mind's eye of a young man. He spoke little of himself, and only once referred to his having won the Nobel Prize for Literature, and this was not in a bragging manner.°

This man, a recluse most of his life, was presently in Hollywood acting as a "motion picture doctor," doing much the same as was usually Fowler's task: strengthening and saving weak scripts which otherwise would have been scrapped by the studio.

I managed to wedge two things out of Faulkner while dining at the Har Omar one evening. One was that until he had won the Nobel Prize, the American reading public did not flock to buy his work, and near the end of World War II, most of his nineteen books were out of print. Although he was looked on as a literary genius in Europe, American critics called him a "fatalistic and nihilistic writer of obscure books." His second confession was that he was in Hollywood doctoring a motion picture "only as a means to pick up some ready cash."

Somewhat in the manner of a guide conducting tourists on a sightseeing trip at Fox one day, Fowler identified the man in the tweeds as he passed the open door with Arthur Robinson. "William Faulkner," he announced. He added, *sotto voce*, "A brooder."

While doing his chores at MGM, Faulkner could no longer tolerate the beehive of activity about him in the Irving Thalberg Building where he was sequestered. "I finally went to Louis B. Mayer," Faulkner said, "and told him I was unable to function under the noisy conditions. I asked the head of the studio if he minded if I worked at home. Mr. Mayer was most accommodating and agreed that this would be permissible."

A week passed. MGM had not heard from Faulkner. An executive put in a call to the home the author was renting to discover that he had disappeared.

A studio publicity man finally did locate Faulkner. He had

° Faulkner was to win the Pulitzer Prize in 1955 for one of his lesser works, *A Fable.*

Faulkner and Hecht in Hollywood

gone home, all right — all the way back to his pre-Civil War plantation, "Rowanock," in Oxford, Mississippi.

* * *

Stirred from their lethargy, American idolaters embalmed Faulkner in a shroud of worship that denied him his right to existence as a human being and to disclosure of the fact that he lived and breathed and drank — like the rest of us. My father once told me a typical Fowleresque story about something that could easily have happened to him, but happened instead to Faulkner. It was a shared experience.

Knowing that Pop had been a sportswriter in the beginning, Faulkner had asked him if he could get tickets for a New Year's Day Rose Bowl football game at Pasadena. Pop got them. Faulkner wanted the total experience of going to the game, so he asked Fowler if he'd mind going by bus.

The only two available seats were separated. Faulkner sat in a two-seater with a seemingly gentle and proper lady. She was alone. Fowler sat across the aisle.

Before starting out, the men had fortified themselves against the possibility of a dreaded New Year's Day chill with several slugs of bourbon.

There were no plumbing facilities on the bus. Faulkner's kidneys cried out to him in anguish. The bus got caught in frequent, interminable delays in the crawling, game-going traffic. Finally, Faulkner's kidneys announced defeat with a smothered, sibilant gushing. His trousers published the news of the disaster. Gradually, the side of the lady next to Faulkner became warmly moist and scented with the fumes of Kentucky sour mash. The floor of the bus confirmed her suspicion. Fowler, always the observing reporter, noted all the details. The lady and Faulkner both maintained the stoical pretense that nothing unusual had happened. Fowler frostily assumed the attitude that Faulkner was a total stranger.

Ultimately, the bus reached Pasadena. It was Faulkner's move. He arose from his seat, gallantly stepped back to let the lady off, and bowed somewhat unsteadily, with all the courtliness of a true gentleman of the old South. The lady nodded in gracious acknowledgment of his courtliness — and smiled — in the finest tradition of Faulkner's own most noble Southern characters, then said, "We're both lucky you didn't have to take a *shit*."

* * *

Many authors of name came to Hollywood to work for the easy buck, but a number were unable to stick it out and left, mainly because the producers were unable to decipher good writing from bad. Besides Faulkner and Fowler, those who experienced disillusionment and frustration were Aldous Huxley, Donald Ogden Stewart, Nathanael West, H. Allen Smith, William Saroyan, Dorothy Parker and Charles MacArthur.

Manuel Komroff, author of *Coronet* and *Two Thieves*, could not understand Hollywood at all. When he stepped off the train in Pasadena, someone was yelling, "Hello, Mike!"

He went to the studio, where he began work on a script. The executives there, trying to be friendly, called him "Mike."

Manuel was confused by all this camaraderie. No one at the Algonquin Hotel in New York ever had called him "Mike."

He finally said to a noted director, "I am a highbrow. I don't know anything about the movies. Would you tell me why you people sent for me to work here?"

The director said, "That's simple, Mike. You must realize you've made a *name* for yourself."

* * *

The most vocal of all about Hollywood was Ben Hecht.

Ben put together the most engrossingly intermingled tragic and amusing book of letters I have ever read. In a modern way, it stacks up to those of Lord Chesterfield and Beethoven in value and interest. But, instead of delving into a single person's missive output, Hecht chose seven. They were Fowler, Sherwood Anderson, H.L. Mencken, poet Maxwell Bodenheim, artist George Grosz, composer George Antheil and his closest friend and collaborator Charles MacArthur. This, the last of his twenty-two books, *Letters from Bohemia* (Doubleday), was published the year of Ben's death, 1964. What made the work more thoughtful than most books on letters was the picturesque tableaus Hecht created, setting up the mood and character of each of his subjects before displaying their correspondence.

In the leadoff segment, Ben reported:

> *In the big studios, Fowler wrestled his way through a score of scenarios. He could write them well if they let him alone. He was still full of boss-loyalty, but he was unable to understand their helpful suggestions, their elephantine clichés, their babykins plot turns, their cold-potato great ideas. He was unable to feed on their "genius."*
>
> *The truth — Fowler was as out of place in Hollywood as a third leg on a rumba dancer. As what man of talent isn't? Except that Fowler was unable to learn the trick of becoming untalented. If you want to scale peaks as a movie writer, you must master this trick. Clichés must come easy. Stereotypes and platitudes must spring spontaneously from your typewriter. And you must crow over them like a diamond cutter.*

As an example of his disdain for Hollywood, Ben received the 1928 Academy Award "Oscar" for his script, *Underworld*. Years following, I recall Ben applied the Oscar in his circular guest house on the west shore of the Hudson River in upper Nyack, New York — as a doorstop.

*　*　*

During his youth as a newspaper reporter in Chicago, it was not beyond Ben Hecht to play a practical joke, but it was usually in concert with the probable instigator, his sidekick, Charles MacArthur.

On a hot summer's day in the early 1920s the two journalists learned that an Abraham Lincoln play was running to a disappointingly small audience. At the same time, Carl Sandburg was laboring on his six-volume Abraham Lincoln biography in that city. He had been at it for two years the night Hecht and MacArthur approached the failing play's title role actor. "Things were going bad for the company," Hecht said, "and they were about to close down. They had been operating in the red for two weeks. So Charlie and I offered the actor five dollars to costume up and slowly pass Sandburg's house a few times. Money was hard to come by, so the gentleman agreed."

The following evening, our hungry Thespian arrived at the theater one hour before curtain time to put on his costume, then accompany the reporters to the area where Sandburg lived and labored.

"It was especially hot and muggy that evening," said Hecht. "The insects were knocking their brains against the street lights directly in front of Sandburg's house. All the doors and windows were open to welcome any stray cool zephyr."

The voyeur reporters hid behind bushes and gazed with their backs to the moon as our actor in black shawl and top hat glided past the front door. The street light silhouetted his bearded face.

"Sandburg's concentration was interrupted while sitting at his typewriter," said Hecht. "He looked up and out the front to see this visage. The historian slowly rose from his chair. He stared at the manufactured apparition, then slumped into his seat after it disappeared. Shaken, he wiped his brow."

When the actor made his second pass, the hobo poet rushed to his front door to better observe the dark figure.

"Sure enough," said Hecht, "I learned later that Sandburg had confided in a few friends. He swore he had actually seen the ghost of Abraham Lincoln pass his home."

On hearing this report, a medical friend advised Sandburg to "take a vacation from work." The author agreed. He did not touch his typewriter for three more months.

* * *

During this time, Ben was covering an execution by hanging in Illinois. Shortly before death's wedding ring was placed about murderer Henry Spencer's neck, Hecht received a telegram from his editor:

PLEASE OMIT ALL GRUESOME DETAILS. SMITH.

Hecht shot back a wire:

WILL MAKE HANGING AS CHEERFUL AND OPTIMISTIC AS POSSIBLE. HECHT.

* * *

When they wassailed together, Hecht's frustration was being unable to keep up, drink for drink, with MacArthur and Fowler. Ultimately, following a night out, the two literally carried Hecht home. On the way, they awakened a country store proprietor and convinced the hick to sell them his entire stock of gelatin. After undressing Ben, they filled his bathtub with warm water. They mixed it with their brew of gelatin and therein placed the nude body of Hecht. Before departing, Charlie scribbled a note and placed it next to a spoon on the tub's running board:

"Eat your way out!"

* * *

Ben Hecht was the only author I had known through my childhood. He and his wife, Rose, visited with the Fowlers at least a few times each year. Mostly, I saw them at their home on Perry Lane in Nyack.

At a special Fourth of July day in the early 1930s Ben set off fireworks and, as a finale, blew up his small boat landing with dynamite. That night we were assigned to our sleeping quarters. I was bedded on a couch in the large mahogany-lined library. It was formal in style, yet comfortable. It seemed to me at the age of twelve that thousands of books were set into the walls, resting on shelves blending with the décor. The bay window afforded a generous view of the Hudson. The couch upon which I would sleep was set near a cupola. A rare Persian rug graced the hardwood floor.

After pilfering about — as does any youngster alone for the first time in a strange castle — I flicked several wall switches until I found one which turned out the lights. As I settled beneath my covers, I noticed several needle rays of light forming frames about eight inches square. They were situated near my cupola, and set into the wall. I hopped out of bed to examine one of these light-rimmed squares. To one side my fingers felt a brass brad. I pulled at it. It was the handle to a small door. Inside was a fully lighted minuscule doll's-house bedroom done to perfection in detail. The vanity table exploited a mirror and brushes and perfume bottles. There was even a delicately laced canopy adorning a four poster bed.

What set this display apart from being an ordinary doll's house were two well fashioned nude figures on the bed, locked in sexual embrace. In each cubicle were two or more dolls in several venery positions. One even displayed an adult woman enjoying her pleasures with two preteenage boys. But the little box I was unable to understand exhibited a female doll lying in bed, her feet touching the floor. And the male doll looked as if he had tripped on the way to greet her. He had fallen, his face landing on her stomach.

I was so entranced by these ravishing displays that I rose a half-dozen times during the night to reinspect my discovery.

From then on, each time we visited Ben's house, I always insisted on sleeping in the library.

*   *   *

In 1947, when the Jewish people were seeking to create their own State of Israel, Ben put his professional efforts into the movement. He sent them all the money he earned from writing scripts. When the British, whose soldiers held reign as protectorates of this Palestinian area, learned of this, Ben Hecht became *persona non grata* as far as writing scenarios for any English studios went. This only caused Ben to double his output. He began exclusively creating original scripts for sale to the English production money men — under a *nom de plume.* Now British producers were indirectly helping finance the future Israelis in their cause, but they were none the wiser. For his efforts, Israelis named one of their ships the *Ben Hecht.*

16

The Reporter from Harvard
and the Dubious Editor

"I always had to touch the stove to make certain it was hot, and then I had to touch it again in half an hour to be sure it hadn't cooled off."

These words typified the inquisitive nature of Fowler's contemporary newspaper star reporter friend, Donald Henderson Clarke, a product of the *New York World*. A unique journeyman of his trade, Don had earned a Harvard sheepskin denoting he held a master's degree in history, philosophy and English. He also possessed the appetite of a gourmet, relishing such dishes as Peconic Bay scallops, Diamond Back Terrapin, Chatham oyster, Southdown mutton chops and lobster fat on toast.

Fowler first met Clarke in 1918 during a Fifth Avenue Liberty Loan parade which traditionally started at Washington Square and ended at One Hundred and Tenth Street. The two followed the parade all the way, recessing at saloons en route. As they walked north, they noticed a very pregnant woman. She was so heavy with child, she looked as though she were harboring a hot-air balloon. After Fowler had made room in front of the spectators for the expectant mother, Clarke looked down and shooed away a remaining group of children, "so her unborn baby could see."

In his autobiography, *Man of the World* (Vanguard), Clarke laid down the basic essentials of a general assignment journalist: "Fundamental requirements of newspaper reporters were sound health, vitality, and an ability to work long hours with little sleep — the same requirements that are necessary for a successful consumer of alcohol."

A veteran who had been discharged from a newspaper more than once, Clarke always had a yen to work for a *Scripps-Howard* sheet primarily because the publisher, E.W. Scripps, was known to have drunk four quarts of whiskey a day, and made two decisions a year. After his doctor warned him that alcohol would kill him, Scripps quit the stuff and now had to make only one decision each year.

Clarke had told me that during his toping days he had screwed himself out of fortunes. "Most guys have screwed themselves into them," he reasoned. "If I had kept my bottles corked and my pants buttoned, I would have amounted to something."

Clarke and Fowler had become such close friends that one often contacted the other's city editor to ask if they might cover the same story together. This was actually permitted them.

The first they covered jointly was the Sing Sing execution of bank robber-murderer Gordon Fawcett Hamby, a meticulous dresser who stooped to murder, but never to profanity. This was the initial night execution is Ossining under the direction of the prison's new warden, Lewis E. Lawes, a man known to be an innovator of humanitarianism toward the inmates. Until then, all executions were carried out at daybreak. Lawes never witnessed an execution. He always turned his back when the electric current was switched on. Nor did he have newspapermen searched for hidden cameras until a *Daily News* photographer, camera strapped to his knee, took a picture of sashweight murderess Ruth Snyder being electrocuted in 1928.

Rather than face life imprisonment in Oregon for two felonies, Hamby insisted he be extradited to New York to stand trial for first-degree murder for killing two employees of an east Brooklyn bank. Hamby called the trial a farce, adding, "I'm guilty. Why this nonsense?"

In an attempt to rile Hamby during a trial recess, Clarke said to the handsome killer, "You're not starring in a three-ring circus, you know. You're being tried because you're a low-down cowardly murdering son-of-a-bitch."

Hamby could not be stired to anger. He even laughed when Clarke and Fowler next saw him enter the death chamber at

Sing Sing. Rather than the usual chalky pallor noticed on a condemned man's face, the svelte gunman showed good color as he walked resolutely toward the chair, smoking a cigarette. He complimented the prison physician, Dr. Squires, on his black tie, then said. "Tell the boys that 'The Little Green Door' is brown." He tossed his cigarette in a puddle of water, water used to moisten his electrified football helmet and ankle straps, then casually sat down. His last words were: "All I wish to say is that no one ever died in front of Grodon Fawcett Hamby's gun without having a chance." After Hamby strained against the chair's leather straps attached to its embracing oak arms, and the medical man in black tie prounced him dead, Clarke rushed toward the executioner. He kissed him on the forehead and said, "A very workmanlike job, my good man." Guards helped revive two young reporters who had fainted, and Hamby's body was placed on a gurney hidden behind the chair. If the electric current didn't kill Hamby, Dr. Squires' autopsy knife would.

* * *

Our unfortunate friend Clarke was sitting on a log washed gray by the sea. Leaning forward and resting his elbows on his knee, he was getting ready to witness an uncommonly bright red Fire Island sunset. But he was not planning to enjoy this prismatic phenomenon, for he had just been suspended for two weeks by the *World*'s publishers for breaking a junior executive's nose while on a toot in the city room. The young man had suggested that Clarke blow some booze money on his ever pressing bills. By this time, Don had graduated from being fired. He was a valuable reporter to lose; therefore, he had been given a professional slap on the wrist and been absented to cool off.

So now Clarke was sitting on a beached log wondering over the "why" of everything. While in purgatorial meditation, he tilted his rump and released a resounding wind. Relieved, he thought, *Why are people always so secretive about farting?* . . . *Of course, burglars* have *to be.* He peered out past the ocean waves, and a boat filled with people came into view. He thought it was too late in the day for this kind of activity in 1918, especially since the Coast Guard had put out a report that enemy submarines might be prowling the shipping lanes.

A champion swimmer during his days as a Harvard student, Don shucked his tennis shoes, dived through the waves and made his way out to the boat.

It turned out to be a lifeboat. Its occupants were survivors from an English freighter that had been torpedoed by a German submarine.

In these days, Fire Island was a sparsely populated sandbar. Ocean Beach had its only telegraph office. An instinctive reporter, Clarke knew the islanders would be heading for the station to alert the mainland about the survivors. After helping the British seamen to the beach, Don listened to a brief recounting of their ship's sinking, then hurried to flash the story to the *New York World*. In order to tie up the wire before he returned to the stricken mechantmen for a detailed follow-up story, Don had the telegrapher start sending the *Holy Bible* starting with Genesis, so he would still be in command of the wireless when he returned.

With his reporter's native luck, Clarke was not only taken off suspension early but received a bonus and a raise.

Yea, Clarke had been cast out to the wilderness in shame, as it were, yet the prodigal journalist was welcomed back into the fold, with manna for the front page.

* * *

About five days before he reported back, Don met with Fowler at the press club to celebrate and brag about his good fortune. Following their extended session of merrymaking, the two visited hotel physician Dr. J. Darwin Nagel. The man of the *World* wished to return to his bosses with clear head and good intentions, and Dr. Nagel was an expert in drying out reporters. But this time, more than sixty years ago, the journalists had a new wrinkle for quick rehabilitation. Their innovation was the *coffee enema!*

In a privately published paper lampooning the medical profession, Clarke and Fowler had announced to their friends that the was on postalcoholic tantrums had been won; that the hangover had met its master. The long-awaited master was coffee, administered as a hot enema. (Applause.)

In this earth-moving White paper, they pointed out that Drs. Holdfhart and Grinn (Fishbein's *A Flyswatter Is No Cure for Crabs*) had used caffeine hypodermically to dispel the toxic coma superinduced by excessive drinking. That technique, the reporters wrote was tedious, offensive to sensitive patients, and could be employed properly only by a skilled practitioner.

The coffee enema, on the other hand, was available to all. It would be given by any tyro, provided he did not try to play roulette with the patient's sphincter. The dosage was such as could be estimated. Very strong coffee, as warm as could be tolerated without sending in a three-alarm call for the fire department, might be entertained, up to three quarts — or *liters*, if the patient was a society woman. (More applause.)

Only a few warnings were necessary. Although the coffee need not be dated, a good grade was preferable. Fastidious persons, who insisted on cream and sugar together with the treatment, were immediately discouraged. Also, those who sought to use French coffee were cautioned against taking such a mixture of chicory, concentrated lye and oxen's urine into their system at *either* end. It was said to be widely known among the professors that there was not a sound bowel in any of the *arrondissements* of France. Indeed, the earlier Gallic obstetricians used French coffee in lieu of ergot during parturition. (Applause. Cries of "Hear! Hear!")

Clarke and Fowler stated that of 7,004 cases observed at the Tannenbaum Clinic, only seven failed to respond to the coffee enema treatment for drunken aftermaths. Of the seven, four were publishers, and the remaining three were almost as phlegmatic:

> *Case 542 — Mrs. M., 52 years old, blue eyes and suffering from hyperacidity. Was resonant on percussion. When brought in seemed to be in state of rigor mortis — or, perhaps, seven months gone. Respiration wheezy, râles in right lung and quantitites of gin in trachea and the bronchi. After three quarts of coffee were spilled by*

nurse, who mistook the target for the Grand Canyon, another dose was managed effectively. Mrs. M. rose screaming from the enema table, started to bid in an imaginary bridge game, chewed up her foundation garment and went singing happily into the night.

Case 234-A — Adolph A., machinist's helper, 36 years old has common law wife and is fond of sweets. Secret drinker. Has boss-persecution complex and Hutchinson's teeth. Found in gutter near fashionable night club. Both hands caught in his own fly. Claimed he was wrestling with an anaconda. Subdued by Patrolmen Schalett and Gordon, and held down while coffee (Maxwell House, No. 4, was used) was siphoned until the colon was distended from sigmoid to cecum. Howled like a castrated mink for two minutes, then got up calmly and began to repair the table in Operating Room B. Claimed it was a Baldwin locomotive that was due for delivery on the morrow. Complete cure.

Case 104-C&D — Emanuel Oblonschoviz, 41 years old, musician. Fell off lady singer while drunk, breaking pelvis and middle finger. Eight quarts coffee (Arbuckle's) failed to bring immediate relief, but when six drops of Coty's No. 3 perfume were added, response instantaneous. Walked out of clinic unaided, except for a note book with telephone numbers on second page (in code). Cure permanent until next Monday.

Case 444 — Armand F——, procurer and organist at St. Ziphany's Church. Rescued from organ bellows, which, in his delirium, he imagined to be his mother. Criticised interns who administered coffee per rectum (the second-grade A&P mocha was given as an experiment) and maintained that somebody was singing off-key. Within two minutes after the stop-and-go method was indulged in, Mr. F—— began to sway his hips and asked the head nurse if she wanted to become a mother. Gratifying cure.

Case 320½ — Marigold P——, 14 years old, a problem

child. Had terrific uncle-father-brother urge. Freud failed miserably in analysing her dreams. Drinks every Thursday night, the maid's evening off, and retires to a closet to play naughty tricks on herself. Juvenile formula No. 7 (two parts coffee, one part circus lemonade) used with amazing success. Little Marigold felt so good she spent night with House Surgeon. Forgot all about her uncle-father-brother and fixed her affections on grand-mother.

Case 50 — Rev. Turk S——, 73, circuit rider for B—— Church, South Norwalk. While drinking for medicinal purposes to ease asthma found himself suddenly committing a carnal sin with an inkeeper's niece. Overcome by shame and venereal troubles, arrived voluntarily at clinic, shouting: "For God's sake! Give it to me." Halfway through treatment (Chase & Sanborn's) looked down and thought himself to be the devil, wearing a long tail. A little prayer and an extra demitasse fixed the Rev. S——, who begged attendants to try the same remedy on urethra. Is now respected by all in South Norwalk, and by a few in New Canaan, also. Asthma cleared up, but the Rev. S—— is a bit flatulent during choir practice.

Case 6788 — Wilbur D——, former cabinet officer under President Chester Arthur, 92 years old, militiaman and student of Parsee Literature. Drunk since the False Armistice. When first treated (Lion Brand) imagined he was the man playing the flute in the 1776 picture, and begged everyone to cut him down from the art gallery wall. Several courses necessary to restore Wilbur D—— to a point resembling the normal. He now thinks he is only a copy of the original 1776 picture, but it is encouraging to know that he believes himself to the the drummer, *and not the* flute player.

*   *   *

In conclusion, Clarke and Fowler stated that anyone could try the coffee enema treatment on themselves, but warned not to expect doughnuts with every appointment. And, above all, if they did bring their own doughnuts, for the love of God and Hippocrates, they were asked not to try to dunk them!

Back to reality, and during the emergency to Dr. Nagel, Clarke and Fowler had been expecting another friend to arrive, but they said they would carry on without him. "You can't lay a tube on our tardy friend," Clarke said to Dr. Nagel. "You seem to be out of Maxwell House, his favorite."

* * *

Several years later, as did so many newspaper writers, Don Clarke migrated to Hollywood following publication of his best-selling novel about the New York underworld, *Louis Beretti*.

At MGM, Don found a room where no one worked on the first day he reported in. The receptionist was a prim, well groomed lady who kept a vase for a single rose on her desk. She asked him for a list of the things he might require. "No need for a list," he said. "Tell my stenogrpaher to get me a brass spittoon."

"This will have to be substantiated in some fashion," she said. "Why do you want a spittoon?"

"Most of my friends chew tobacco," he told her, "and those who do not chew tobacco are always puking with hangovers, and I don't want them to get it on the floor."

Clarke and the receptionist became enemies at once; three months later, his producer informed him that he had fired the lady.

"You didn't have to do that," said Clarke.

"I had to," said the producer. "Every morning she came in and told me that you had alcohol on your breath. I got tired of hearing this and said, 'I wish that all the writers had alcohol on their respective breaths if they could deliver the amount of work that Clarke does. . . . You're fired.' "

* * *

Shortly after Fowler mailed his critique along with a foreword to Clarke's final book, his autobiography, he enclosed a letter to the publisher warning him not to have his editors "emasculate the manuscript, else you shall have corrupted the very essence of the work itself."

The Reporter from Harvard and the Dubious Editor

Having read a copy of the letter, Clarke wrote to Fowler:

> *Your letter gave me the same pleasure I derive from the so-called classics — the orgasmic response to wisdom with modesty, insight without parade, and the divine spirit without the dogma. I have re-read your words several times which is the highest compliment I can pay to any writing.*

In the days when many well-put-together magazines were available to a selective reading public, Burt MacBride was respected by contributing writers of national and international esteem. During his editorship of *Cosmopolitan*, and later as a senior editor of *Reader's Digest*, MacBride associated on a personal basis with the likes of John Steinbeck, Ernest Hemingway, Ben Hecht, Bruce Catton, Lowell Thomas, Robert Benchley, T.S. Eliot, Sinclair Lewis and J.P. Marquand. And many more took editorial advice from this man.

But along the line, Burt told me in later years, he heard the call of Hollywood. He had written to Fowler, asking the author's opinion as to whether he should travel west for the big money and write for the studios.

Although Burt and I had never met, we began our correspondence when I first submitted a story about a little boy who died through an accident when convinced that it was possible for him to fly. He loved the story and in the early 1950s wrote from the *Reader's Digest* to tell me so.

It was not until 1961, when I was writing my first book, *The Young Man From Denver* (Doubleday), that MacBride sent me a copy of the letter my father had written him in 1935.

> *You place me in the position of a Lord Chesterfield communing with his son. I know quite well that sooner or later you will come out here and that you will succeed. Notwithstanding, I must give you my Jeremiacal impression of this and that.*
>
> *I need not point out that you are now occupying a decent position, and that you have professional intercourse directly or indirectly with articulate folk. When you fi-*

nally have put New York behind you, have stepped on
and off the "Chief" and have arrived in Hollywood, you
will have climbed up the rainbow, coasted down the
other side and wedged your posterior in the pot of gold.
But it is fool's gold — the iron pyrites of spiritual dam-
nation.

It all seems entrancing, from your distant fortified
position, but I assure you that Hollywood success will become bitter in your mouth. In your position as editor,
you at least deal literately with a semi-literate public. In
short, you and your colleagues are able to read, and it is
conceivable that your subscribers can pick out a word
here and there. The situation is immeasurably different
in Hollywood. The mumping hyenas who control this
abysmal "industry" cannot read, write nor converse intelligently. They throw all men's sprigs of laurel into a
sort of witches' broth and give their public a Mickey
Finn.

It will be a great shock to you. As Burt MacBride, editor of Cosmopolitan, you have prestige and command the
ready ear of those who regard your position as something
respectable. As Burt MacBride, employee of Simon
Glutz, President of Herringbone Films, you will be
looked upon as something won at a Chinese carnival.
Once you have entered a Hollywood "story conference,"
every legitimate molecule of your intelligence will fly
out through your ears. And if molecules have the habit of
vomiting, I'm sure yours will retch until the mystery of
releasing atomic energy will have been achieved in the
gutters of Sunset Boulevard.

I am reminiscently aware that the glitter of Hollywood gold blinds us all at the beginning. We amass a
stack of obligations; our ambitions sink a spear in our
flanks; we feel that we must "get the money" and Hollywood seems to be the only town full of payoff windows.
However, you will have to sleep with a fellow named
Burt MacBride each night, and on some nights you will
be unable to rest, because you will have sold a birthright.
A woman raped by a Senegambian leper is much better
off than the man who has yielded to the gilt phallus.

Some of our brighter young citizens have come here

full of strange excitements and the will to improve the
motion picture medium. Most of these precocious lads
now are hiding behind rubber plants hoping to escape
from their own shadows. Your well-seasoned editorial
brain will be set upon by golden blackjacks, split infini-
tives, ten-cent suggestions and superlative disregard for
anything that resembles a constructive idea. A bogus
chastity belt, studded with clichés, stolen ideas, claptrap
formulae, will be riveted on you. A censorship that stinks
like the seventeen streets of Jerusalem, will oppress you
until you swim in your own night sweats. The horizon
that seems so bright and shining from where you sit
overlooking Broadway actually is full of mirages.

I came out here because I needed money and had a
great many obligations. I assume that your reason for
wanting to sample the urine-flavored nectars of the cinema include this same financial urge. But please think on
it. You certainly are not starving. Your magazine is a
leader, and you have had an excellent training in the
field which now sustains you.

My God, Burt, I have been a prisoner in the Hollywood
Bedlam for almost six years! I dare not go to the Hollywood parties. I dare not mingle with the once gallant
lancers who have busted their asses on the rocks while
cocking an ear for the song of the Lorelei. Each day is
like coming to the Big House — only the wardens of Hollywood lisp. Soon (when the breath of Uncle Sam leaves
the nape of my neck) I shall retire on a small income and
begin to inhale the air of literacy one again. I willingly
shrug off the fortune that is here — for I cannot bear the
platinum chains longer. . . .

You will forgive me for a ham reference to a book
which I am doing, but in which one of my characters
says: "You may pin great handpainted wings on a louse,
but that does not make it a butterfly." . . .

You have a wife and children. I am sure she is a fine
woman and that the children are great people. But no
matter how firmly entrenched you are amid the ties of
domesticity, your wife either will be lonely out here —
terribly lonely — or she will be compelled to associate
with the God damndest tribe of green-eyed monsters,

festered critics, loud-mouthed destructionists, home wreckers, victims of decadent romances and the greatest congress of concentrated scum that ever has been surveyed since the time when Babylon fell off its trestle and was buried by the sands.

You will be able to buy Mrs. MacBride a mink coat, and soon she will wear diamonds and command four maids. But this will not make her happy. Any day one can go to Santa Anita race course to see the melancholy wives, who wear so much jewelry that it seems they are carrying brass knuckles and the trays of Frigidaire on each hand. But they are not happy. They mince in a sad minute.

The fact that you will be successful out here . . . is all the more reason for you to stay where you are. A Hollywood "success" is a hot house of man-eating plants. The stenches of this botanical display are hidden beneath a Niagara Falls of Coty's perfume. But the underlying decay is still there.

For Christ's sake, Burt, unless you are sentenced by a Federal Judge to exile in this artificial paradise, keep on producing magazines. Kick desire in the balls and stay reasonably content.

* * *

In each of his letters until he died, Burt found a way to refer to Fowler's letter of warning not to come to Hollywood.

MacBride felt that Fowler had talked him out of the greatest chance of his life.

17

Red Skelton: The Complex Clown

Before he died, my father presented me with thirty-five tapes he had made with Red Skelton during an intensive session which lasted throughout the months of April and May of 1951. Born July 18, 1913, in Vincennes, Indiana, Red was nearly thirty-eight at the time, and it was the intention of both that Fowler would write a Skelton biography. But when the two completed this marathon of talks which, transcribed, ran about five hundred pages, it was Fowler's opinion that the comedian had not yet lived long enough for the author to translate a full spectrum analysis of the man subject.

I visited my parents' home in 1944, shortly after *Good Night, Sweet Prince* had taken its perch as the number one national best-seller, there to remain for about a year. Demand for the book was so great during World War II that it was necessary for Viking Press to purchase two small printing houses in order to acquire their rationed paper allotments.

I answered the door to meet this tall (six foot three) man with the bashful smile. He held the Barrymore biography under his arm. "My name is Red Skelton," he said. "Is this the home of Gene Fowler?"

I invited him, then called upstairs: "Hey, Pop! Come on down! Cousin Delfred is here!"

"Cousin who?" Skelton asked.

"Cousin Delfred was our drinking cousin," I told the comedian, who at the time was riding the crest of success with his radio show.

"I've got to find out some more about this Cousin Delfred," he said. "Can I use his name on my show?"

"I don't see why not. Cousin Delfred drank himself to death a few years ago,"

Pop arrived at the upstairs railing. "Well, I'll be damned — Red Skelton. Come on up." I followed Red up the grand staircase to my father's workroom.

After he autographed the book, Fowler asked Skelton if he might get him a drink. Red declined. He was still married to his first wife, Edna, and had not yet taken to the bottle. "I wouldn't mind having one," said Fowler, "but certain members of the household have a dislike for the stuff, especially if it's going into *my* belly."

This was the beginning of a friendship that grew between an older man of some prominence and the younger, who then stood at the doorway of fame through which he would march until he was a dominating force in the medium of television.

Until his death in 1960, Fowler became one of the few people Skelton would trust. It was more than a surrogate father-son relationship. Skelton's father had died two months before the comedian's birth.

On his following radio program, Cousin Delfred debuted (via Red's voice). Members of Delfred's family, listening to same, asked Fowler if the comedian could possibly be referring to our own departed cousin. " 'Delfred' is not a common name," my Aunt Etta pointed out.

In the tapes which Red shared with Fowler, he remarked that his father had been a clown with the Hagenbeck and Wallace Circus. Later, he opened a grocery store in Vincennes. "My grandmother and half-uncle, due to the fact that my mother [Anna Fields] couldn't read or write, beat my mother out of everything," Skelton said. "The store, three houses in Vincennes and a farm in Robinson, Illinois. My half-uncle set fire — came into the store — and gave my Pop — who loved the booze by the way — a big slug of whiskey before breakfast, and that afternoon they carried him up to the house and he died two weeks later."

Telling of the store's fiery end, Red said his half-uncle, Chris,

"came around and got . . . the big kerosene can that stayed behind the store . . . set fire to this thing, and the tank fortunately
blew the opposite direction and burned down the store. . . . He
had it all set so that it would blow through the house and kill all
of us."

Red's grandmother, the second party who "beat my mother
out of everything," Ella Cochran, lived in Washington, Indiana,
"and by the way, ran the biggest whorehouse in the State of Indiana," sent for the Skelton boys to visit with her. Red said that
"these girls would keep coming and and I'd see all these strange
men coming in and out of the place. They were all friends of
Grandma's. And she was an atheist by the way. Grandma used to
stand out in the back and yell, 'You goddamned son-of-a-bitch!'
she says. "If you're up there, hit me with your fucking lightning!'
And boom! It took her. She died. She was paralyzed. One day it
hit her. The lightning hit her. . . . That's my father's mother."

* * *

Red had three older brothers: Ishmael, Chris and Paul. Red said,
"They used to do everything they could to try and kill me . . .
used to stand me in a corner for four and five hours at a time,
and if I turned around they'd belt me one, you know."

Red said that his family often moved from one city to the
other. "It seemed like every month we would move to another
house. It was cheaper than paying rent. You could get somebody
to move you for a dollar, you know."

Following one of their commuting moves between Indianapolis and Vincennes, Red spoke of his brief encounter with a public
school. "I was only six years old, had been in school for just one
year. And the second year I had already passed my other two
brothers. I got double promotion. But then when we moved back
to Vincennes, they says, 'How old are you?' I says, 'Why?' And
they says, 'Well, because you're not old enough.' So I says, 'Well,
give me the examination.' So that meant nothing, and they put
me back in the 1-A. Well, I lost all interest in school." Skelton left
school, never to return.

While taking advantage of free rent in Indianapolis, Red's
mother operated an elevator. She was also a scrubwoman at the

Lemke Building. Finished with these chores, she then labored two hours in a bakery. There was little time for sleep and watching over her sons.

There was enough money to place Red in a nursery school. It cost fifty cents a day. To our comedian, this seemed yet another downgrading until he suggested that he could put on a show for the other kids. The teacher then stood Red up to preach the Bible. "They'd always have to wrap an American flag around me," Red said, "around the highchair, or whatever I stood on, and I'd entertain the kids all day long."

This gave Red the idea of constructing his first stage. On Saturdays he would hitchhike to town such as Bicknell and Washington, Indiana, where he would pick a conveniently trafficked sidewalk to erect his stage. "I would take this little ukulele that I had. It was never in tune. All I knew was 'My Dog Has Fleas.' And no matter what came out, if it was too low, I kept singing lower. And then I would blacken up. And I'd take my own cork, burn it, go up an alley somewhere, blacken up, and then come out on the street. Yuck! Yuck!"

Following his performances, Red would return home and hand over the money he earned to his mother. Then she would give it to his older brother, Paul.

"He was the favorite," Red said. "They all hated me, because my mother told them that a woman came and left me on the doorstep and gave her five dollars to take care of me." He was the only member of the family with red hair.

"At Christmas time," he said, "they used to put coal in my socks. Or they'd get a horse-apple, and they'd tell me that I got a pony but he ran away."

When his mother couldn't afford to send the boy to the day nursery, she used to leave him in the house all day by himself. "I remember she used to turn the bed mattress back — this one mattress. And she says, 'If you have to go, you go there.' Because my next-to-the-oldest brother had weak kidneys to begin with, and he used to wet the bed all the time. And she says, 'Just go there and it'll be all right.' "

When his brothers came home, they would open the front door and allow him to go out for some fresh air. At the same time, his mother would warn him, "Don't let anybody in, because if you do, they'll put you in a orphans' home."

Most of the time the family subsisted on beans. Red's mother tried to make this an appetizing experience. She used to say, "We're going to have beans tonight. Ummm," and she would rub her stomach. "Oh, boy, beans." Red said they ate beans morning, noon and night. "Nothing but beans. It was the noisiest part of town."

* * *

Before entering show business, Red landed a job killing rats beneath the main floor of the local theater. He used a rifle and was awarded twenty-five cents for each dead rat he turned over to the manager. He was a good shot and made enough to help keep the family in beans.

With some of the money he purchased a packet of writing paper in order to correspond with a girl he had fallen in love with. "I remember this letter that I wrote to her," Red said. "And I've been always ashamed of it. Maybe that's why I don't write letters. . . . And I looked through the dictionary, and I found the biggest words. . . . And I said, 'I am sitting here in Mother's sanctuary, the library where she rests. She's gone to the bank now and that's why I'm writing this.' Actually, I'm sitting there freezing to death in the dump. Right on the railroad tracks in Vincennes."

His girlfriend was a waitress in a restaurant across from the Fort Smith Hotel in Arkansas, "which," Red said, "is a hook joint, by the way." Red later told this to director Frank Borzage's brother, Lou. He didn't believe it.

Red told Borzage that he had one girl there who made him a "creeper" in this panel joint. This is an establishment where a prostitute takes a man to bed, and, during his act of bedroom polo, her male confederate sneaks through a concealed panel to relieve the passionate fellow of his valuables. Skelton said, "She'd get a guy in there, and I'd come through this — slide the panel back in this big chiffonier, and while she was doing the business, I would pick the pocket, and then she's beat the hell out of the guy because he wouldn't pay her, see? He'd be half drunk any-how. And then we'd split."

* * *

Skelton was not quite twelve when he landed a showboat job in Cairo, Illinois, birthplace of humorist H. Allen Smith. It was in Hitner's Mississippi floating palace, the *Cotton Blossom*. Run by Captain Happy O'Kern, and Red sold candy there. It was a typi-cal scam. But one night the sales were so bad the young vendor exclaimed, "There's a man over there just won a Ford car." Red went down to where the customer was sitting. "Ladies and gen-tlemen, I've been on this river for years, selling candy. And if you think I'm making money, you're full of shit!"

Red fell in love with a girl working on the boat named Posey. She was fourteen. "So I'm watching her," Red said, "and, oh, God, I've really got a yen for this gal. And I pass the word that I've been around. I talk loud about the hook joints I've lived in and all the girls I've known. I figure, well, she may want some experience."

He followed Posey after the show one evening. "She goes down off the boat, and she says, 'I'll be right back. I'm going to take a little walk.' So I follow her. She gets into a car. So [later] I say to her, 'Why don't you keep it in the family? There's a way of working this out. We'll take the mosquito netting off the win-dow. . . .' So we take it off, and she tied it onto her bunk post. And I pulled myself around like a gallant man, you know.

"Now when everything's through, I want to enjoy it for an hour or so. So five minutes after laying there, telling her how beautiful and how lovely she is and everything, because that's one thing I was always taught. Also help them dress. They appre-ciate it. So all of a sudden I hear a voice yell, 'God damn! It's hot on this boat tonight. Why don't you open up them doors? Why you got them closed?' Now I gotta get back and I miss the rope and I go in the river. The next thing I know, here comes my wigs and my makeup and my wardrobe — everything — right out the window. He must have peeked in the door."

Taking the next step in furthering his career, Skelton joined the circus. *Billboard Magazine* carried an ad:

CLOWNS WANTED:
HAGENBECK & WALLACE, SELLS-FLOTO

When he walked in to apply, Red was asked, "What's your walk-around?" He was unaware that this was a routine clowns perform between major acts. In burlesque, they are called "bits." Nevertheless, he got the job for $20 a week.

Another circus tradition he was unaware of was that all entertainers were fined if they didn't adhere to rules, or were accepting undeserved privileges. As to the latter, an entertainer had a quarter taken from his salary; fifty cents for receiving mail, another half dollar for ketchup on the table — and there was a slot machine in the Privilege Car one could play if he had any money left.

The most serious offense for which a fine was levied on a clown was to turn around and look back during "the 11:45," the show's starting time. Supersitition rules that no one look back after passing his starting point. If one did, he would have to pay two dollars. This money would go into "the Hotel box," the tent where performers ate. Even today, the clowns wave only to the audience ahead of them.

Red had always wanted to own a trunk but, because of his lack of finances, was unable to buy one.

In the Privilege Car, Skelton said, "They would always have one fellow who would get up and say, 'Would you read a chapter?' And they would read a few paragraphs [from the Bible], and then they would all sit down and discuss it, see?"

Oddly enough, members attending their Sundays in the Privilege Car, also drank whiskey while discussing the Scriptures. "Some guy would disagree, and the guy would say, 'Why you silly bum, for Christ's sake, what do you know about the subject?' This would usually lead to a trading of words and often end up in a fistfight."

Becoming wiser, Red told the clowns that his father, Joe E. Hart, had also been a circus jester, traveling with the Hagenbeck and Wallace outfit. From that time on, his fines became less severe.

The clowns took a liking to the teenager and when he departed the circus after the first season was completed, they chipped in and bought him a trunk with his name on it.

* * *

Claiming he was "broad-happy," Red decided to join burlesque. It was necessary to have his birth certificate updated one year because the law required one to be sixteen to work in a burlesque house. His first job with a strip joint was to stand outside the theater seven days a week and deliver a spiel to corral customers inside. Yearning to be inside, performing, Red again searched the pages of *Billboard*. He found an ad seeking a burlesque comedian. Answering, he wrote, ". . . Do black face, Tobey comedian, nut comedy, and I'm sixteen years old."

During this time Skelton learned "delivery," "reaction" and "timing."

He started studying the professional comics' delivery.

"Timing is the exact delay — the timing of the pause," he said. "We'll say a guy, Ken Murray — they all use tricks in timing — Ken Murray has great timing but no delivery, see? Now his timing is — like you'd say, 'How do you like this suit? Paid $90 for it. Got fourteen pair of pants and a radio with it.' Now his timing is with a cigar. He will flip it as he's talking with it in his mouth, and then, when he takes it out of his mouth again, he delivers the punch line.

"Ted Healy has the greatest timing, I think. Ed Wynn, from figuring out their little quirks and stuff. Berle has no timing whatsoever. He just rides over it. Hope has a timing that he stole from Henny Youngman. Henny Youngman has one of the greatest timings, and is one of the greatest comedians that came along. And he was the first one to get on the air with this.

"Now, Ted Healy — he would come out and he'd say, 'All right, back up.' Now with his coat sleeve, by just grabbing up and straightening out his coat sleeve, he filled in just that amount of time that he needed.

"Now, Ed Wynn — he is a fellow that will use his hands. He

says, 'We're bluebloods. When you get mad, blood will just surge to his face. Blue serge.' Well, he does it with his hands. But if you'll notice, every one of these comics, they all do the same thing. They actually time off maybe one, two, three. Now every comic — basically, this goes for Durante, myself, and anybody — will say, to set up a joke, will go in threes. Everything is in threes. Like he says, 'A fellow was walking down the street, and a car knocked him down, so he gets up and he starts across the street and then another car knocks him down again. Then as he walks out again, he sees the car coming, he backs up, and he says, 'This is my lucky day,' and he got hit in the ass by a truck. I mean that's not a joke, but you get the idea.

"Now with me," he continued, "my timing is in a different way. I start to do a joke, and I always sort of shy like with my foot if you'll ever notice. I count off 'One, two, three, bam!' Like I say, 'Well, here we go, up to the lips, and over the gums, look out stomach, here she comes.' Then I drink. But I've actually counted three. . . .

"Now Fred Allen had a different technique, but which doesn't get over actually in person. It does on the air. Someone says something to him, and he will look away, and then come back more stern than he was before.

"If there's a hysterical woman in the audience they will bring along the rest of the audience with them — like Milton Berle carries his mother, see? She's got this 'Haw! Haw!' He plays on that.

"Like I always get one at my broadcast, when I say to the lady, 'Where were you during the broadcast?' Then I do the joke. I said that to a lady a couple of weeks ago. 'Where were you during the broadcast?' and she says, 'Where were you?' So now I come back and put the audience above me again. You have to keep yourself beneath the audience."

Referring to radio again, Red said, "Jack Benny's timing — if you've ever seen the broadcast — he will say something, and then look at the audience and then look back again. So again you have the motions of three. The look, the hold and then back again.

"Jolson went — always with his head. And all the time they're talking they time themselves by shaking their heads fast, back and forth, while half looking at the audience and half not. Even in their singing. Cantor is a guy that would look from one side to the other. Like to the right wing, then to the left wing, then to the audience again before he'd tell his jokes. Ted Healy not only did this, but before he'd tell his jokes he says, 'Ah . . . heh, heh, . . that's what I said to him.' See, he put a chuckle in. . . .

"Now W.C. Fields was a guy that would say, 'Aw, yes . . .' Then flip open the bottle. 'My dear . . .' He would pour. 'I was coming straight, all warm . . .' Now he stirs. But he never lets his dialogue, his expression, or his motions or his prop detract from each other."

Skelton remembered Danny Thomas. "I was going to tell you about Thomas' timing. This man was the closest thing to a religious timing — that is, like a priest — than any man I've ever seen in my life. Before he delivers his joke, he steps back, and with his hands out — like the statue — always with the hands out. With the palms to the audience. You feel he's deserving of something. . . . He isn't demanding it, just saying, 'What do you think?' "

Among other comedians he admired, Red singled out Jimmy Durante as a superior prop handler. "The other guys around him like the drums and stuff, take away from Jimmy, but out of loyalty . . . he holds onto these things."

Red called Bert Lahr "a warrior" and held Joe E. Brown and Edward Everett Horton near the top.

He admitted that Bert Williams and John Barrymore's "Uncle Guggin," and Jack's grandmother's illegitimate son, Sidney Drew, were before his time.

Last, he talked about Charles Chaplin: "I would like to see him go out into a picture that he didn't produce . . . and on his own, win over the audience right from the beginning and then get a big reception at the finish without going back and taking it over or — I mean — just on the spur of the moment."

Then Red reflected on the old circus days, saying that it was meant for kids, not adults. He compared it to his radio show. "People listen and say, 'Aw, that corny crap he throws out there. Jesus Christ! That mean little kid thing.' And yet if I leave him out, I get letters, people say, 'I let my little boy stay up until nine o'clock to hear Junior and he wasn't on.' They resent it."

He had a hangup while he was in the circus which carried over to his radio show: someone would tell him they just heard a good joke. "And I was always afraid to say, 'This is my joke.' So I gave it to somebody else. I'd say 'Jesus! Edna's [his first wife] coming up with a wonderful idea next week.' And for fourteen years, Gene," he said to Fowler, "everybody says, 'Jesus, too much on your shoulders now. The writing.' I've been doing it for fourteen years and I've been giving it to somebody else which is a credit for her [Edna]. I give all these ideas, and boom! But then when I come up and I say, 'Hey! Is this funny? and accidentally say it front of somebody else, *she* would always say, 'Well, it *should* be funny. I wrote it.' Well, then, that's what started beating me down. So in 1942, I said, 'Well, fuck this.' "

Shortly after this run-in with Edna, Red took up quarters in a legtimate hostelry. It was the Aladdin Hotel in Kansas City. "The rest of them were either combination hook-joints out-and-out hook joints." For his hotel room, he paid $10 a week.

One evening Skelton received a phone call at the Aladdin. It was a man who said his name was Tibbetts, the Walkathon promoter of Seltzer and Tibbetts. He said he had caught one of Red's stage shows and liked it, and he wanted to know if the comedian would work for him. He offered $150 a week. Red said, "I'll tell him when he comes in. You'll have to speak to my manager," and hung up.

Red told Fowler he had a man sitting in the room with him, "and we both had dames." Red's acquaintance asked what he had been offered to do for $150 a week. Red said, "A walk-athing. What's a Walkathon?"

His companion explained that it was an endurance contest where couples walked and/or danced, with the winners getting the purse.

A few days later, another agent approached Red with the same deal. Again, Skelton asked, "What the hell is a Walkathon?"

"Well, between your shows," said the agent, "would you like to go out and take a look at it?"

"Now, at the time," Red said, "I'm going with this Ada ———, and I had two other gals, one whose name was Mary June————. Oh, just out of this world, you know. My God! Every movement was elocution. Insincere moans, you know.

"But I said, 'Well, now wait a moment. If there's any such work around maybe I can knock off both of these gals at one time, you know.'

"So I go out and see these people walking round the floor, and boom! I recognize one girl who is a contestant, which is Edna. And I says, 'Well, now I know her from somewhere.' And I started to think back, and I remembered that about six months before the manager of the Pantages Theater at Kansas City came down to the burlesque house and said that one of the acts had failed to show up, and would I like to fill for the week, for a yard and a half."

So Skelton became acquainted with Edna Stillwell. He also had complained to Edna that he was not making his full salary.

Edna suggested she become the Walkathon ticket taker and hold back on her new boyfriend's salary, then give the company their take. This worked well, and both their salaries were collected first.

Shortly before he became a Walkathon master of ceremonies, Skelton sold illegal alcohol for a Greek restaurant operator in Indianapolis. "I had these pints with me," he said, "these half pints and pints. And it was half wood alcohol, half water with brown sugar for color. We were selling them for two and a half a bottle. So I got fifty cents and he got the two. So I said, 'Well, Christ! Why should I mess with this guy? I'll go in the business for myself.'"

Red saved up $38, purchased a gallon can of wood alcohol, bought some small bottles and went upstairs to his hotel room. He mixed his concoction and poured the fresh booze into bottles, then hid them in his bottom dresser drawer. Later that evening, when he was ready to deliver the goods, Skelton discovered the bottles had been stolen. "I've been hijacked," he said. And that was the end of his illegal liquor venture.

* * *

Red Skelton: The Complex Clown

The Walkathons started in Kansas City. "It's an endurance contest," Red said. "The thing goes for four and five months at a time.

"Edna walked for twenty-eight hundred hours. She won $500. When she went to sleep, the promoter stole the money."

But Red became one of the most successful Walkathon masters of ceremonies. He had the gift of drawing large crowds, especially when the event branched out to be covered by radio. Edna came to like Red and he started using her in several of his comedy bits, because of her good memory. Soon they were engaged on the Walkathon floor. Red said he had to borrow two dollars from Edna when they were married at City Hall. "She didn't have any shoes on at the time. She took them off because her feet were killing her, you know."

*   *   *

When Red first hit New York, he made an appointment with the William Morris agency office. "I did an imitation of John D. Rockefeller playing golf for young Bill Morris. I did this imitation of this old son-of-a-bitch playing golf and giving somebody a dime. And Morris says, 'That's pretty good. I'll tell you what. Not much I can do, but you step right through that door and you talk to somebody there.' So I walk through the door and I'm in the hall."

Red eventually landed a job at Proctor's 125th Street Theater doing impersonations with a comic named Johnny Woods. Red's agent talked George M. Cohan into catching their act. Following the performance, Cohan said to Skelton, "You want to be smart? Get out of this act."

Red said, "We'll, I've got to eat."

"What would you rather do?" Cohan asked. "Eat now and starve later?"

This ended Red's brief partnership with Woods.

That year, 1934, it was arranged for Skelton to take a screen test by MGM at Fox's New York studio. But, instead of a comedy rountine, he was given a serious role to play. It was a flop. But they did offer him a contract for $75 a week.

Fowler asked Red if he got his contract with Metro. Skelton

said, "No they wouldn't even consider it. But," he added, "now I got them for $150,000 a picture, see?"

Edna and Red were successful as a team. She played straight and sang. They appeared in several of the big houses.

A booker, Eve Ross, asked Red if he had ever done a nightclub date. He said he hadn't. In any event, Edna sent him to work the Lido Club in Montreal. "And the first show that I walked out in," Skelton said, "I laid the biggest bomb that's ever been laid. I had a straw hat, cane, cigar, spats.

"Edna said when I came off, 'You know what's wrong with you? You don't know who you want to be. Harry Richman, or Ken Murray, or Ted Healy, or Bobby Clark.' " She said he didn't need all those props, and to get rid of them. He did, and Edna talked the nightclub's manager, who nearly canceled him out the first night, into letting Red finish the week. Skelton made his second appearance in tuxedo, minus all the props. "First time I'd ever had a tuxedo," Red said. After he delivered his first joke, a customer in the audience shouted, "That's old."

"Oh, you don't like anything old?" Red asked him.

"No," came the answer.

"Where in the hell did you get that face?" For the first time, Skelton had the audience with him. He packed the Lido for six weeks.

* * *

If it was possible, Skelton's life became even more frustrating near the end of World War II. He and Edna were having marital troubles. He was infatuated with a girl named Muriel. And then Georgia Davis came along. She was studying art and modeling from Tom Kelly and Paul Hesse. The redheaded girl's fresh innocence took his mind off Muriel.

"Red and I had a date one afternoon," Georgia reported on the tape. She had met him at the Beverly Wilshire Hotel where he was living, "and Edna drove us downtown in her big limousine." On the way to purchase an antique dining room set, Georgia noticed how elegantly Edna was dressed. Red asked his wife, "**Mummy,** how much did you pay for your suit? Can't I get one here for Georgia? Can I take her in to see Irma Beal, your dress-maker, and have her fit Georgia?" He had figured, *Give any-body $50. . . . I didn't know what clothes cost.*

According to Georgia, Edna said, "Well, *Junior*, I'm afraid these suits cost a little more than you realize." But Easter was coming, and Red insisted that Georgia have a new suit.

Irma Beal designed a suit for Georgia. It was to be ready for Easter when Red promised to take Georgia to church.

Easter Sunday arrived along with the new suit, but Red did not show up. Georgia contacted Edna on the telephone. She wanted to know if Red had forgotten their date. "Haven't you seen the papers?' Edna asked. And I [Georgia] said, 'Why no, I haven't been out.' I was afraid to leave the room for fear I'd miss his call.

"So she said, 'Well, you better go down and get a paper be-cause he's in Beverly Management with Uncle Bö [Bö Roos, Red's business manager] and Muriel, and they're getting a blood test, and they're going to be married.' "

"I kept getting in deeper, and deeper, and deeper, and really thought I was nuts about this broad [Muriel]," Red said. "So the next thing I know I'm buying her a fur coat, a Plymouth car, set her up in an apartment for a year.

"Edna says, 'Well, if this is what you want, okay.' She walks out. Edna is protected. She has a ten-year contract to work for me. Edna wasn't gonna budge at all, and you should see some of the letters. . . . When you look back now, you say, 'Holy Jesus! What a stupid son-of-a-bitch I was.' So anyhow, I take this gun and I fire it through the wall, see? I says, 'I'm ending it all. . . .' And Edna came running. She says, 'Oh, God, if you're really that desperate then I'll give you the divorce.' So Edna gave me the divorce, and then I kicked my ass for it.

"Then I'm giving her [Muriel] all my allowance every week. She's working in pictures, and at the same time she's humping on the side, and she's a Lesbo. All directions.

"She came up to me one day and she says, 'I'm going to have a baby.' I says, 'Oh?' and she says, 'Of course, I will be willing to go to one of these doctors to knock it off, but it's going to cost you a couple hundred dollars.'

"And I says, 'Well, gee, I'll try to get that.' So I saved my allowance and gave it to her."

"What was your allowance?" Fowler asked.

"At the time? Fifty bucks a week."

Three months later Muriel approached him a second time with the same problem, but the price had gone up another hundred dollars. Red confided this to a friend, who told him that this was a scam and that Muriel had never been pregnant.

Muriel approached Red again, this time for a diaphragm.

"I says, 'Well, what does this do?'

"She says, 'Well, you put it up in me and I can't get pregnant.' "

Red asked her how much this could cost and she said, "Oh, around a hundred dollars."

"Well, when Little Red [Georgia] went to have one made," Skelton said, "they're ten bucks, see? She was a real honest-to-God vulture, you know."

Red told Fowler that "another time she says, 'I'll embarrass you, you son-of-a-bitch.' And she runs out in the middle of the street without a thing on, yelling, 'Look what he wants to give up!' And I ran like a son-of-a-bitch. I hopped in my little car and I blew . . . She had a key to my house. The door opens, and here is a mad-looking woman standing there with a flashlight, and she's got it showing up underneath her, see? And she's got a butcher knife in her hand. . . . So I says, 'Now, I don't know who you are, but by God you ain't gonna be there long.' And click! . . . I had these guns all over the place, see? And boom! Zoom! . . . She says, 'Don't shoot me, don't shoot me!' . . . Big hysterical broad."

Georgia interrupted the tape to tell Fowler, "The only reason he wanted you to know this is how confused the poor man was when I got him."

"I went downstairs into the trunk and I opened it up and I got a fresh bottle of Vat 69," Red went on. "Well, before that time I thought Vat 69 was the Pope's address. . . . And I take a big slug of it, and I threw up all over the place. Well, I've gotta learn sometime. So I take another big slug. And I'm drinking this water real quick on the side. And two of them's all I needed. Now

Red Skelton: The Complex Clown

I'm sitting around like this, just stupid." This signaled the time when Skelton would start drinking heavily on a steady basis.

* * *

On May 2, 1951, red received the news that, at that moment, he was the highest priced actor in the country. This included the pay he received for starring in pictures for MGM, and from *The Red Skelton Show,* which debuted in 1941 on NBC. Red and Edna created the six radio characters: Junior (The Mean Widdle Kid), Clem Kadiddlehopper, Deadeye, Willy Lump-Lump, J. Newton Numbskull and Bolivar Shagnasty. The show was replaced for one season by *The Gay Mrs. Featherstone,* starring Billie Burke, while Skelton served in the army as a buck private. This was 1945, when Red married Georgia.

In 1951 Skelton adandoned radio to debut on his television progam, also for NBC. Along with his other holdings, he would be taking in at least one million a year. This amount would grow substantially during the ensuing seasons.

* * *

Although I had known Skelton since 1944, I had never visited him at his house on Bellagio Road in Bel Air until just before he and Fowler started making the 1951 tapes.

The first time I was accompanied by George Putnam, the dynamic television newscaster. George was then the highest paid newsman in the country, at $300,000 per annum. George and I spent the evening with Skelton. The two struck up a friendship which, publicity-wise, helped Red's career during the comedian's meteoric climb to the top of the entertainment world.

* * *

Until he arrived, nothing had such a comedic impact on television as Red's show. It rose to the number one slot in the national rating charts. He was invited to entertain in London's Palladium.

* * *

When Skelton hired me as a writer in 1952, I had been accustomed to rising at four in the morning in order to get downtown by six and go to work on the *Herald,* where I was still functioning as a reporter. Now there I was with time on my hands. I found myself sleeping late with three days off before my personal deadline when I would write my material for the next show.

During the first writers' meeting, I was aware that everybody else knew what they were doing. I didn't. This was my first meeting with John Fenton Murray and Ben Freedman. Murray, who had just returned from a Hawaii vacation, sported a rich tan. He was the only one who had written anything for the show.

After a few shows, I began to feel more at ease in the writers' meetings. My father and mother visited Red's house just as we finished one week's session. Murray, an admirer of Fowler, stayed on to talk with him. Another Murray, Ken Murray (no relation), arrived shortly after the Fowlers. The comedian had just heard a funny joke, but it was a "little dirty, and I wouldn't like to tell it in front of Mrs. Fowler," he said. My mother gave no response. Murray persisted, again adding that the joke was too risqué. At long last, this tea cozy of a lady looked up at Murray and smiled.

"I'll set a joke level for you," she said. "Shit."

The comic went down to defeat as the rest of us cried with laughter at my mother's rejoinder.

Ken Murray never got to tell his joke.

* * *

We writers attended rehearsals and the shooting of the Kinescope show. Then I began to notice inconsistencies and intrigue attached to behind-the-scenes operations.

It was politely passed on to me that it would be advisable to be present when we filmed, in order to laugh. Laughing loud near the audience reaction microphone was a must. Today, when I watch a television comedy show, I can usually pick out a particular manner of laugh and identify it as that of a writer. The secret is that if the joke is weak, the writer's guffaw is far louder than that of the audience reaction — especially if it is *his* joke.

Toward midseason, something alien seemed to be in the offing. Red was outwardly dissatisfied. Too many men in business suits were trying to run his professional affairs to think for him. Bö Roos traveled the hill several times a week. Freeman Keyes, Red's personal manager, flew out from his Russel M. Seeds advertising agency offices in Chicago to confer. Following these meetings, I observed that Red became moody and had a tendency to fly off the handle with his friends.

These burdens took their toll. Prior to his physical breakdown, the comedian would retreat to the privacy of his dressing room where I could hear him groan. Several times, when I saw him holding his chest, I was afraid these outside forces might cause Red to have a heart attack. He was finally taken to St. John's Hospital in Santa Monica where he was diagnosed as having a diaphragmatic hernia. The show was shut down and Kinescopes were rerun so often that the ratings suffered.

Fowler was against surgery for the hernia. He had been in contact with the country's leading authority on the procedure. It was this Boston doctor's steadfast opinion that Skelton's operation was not indicated; that it should not be undertaken unless it was an emergency. The physician said that "one should learn to live with the affliction."

Red's spirits were high the morning of the operation. He even had a piece of adhesive tape plastered on his chest which read, "Don't open till Christmas."

Skelton's personal physician stood by in surgery while two others "ghosted" the operation. One was a chest surgeon, so instead of entering through the front door, a lung was collapsed and an incision was made about halfway around the side of the body. Fowler's last words to Red before they wheeled him away were: "Is this trip necessary?"

Through his great physical strength, Red survived. He healed quickly, but was unable to work for some time. Because of unethical medical procedures, the personal physician was barred from then on from even entering St. John's Hospital.

During Skelton's period of recovery at his home, I, among other friends, visited with him in the evenings, when he would have his Kinescopes projected out by the pool. This was trying at times, but what the hell, we *were* being paid.

Now Freeman Keyes leaned on Fowler with an inquiry about

what he, Fowler, thought might be done to bolster the show's ratings.

Fowler returned a detailed letter of more than three-thousand words which, in essence, advised Keyes and all others to get off the artist's back until he had recovered. He added that Skelton was in the prime of life, but that he had to have time to get his strength back and reorient himself. Fowler also said that, during his association with Skelton, he had observed two rules: (1) not to interfere with his business relationships; and (2) not to take sides in his private life.

Fowler added that, with so little time left for himself, it became increasingly certain in his mind that the employment of one's time was of the greatest importance here on earth. He said that the usual procedure for almost anyone near a star, whether Skelton or anyone else, was to enter wholeheartedly into the success of that luminary sharing his glory *as well as his proceeds.* "But when anything untoward happens, such as an act of God, illness, or what-have-you, the tendency of most human beings, I regret to say, is to leave that star to a condition of panic and loneliness, and fail to show a constructive willingness to share the grief or defeat. Then, when success returns, the same ones who deserted the star suddenly troop back as though a Pied Piper were playing an old, sure tune."

My father told me that only by dint of character and stout philosophy could any of us endure the evening of our respective careers. He had insisted to Keyes that Skelton was too young and too near his noontime even to consider that he was through, or that his basic talent was impaired.

For Keyes' edification, Fowler had listed the specifics of this comedian's life. He suggested that Skelton should know exactly how much he was worth in actual money terms, and at any time.

Mr. Keyes had commented upon Skelton's excessive drinking, adding that his illness had imparied the comedian's value as an investment. To this, Fowler responded that "Gleason drinks. . . . Godfrey drinks. Joe E. Lewis drinks. Bing Crosby used to drink. But we control it, in a measure. I do because I have to. I cannot stomach a drink the next day after."

In summation, Fowler said, "I feel this might not be a popular suggestion, but the evidence is preponderant that Skelton should do but one television show a month."

Before the rerun season had concluded, Skelton returned to work.

Some years later it was necessary for the comedian to have this surgical procedure repeated.

* * *

Tragedy struck in 1956. Red's fragile nine-year-old son, Richard, developed leukemia. During this long illness, Red took time off to travel about the world with Richard. The two were granted a private audience with Pope Pius XII in the Vatican.

The little boy finally died May 12, 1958. My father, who dearly loved Richard, wrote his eulogy.

* * *

> *This is the end of the glad hours we have spent with this bright and shining child. . . . Somehow we sensed that a saintly child had been lent to us for a little while. . . . When he reached the last moments of his long ordeal, Richard kissed Valentina, whom he loved so dearly. He seemed to know that it was goodbye. He spoke calmly and lovingly to his grieving mother and to his great father. Then he clasped his small, wasted hands, as though in prayer. And now he has lived out the time, the so-little time he had been lent to us all.*

* * *

Crestfallen, Red returned home. He never took a drink from that day on.

* * *

The last time I visited with Red and Georgia was in 1961, the spring after my father had died.

* * *

In 1971, Skelton filed suit for dissolution of their twenty-six-year marriage. In October of 1973, he married Hollywood photographer Lothian Toland. She was thirty-five. Red was sixty.

In 1976, Georgia, who was suffering from a rare blood disease and had endured loneliness, despair, and a heart attack, walked into her garden in Rancho Mirage near Palm Springs and shot herself to death with a thirty-eight-caliber pistol. She was fifty-four. She left no note. It was May 12, the eighteenth anniversary of her son's death.

18

Top Man on the Totem Pole

When H. Allen Smith left us one February afternoon in 1976, it was as if the fading light at the end of the tunnel of yesterday's eminent humorists had finally flickered out. In the 1940s, Allen nudged elbows with the likes of H.L. Mencken, Franklin P. Adams (F.P.A.), Arthur "Bugs" Baer, Thorne Smith, Fred Allen, James Thurber, Nunnally Johnson and Henry McLemore.

"There were so many great humorists when I was a young writer," Allen told me when I visited him at his Alpine, Texas, home in 1974, "that you couldn't walk down Park Row without tripping over one. Today, there are only two left of my ragged persuasion: S.J. Perelman and me. . . . And Perelman ain't writin'."° At the time I was working with Smith on what was to be his last book, *The Life and Legend of Gene Fowler* (William Morrow).

There may have been some satirists better than H. Allen Smith in my time. And there may have been some who were not as good. But there was never one exactly like him.

Smith had four and a half million copies† of his thirty-eight books distributed during his nearly forty years as a professional journeyman. He was a bona fide product of the old Southwest,

---

°He did mention at another time that he admired the wit of Russell Baker and Erma Bombeck. But, as with most authors, his mind kept changing.

† He had 1.4 million copies published during the war years between 1941 and 1945.

which was originally accepted as being in the area of western Kentucky, southern Illinois, Tennessee and Hannibal, Missouri, the last of which was the crucible that whelped Mark Twain.

Smith was born in 1906 in McLeansboro, Illinois, just two hundred miles from Hannibal. He received no formal education past the eighth grade and firmly stated he never learned anything there but spelling. He often told his friends that he was probably one of the few who could write before he became literate. Smith was fond of practical jokes (as long as they didn't hurt anybody physically), dirty stories and plain old-fashioned cussing. He said that of his four favorite cussers, his father Henry was the champion. "Then there was Gant's father in Thomas Wolfe's *Look Homeward, Angel*, and Huckleberry Finn's daddy, Eugene. Pick anyone from second to fourth," Allen said, "and that'll be *me*." Claiming his paw as his primer, H. Allen Smith° said he received his postgraduate course in fine tarnished grammar while cleaning up barbershops and pool halls around southern Illinois.

After moving to Huntington, Indiana, Smith landed a job proofreading for the local newspaper. He was fifteen, but old enough to graduate to the status of reporter. While covering stories, he indulged in growing-pain humor columns under the by-lines of Miss Ella Vator and Al T. Tude.

Having been a full-blown reporter for nearly two years, Allen found himself drunk with a friend in the city room while talking about the sexual mysteries of young girls. This encouraged Smith to bang our an essay entitled *Stranded on a Davenport*.† It recounted a fictitious and lustful adventure he shared with a juvenile wench on the title's furniture. So elated was Smith's friend with the short story that he made copies of the piece, stuffing his typewriter with carbons. These circulated around to both boys

---

°The "H." in H. Allen Smith stands for "Harry." Although in a letter to me his wife Nelle vehemently denied this, I must stick with history, sic: *Low Man on a Totem Pole* and *Life in a Putty Knife Factory*, both Doubleday, Doran, and written by Harry Allen Smith.

†Smith spent the remainder of his days trying to come up with a copy of this piece. His search was in vain.

and girls attending Huntington High School. It was fated that
the principal would get hold of a copy, just as it was inevitable
that the school's leader would call in the chief of police to ferret
out its author. Smith had already developed a shadowy reputation. He was the first called in for interrogation.

"Did you write this thing?" the chief asked Smith, waving the
evidence before him.

"Write what? I didn't write anything," said Smith.

"If ya admit ya did," said the chief at the principal's urging,
"there's nothin'll happen to ya."

This sounded equitable, so the young man confessed.

At this, the chief hauled Smith away to jail. From then on, our
Harry placed little trust in law enforcement personnel.

"At the trial," Smith recalled, "all these girls were put on the
stand to testify. They admitted they had read *Stranded on a
Davenport*, but added that, 'Oh, no,' they didn't understand a
word of what it meant. The hell they didn't!"

Young Smith was unable to fathom the vastness of the crowd
accumulating in front of the courthouse. "Just a few words I
wrote on a piece of paper caused all this commotion," he said.
"There hadn't been this many folk gathered since old man Twi-
ford got locked in his two-seater with the new moon on the door
when his barn got burnt."

Fearing nothing less than a death sentence, Allen was relieved
to be fined only a few dollars. At seventeen, he left the area to
work as a reporter on small-town newspapers in Kentucky and
Indiana.

Pulling into Florida, he landed a job as editor of a daily, the
Sebring American, at the age of nineteen. There he met the paper's society editor, Nelle Simpson. He had never owned a book,
and Nelle opened his mind to the likes of O. Henry. She made
him a present of the author's works.

After the Florida land boom fizzled in the mid-twenties, Allen
left for Tulsa. When Nelle arrived shortly thereafter, they were
married on April 14, 1927.

Denver was the next stop for the couple, and Smith took a job
on the *Post*. While working for the notorious publishers F.G.
Bonfils and H.H. Tammen, he listened to his contemporaries

talk about such authors as H.G. Wells and H.L. Mencken. They discussed the principal events that changed the course of history. Smith didn't know what the hell they were talking about. He decided to educate himself and asked his friend Morris Watson, founder of the Newspaper Guild, what he should read. Morris told him, "Wells' two-volume *Outline of History*. Remember every date therein, and write down every word you don't understand." Then Smith devoured the works of Anatole France and Charles Dickens. Next to Twain, Mencken was his guiding light.

Shortly before the stock market crash of 1929, Smith left Denver for New York. A honed writer now, he concentrated on feature stories for various papers during the next twelve years. He was discovered by a weather-reading public with his clipped one-liners displayed on the front page of the *New York World-Telegram*. When the temperature dropped below zero, his remarks beneath the subhead, *Cold*, would read, "Sure is!" or, "Colder than a well-digger's you-know-what!" Or, "All brass monkeys had better go inside." Not eye-raising today, but in the early forties, wow!

His United Press wire service feature profile stories on famous personalities grabbed Smith his first national reading audience. I once asked him if he had any special technique with his interviews. "Hell, yes," he said. "I'd usually give them a goose, and they'd be so goddamned surprised, they'd start talking a blue streak. They'd tell me anything I wanted to know . . . that is, while they were trying to compose themselves."

A soberly shy man, John Steinbeck was said to be uninterviewable. When his novel *Grapes of Wrath* was first published, Allen intended to get an interview with him. When Steinbeck hit town, he would usually drop into the offices of his publisher friend, Pascal Covici. Smith managed to be there when Steinbeck dropped in. The two cracked a bottle of cognac — and a second. They hit it off well, and Smith emerged from the drinking bout with a sparkling interview.

Two of Smith's goosees were Marlene Dietrich and Simone Simon. Smith turned J.P. Morgan's klaxon-horn nose a shade redder when he greeted the man of high finance with a "Hiya, toots!" Going to any length for this particular interview, he kidnapped Albert Einstein. At the time, the fiddle-playing father of the theory of relativity was being honored at a dinner party.

When there was no chance for an interview, Smith was capable of creating one. "The most revealing interview I ever had," in 1934, was with Primo Carnera, just after he had lost the heavyweight boxing championship of the world to Max Baer. Before he was knocked out in the eleventh round, the Italian giant had been pounded to the canvas at Long Island City twelve times. His jaw and cheek and nose had been broken. His eyes were swollen shut. Carnera looked like all the St. Valentine's Day murder victims rolled into one as his seconds guided him to his dressing room. He was the gladiator after the fact. The Romans had given him a thumbs down. His face looked like a chimpanzee's bloody backside. Reporters were so shocked at the appearance of the blinded six-and-a-half-foot pugilist, they were struck dumb. They just stared. But H. Allen stepped forward:

"Did Baer wear you down?" he asked.

Carnera's lips moved faintly: "Holy Jesus!"

"What about the prospects of a rematch?" Smith continued.

"Holy Jesus!" the Tyrolean Timber again mumbled.

"Do you think you could beat Baer next time?"

"Holy Jesus!"

"Does your head hurt?"

"Holy Jesus!"

"Do you think Baer can lick Max Schmeling?"

"Holy Jesus!"

The reporters were finally ordered from the dressing room, and for what it was, Smith had gotten his interview.

* * *

Allen's first two books, *Robert Gaer: A Study* (Dial) and *Mr. Klein's Kampf* (Stackpole), made little noise. The initial one was an ego trip potboiler for a man who had made a fortune in the paper manufacturing business. *Kampf* had a humorous bent with its main character, Orson Klein, playing Adolf Hitler's double.

Then, in 1941, came his best-seller, *Low Man on a Totem Pole* (Doubleday, Doran). It contained his hilarious interviews with a gallery of the famous and fantastic while writing for the *World-Telegram*. In a capsule autobiography, he led off: "When I was five years old I fell head downward into an empty cistern and was not found until six hours later, at which time I was quietly eating dirt." Thus was formed the pattern of a humor fount which would pour from his ribald mind. In the introduction, his friend Fred Allen, who referred to H. Allen as "the screwballs' Boswell," wrote:

> *Smith is a waste of skin. . . . There isn't enough meat on him to glut a baby buzzard. . . . His legs have no calves and appear to be two swans' necks that have been starched. . . . His arms dangle from their pits like two limp buggy whips. . . . If Smith were an Indian he would be low man on any totem pole. . . . His suit is a rhapsody in rummage. . . . His Elk's tooth has a cavity in it. . . . He enjoys people who are looking at excavations. He stands in long lines outside the movie theaters and, at the crucial moment, doesn't go in. Displayed prominently in his study is an old-fashioned pot (with handle) which bears the sign: "I'm going to get this full of money."*

Low Man's success allowed our friend to quit his job at the newspaper and move to suburban Mount Kisco, New York. There, he completed his best-seller triple play with *Life in a Putty Knife Factory* and *Lost in the Horse Latitudes* (Doubleday, Doran). They followed *Low Man's* pattern, and guaranteed that he would be remembered in literary granite.

H. Allen always yearned to up and travel. He did, and he wrote about it. A trip to Mexico produced *The Pig in the Barber Shop* (Little, Brown). *Waikiki Beachnik* (Little, Brown) followed a visit to Hawaii. Then came *Smith's London Journal* (Doubleday) and a long visit to Tahiti gave us one of my favorite travel yarns, *Two-Thirds of a Coconut Tree* (Little, Brown).

* * *

Little did I know, after I had become a communicant to the shrine of H. Allen Smith, that I would also become a member of his *Brotherhood*. The other five fellahs in this exclusive social organization are/were men of brain and wit: Fred Beck, Rufus Blair, Ed Sheehan, Joe Bryan, Jr., and Bergen Evans — all a cone pine's age older than me. Our main function was the exchanging of letters, all specifically and simply addressed to "The Brotherhood," and intended for general circulation. Over a period of sixteen years Smith and I corresponded, I accumulated a round thousand pages of letters. In his landmark collection of jokes, quips, one-liners, buffoonery, hoodwinkings and justification of the pornographic mind, *Buskin' with H. Allen Smith* (Trident), Allen noted:

> *Gene's son Will is an adequately salacious contributing member of* The Brotherhood *and has his Paw's lusty attitude toward life. Will Fowler, if I may speak metaphorically, doesn't own a decent bone in his body and wouldn't know what to do with such a bone if he had it.*

This was in introduction to a letter I had written to him which eventually appeared in his successful collection of *Rude Jokes* (Gold Medal). The letter had to do with the days when we young reporters were not allowed to use the word "rape" in our copy — even after a girl *was* raped. An excerpt explained the point:

> *As she was walking through a dark alley, Charlotte Dussag of 614 Morrison Street, Bel Air, was struck a stunning blow on the head with a blunt instrument. Then, as she lay helpless on the pavement, she was kicked and stomped upon and hit with rocks. When she tried to struggle to her feet, her assailant knocked out six of her teeth, tore her clothes from her body, and began to pound her in the stomach with his fists until she fell once again. Just as she was lapsing into unconsciousness, her assailant proceeded to attack her.*

In consideration, I sent a copy of a now former version of my H. Allen Smith chapter to his widow for any possible corrections. Nelle's return letter put me in shock for a full ten days. My stomach ulcer reappeared and, while attempting to subdue the trauma, my physician had to place me on a skimmed milk diet along with prescribed medication. Think you take things hard, baby? Hell, gigantic trifles like opening a can of tomato soup scares me: I'm afraid the nectar inside spilling over on my hand might turn out to be my blood.

What a helluva jolt it was when Nelle laid it on me that, with the exception of the *Medical Memo to the Brotherhood*, she would not allow me to reprint any of the other Brotherhood letters Allen had collectively written to all of us. She even held a hook on the reproduction of the aforementioned letter in that I was to delete words such as a——h——e, p——er and p——y!

Allen's daughter, Nancy, was visiting Nelle when I received Mrs. Smith's letter. Nelle wrote that Nancy saw no objection to reproducing the letter, nor, probably, would Allen. At this late stage, I realized that a single-handed, posthumous attempt was being made to clean up the H. Allen Smith literary image.

When I passed this information along to my literary friend Robert Young, Jr. (no relation to the actor), he wrote:

> *Why is it, regarding Mrs. Smith, that the dead suddenly become paragons if anyone is to write about them post-mortem? Pop [Gene Fowler] was right in those words Allen quoted at the front of his book.° Warts and all, damn it. Anything less is gilt! Allen certainly did not white-wash Pop. For that matter I don't think Allen white-washed himself in his books, so why the hell should he be painted something he was not? Mrs. Smith wrongly does the Mary Hemingway bit, I think.* Oh, these keepers of the flame!

Possessing one of the most prolific minds of any writer-director-producer in radio, motion picture and television, Hal Kanter won an Emmy award for writing the George Gobel TV series. That and the Ed Wynn show also chalked up seven Emmy and two Peabody awards. As an artist, he sold his first cartoon at the

---

°In the front of his final book, *The Life and Legend of Gene Fowler* (William Morrow), H. Allen Smith quoted Fowler as saying: "Set things down fairly, and honestly, and without pulling punches . . . unthinking persons blush to recall, but which are the very essence of true biography."

age of fifteen to the *Long Island Independent*. He traveled to Hollywood where he ghost-wrote comic strips before becoming a comedy writer for the Eddie Cantor radio show. From then on, his credits were too many to list, but he had written for Jack Oakie, Jack Haley, Alan Young, Danny Kaye, Don Ameche, Jack Paar, Bing Crosby and Amos 'n' Andy in radio. And he wrote for almost everybody in television, including Arthur Godfrey. Among the pages of credits for motion pictures, he wrote for Bob Hope, Joan Fontaine, Shirley Booth, Martin and Lewis, Marilyn Monroe, Bette Davis and the *Rose Tattoo* adaptation for Burt Lancaster and Anna Magnani.

Answering my letter regarding Nelle Smith's attitude about her husband never having written anything profoundly off-color for publication, he answered: "Freud did cover it, as I recall from some early reading. He said the one thing that had baffled him all his life was the perplexing question of what exactly do women want?"

Thank God that geniuses like Geoffrey Chaucer, Rabelais, Giovanni Boccaccio, François Voltaire, Sir Richard Burton, Benjamin Franklin, Mark Twain, James Joyce and Gene Fowler did not have lingering widows who would have cheated the reading world of their magnificent, wholesomely base language used from the barns to the castles when a man wishes to explain himself in the grand manner.

Forty years have passed during which time Allen quoted my father and myself. As for me, I went a bit further, researching areas for his many books. And not once was a letter passed between us to ask permission to use or copy this-and-that. Drat on you imposters who have secured the keys of one's mind, but are unfamiliar with the locks!

At the outset, to say that H. Allen Smith never wrote anything pornographic for publication, I believe that this is either an irresponsible statement, or that Mrs. Smith did not read all of her late husband's published books. *I have.*

As an interesting example, let us take *The Life and Legend of Gene Fowler:*

At the beginning of the book, it is related that reporters in Denver used to take time off from work to look down and across the corner where, every workday-end, a beautiful lass stood for a while until the streetcar picked her up. After conjecture about her virginity, a challenge came: Who could lay her? Young Fowler was obviously not the obvious one to perform, but the gauntlet was laid down and bets were made. That evening, Fowler had a hundred and one eyes on him as he approached the lass on the corner (one man had a glass eye). Fowler whispered into her ear. She nearly swooned, but walked away with young Fowler. After picking up the betting money the following morning, Fowler was asked by the amazed gentlemen in the city room about the magic he possessed. According to H. Allen Smith:

> *"I simply walked up to her and tipped my hat," said Fowler, "and I said, 'Young lady, would you mind telling me if you fuck?'"*

Also, one should take a look through Allen's *Buskin' with H. Allen Smith* (Trident), which he so generously dedicated to The Brotherhood. Take page 189, where Allen described a wound my father suffered on the penis:

> *... the water glass slipped from his hand, hit the edge of the basin, broke in pieces, and one fragment struck him viciously in the peter and lacerated same.*

Then there is Allen's *The View from Chivo* (Trident). I had suggested the main gimmick, its use and application for the seventh chapter. The gimmick was a *merkin*.

Allen wrote back that he did not know what a merkin was. In the return mail, I explained that a merkin is/was a false hairpiece dancing girls and the like wear.

"Why?" Allen asked me.

"Because several men enjoy looking at a freshly shaved woman's part."

"Amazing."

Allen became so overjoyed with the idea of using the merkin for his seventh chapter in *Chivo*, he even named the craftsman "Bill Flower, The Merkin Maker."

Let us also not forget that Allen edited Gene Fowler's scatological book, *Lady Scatterly's Lovers* (Lyle Stuart). In my opinion, this book is not only equal to, but surpasses, Mark Twain's *1601* both in style and invention.

* * *

Finally, we should dwell upon one of Allen's last books, *Rude Jokes* (Gold Medal). Prior to its publication, Allen told me of his reluctance to put it out because it was laden with four-letter words helping to describe scores of scatological and pornographic vignettes. "But both my son, Allen, and daughter reassured me that in these permissive times, there was nothing to fear about using such material along with four-letter words. "Hell," he added, "most of my cuss words usually have six-to-eleven letters long."

In conclusion, I would like to report a letter in answer to the widow of Russia's magnificent basso, Feodor Chaliapin (the man John Barrymore claimed was the world's greatest actor). The presumably fine, yet uninformed, lady wished Fowler to "collaborate" with her on the life story of her late husband. In refusal, he kindly yet firmly wrote:

> *It has been my experience that wives who write concerning their husbands have an objective that stands in the way of solid literary accomplishment and really results in destroying a great character in print; this is the almost universal tendency of wives to stay "mum" on all questions having to do with the faults of great men. Their romantic wish to tell all that is good and hide all that the world calls bad makes the terminal event, i.e., publication, a flat and saccharine occurrence with no hills and valleys, no sunshine or shadows, no blood, no soul.*

The *Brotherhood* memo Mrs. Smith allowed me to reproduce follows:

> *In case anybody has been wondering where I have been lately, this is the report that yesterday I emerged from the hocking fusspital.*

Top Man on the Totem Pole

Transurethral resection for benign prostatic hoper-
thropy. Benign, my a——. What they did was they
rammed some kind of a periscope, of the type used to
look at parades when there are a lot of other idiot
parade-lookers jammed up in front of you. . . . They
rammed this here periscope clean up and all the way
through my whammadoodle . . . and some distance be-
yond, I suspect. The object they were after, as I get the
word, was a thing the size of a Land Rover snow tire, a
mean antisocial son-of-a-bitch that had wrapped itself
around the neck of my bladder, and then started tighten-
ing in on me like a boa constrictor. This made it all but
impossible for me to p——, a procedure which the doc-
tors spoke of as "void." The nurses also called it void.
They'd come into the room and say, "Did you void yet
this morning, Mr. Smith?" These were nurses to whom I
had been telling a whole series of dirty stories from time-
to-time, with huge success — stories with words in them
like a—— and p—— and p—— and the like. So I would
reply to them, "If you mean did I p—— yet this morn-
ing, well, I . . ." By this time they would have flung up
their hands in despair and fled from the room. There is
no understanding women. . . .

Anyway, I am now home, filled with plenty of void,
but very little vinegar. It was all quite enlivening and I
have no criticism to make of anybody, except maybe a
small general quibble against the doctors. I wish they
would improve their penmanship and learn to say s——.

Despiser of the hollow-minded, Allen forwarded a letter that
had been sent to him by a publisher. It seems our Smith had
written a humorous piece for the Smithsonian Institution's
monthly magazine on the history of the bagpipe. A mind-wart
enamored with the plaid octopus wrote a highfalutin letter of
objection to the publication's vice president in charge of bag-
pipes and douche bags. The stuffed shirt from La Jolla claimed
Allen's article was "unintelligent and insulting," and straightway
canceled his subscription.

The admonishing letter had been forwarded to H.A.S. while I
was visiting him in Alpine. Allen had laughed and said to me,

"An author is never supposed to sass back when he is criticized. But I have observed elsewhere that after a person passes sixty-five, he is entitled to speak his mind forcefully under any and all circumstances." He snickered, sat down at his typewriter, then dashed off something very swiftly. I asked him what he had written. He said. "In essence, I told the bastard that he must be an insufferable old thunder-jug, and knowing that La Jolla was filled with insufferable old thunder-jugs, he must be the *Captain!*"

*   *   *

A Xerox missive was circulated among the Brotherhood. Its genesis came from some magazine editor with the news which could have displaced the earth's poles, thusly replacing our icecaps in the middle of Java and the center of Majorca's bullring!

> *I was down in the Bahamas with a group of doctors last week and one of the wives, a very lovely Hawaiian lady (who now lives in Jersey), told me about a recent research project which had come to her attention. She said that after a dimensional survey of the genitalia of the American male and female, it was determined that the average male penis was six inches long and the average female vagina was eight inches deep. These figures were fed into a computer, along with population estimates for the entire country, and the computer came up with the information that there were about twenty-five thousand miles of unused vagina running around in the United States.*

Regarding the U.S. male's deficit, I can only recall that Allen said that we had to "retool."

*   *   *

What started out as a Brotherhood letter sometimes metamorphosed into one of Allen's many magazine pieces. I recall that, on one of his Southern California visits, I was showing him off to today's nonpareil comedy writer-producer-director, Hal Kanter, at my former favorite Encino watering hole, the Samoa House.

Top Man on the Totem Pole

Hal was interested in having Smith do an around-the-country television oddity series. When Allen said he had become too old for this rigorous kind of exercise, we traveled to other pastures of thought. Allen hit upon English misusage, and the three of us came up with interesting tidbits.

First at bat, Allen said he suffered from high-paid newscasters incorrectly pronouncing the *Carib*bean with the accent on *be*. . . . He then alluded to his thirteen-volume set of *The Oxford English Dictionary*, adding that the British called the halfpenny a "hayp-nee."

Then I pointed out that Red Skelton pronounces the word "pantomime" as being "pantomi*ne*."

'The hell with that," cried Kanter. "Horace Greeley never voiced the expression, 'Go west, young man!' "

"Who the hell was it?" I asked.

"It was an editorial writer in the *Terre Haute Express*, John B.L. Soule, that said it three years before that pastepot Greeley."

"What about everyone who quotes Mark Twain as saying, 'Everybody talks about the weather, but nobody does anything about it'?" Smith asked.

"Everyone takes credit for it," Kanter offered.

"And for that matter," Smith put in, "who . . ."

As usual, I interrupted, raised my glass and said, "I'll drink to that."

Smith continued: "Who originated *that?*"

Kanter smiled. "Probably someone who was cold . . . the night after his gas was turned off."

*   *   *

In one of his many phone conversations with me, Allen mentioned that a ferocious Babbitt he had met in New York indicated that he did not believe him when Smith told him there was a tribe of people living there with the delightful surname of Pecker. The disbeliever also raised his brows when Allen said there was also a mystery novel writer named Jack Dolph.

As to the long-and-short of it, Smith told him that when he had time he might look up the name of the founder and head of the

Korvette discount stores. A gentleman by the name of Gene Fir-koff!

And, after that, Allen suggested the doubting thomas inspect the phone book for people named Zass, and speculate upon names for their baby girls.

Try it on your own home phone book if you are so inclined, and if your mind tends to be dirty — like mine.

* * *

A fellow author told Allen *she* had no trouble at all starting a book. Now, you know how frightening that first blank page looks. My late friend, World War II correspondent Ernie Pyle, once told me, "God damn it, one day I decided I was going to write my first book, so I regimented myself. I gave up the booze . . . which took me about two weeks to think straight without it. I sat down at the typewriter exactly at eight o'clock in the morning, stared at the blank piece of paper until noon, then quit. This went on for five months if you want a grab at tenacity. But all the time I was sitting there, I was thinking. Then one day, the words slowly started to come. A year later, I'd finished my first book."

* * *

One critic had had the gall to say that Smith's book titles were "lacking." I wish I could come up with the like. How about *Rhubarb, Desert Island Decameron, Larks in the Popcorn, Let the Crabgrass Grow, To Hell in a Handbasket* and *How to Write Without Knowing Nothing?* My favorite Smith title, about his Tahiti visit, is *Two-Thirds of a Coconut Tree.* The Tahitian Building Code is explained thusly in the front of the book: "And in furtherance of the scheme to Keep Tahiti Tahitian, it is decreed that no building shall be higher than two-thirds of a coconut tree." That was in 1963. When I traveled to Tahiti nearly thirty years ago, there weren't any buildings over *one*-third of a coconut tree high, much less airplanes flying about. In those days large ships, which were actually guided through a dangerously narrow coral channel by a dolphin, visited the island only twice a year. In celebration, the place closed down and everybody had

fun. I even fell in love with two sisters. We swam bare-assed naked by the black volcanic sands, and I didn't know which one I
wanted to marry. They said, "That's all right . . . makes no difference . . . we all live together . . . one happy family." Neat
folks, these Tahitian girls. . . . My ship sailed. I never returned.
What the hell, who wants to see jet airplanes landing on my once
romantic tropical island?

* * *

One-liners, and such, Allen and I used to throw back and forth to
one another throughout the years. I'll take credit for the first
one, then you can take it from there:

> *When the devil was given his due, God told him to go to
> hell.*

> *That guy was so ugly that when he was a kid his momma
> had to hang a pork chop around his neck to get the dog to
> play with him.*

> *That sumbitch has got a pecker as long as $50 worth of
> shoestrings.*

> *George Raft to Marjorie Rambeau: "If we could find a
> bed around here, I'd give you one of the greatest experi-
> ences you ever had."*
>   *Marjorie Rambeau to George Raft: "What's the mat-
> ter with the floor, you a dude?"*

> *John D. Rockefeller, Jr.: "Operator I didn't get my nickel
> back."*
>   *Operator: "Sorry, sir. Please give me your name and
> address and we will refund your nickel."*
>   *John D. Rockefeller, Jr.: "Just forget it, miss. You
> wouldn't believe me anyway."*

> *Q. What's that white stuff in bird shit?*
>   *A. That's bird shit, too.*

> *John Barrymore: "Lost: one gold cufflink. Will buy or
> sell."*

Top Man on the Totem Pole

Groucho Marx found himself in an elevator surrounded by Catholic priests. One of the cloth said, "Mr. Marx, I want you to know the enjoyment you bring my mother." Groucho replied, "I didn't know you fellows were allowed to have mothers."

A postman carried a pile of Christmas cards to the front door to find the lady answering in the nude. She invited him inside and proceeded to give him an equally beautiful screw. When he departed, the nice lady handed him a dollar bill, which baffled the postman. The following day, came the postman with another pile of Christmas cards. After handing her the mail, he inquired why she had given him a dollar the day before. "Oh," the lovely lady said, "my husband and I were talking the other night about what we should give the postman for Christmas, and my husband said, 'Fuck 'im. Give him a dollar.'"

Guy quietly asked gal at the bar if she'd like a drink. With a stage voice, she answered: "Go to a motel with you?" "Just a little drink," said the guy in a whisper. "Go to a motel with you? Certainly not, you terrible man!" Shamed and shattered, our poor fellow retreated to a booth at the other end of the bar. Then the young lady walked over to him and explained, "I'm just a psychology student. I didn't mean to embarrass you. I just wanted to see what your reaction would be." At this, the guy screamed, "Seventy-five dollars?"

Human meets Tarzan for first time. "Hey Tarz, what's your wife's whole name?" Said Tarz, "Her whole name is pussy!"

True: A guy worked twenty-eight years for one company. Never had a sick day off. When he retired, his empty lunch bucket had paid off. Each day, he stole only one brick, and when his sixty-fifth came along, he had enough to build himself a strong house.

You know the definition of the phrase bar stool? Some-

thing Daniel Boone stepped in. You know how to find a good whorehouse in France? Go to the one where the truck drivers eat.

Tell businessmen with no sense of humor to go to hell.

* * *

There's stuff still sticking around worth mentioning when one winds up two years' work on a book. I have a friend who is a complete nut. He is a newscaster and makes money in several other ways. He is Larry Burrell. Actually, the original spelling is something like "Berill," "Berhill," "Bumpop," or "Berrrr," like in as if you are cold.

Larry, the only spelling of which I am certain, has a quick and dirty wit. On occasion he writes to me, usually with some sixteenth page subheadline, as follows:

MAN ARRESTED FOR SODOMY WITH DUCK

Suggested subheads came to me in this disgusting manner:

COURT CLAIMS CON COPULATES CAPON

TRUCK DUCKFUCKER DIPS DICK IN FEATHERED FRIEND

HE WAS A GOOD EGG, SAYS MAN WHO FUCKS DUCK

DUCK GIVES BILL TO MAN IN BACK SEAT

MAN MAKES LOVE TO QUACK

MAN SEDUCES DUCK . . . THAT'S NO YOKE

Funny letter from a man who can't even spell his own name.

* * *

Gene Fowler wrote about several examples of gallows humor, his favorite being at an execution in Chicago. Fowler's friend Ben Hecht was present and recalled the victim's parting words. When the sheriff asked the about-to-be-strung-up victim if he had a farewell statement to make, the man replied, "I have nothing to say at this time."

*   *   *

Nicknames of sorts:

Allen went out of his way to collect nicknames, such as the one given a North Carolina man some years back called Psm C. Jackson. His folks got it out of the Bible — Psm C. (for Psalm 100). His late friend, author James Street, was plagued throughout his life by funnymen who alluded to him as Forty-second, One Way and Dead End.

One of my favorite stories had to do with a government worker named R.B. Jones. His initials stood for absolutely nothing. To clarify this on his work application, he wrote, "R (only) B (only) Jones. His first paycheck was made out to Ronly Bonly Jones. It stuck.

Another Jones wished to have his name perpetuated. He lived in a small Idaho town surrounded by a hundred creeks, such as Wexler Creek, Carey Creek, Elmendorf Creek and Velardi Creek. But there was no Jones Creek, so he decided to find one and name it after himself. He soon found it wasn't all that easy. The years stretched out, the search continued, but there was no unnamed creek he could put his moniker on. Folks began to call the frustrated fellow *No Creek Jones.* When No Creek Jones was about seventy-five, he found a little creek that had never been given a name. "It was the end of his rainbow," Allen told me. "To this day, that stream is called *No Creek Jones Creek!*"

*   *   *

By the time Smith's children, Allen W. and Shirley, married, he considered that Mount Kisco had become "people polluted." He wanted to move to a small town. He had visited the college town of Alpine, Texas, about twenty years before. He still liked it in 1967, so he decided to build a fine home on a hill overlooking Sul Ross State College. His disenchantment with the place came when local contractors "started rooking me with construction costs. And just after moving in, some local gal asked, 'Mr. Smith, just what does a writer do?' All at once, I discovered only about three people in Alpine read books, and I was its only author. They have only one dentist, but they got seventeen churches, which don't help an old agnostic like me." He referred to this period in his life as "The Trouble." A local newspaperman said the Alpine folks learned that Smith had money, and set out to part him from all they could. When Allen tried to buy a parcel of land adjacent to his house, the price doubled. Only as small-town people can, Smith was condemned by those who said the author had expected them to "bow and scrape." The local radio station, KVLF, ignored his presence. He called the Alpine newspaper the "Weekly Gut Rumble," and claimed the radio call letters stood for "K-Very-Loud-Fart."

Not knowing he was going to be quoted in a news magazine, Allen said he had never seen "such a goddamned bunch of bigoted, pious, lying, cheating bastards than in Alpine." It caused quite an explosion when Allen refused to take back what he had said. He'd get anonymous phone calls. "Is this H. Allen Smith?" Allen would confirm and the caller would say, "Screw you," and hang up. A concerned friend from a neighboring village called to tell Smith there was talk about some people heading for his house to tar and feather him. "Let 'em come," he said. "I'll be waitin' with a loaded shotgun." Armed, he stood outside his front door till midnight, but no one showed. He kept the shotgun within reach, as though he wished they would turn up.

"I am generally referred to as a humorist although a good many people think of me around here as a suppuration, or worse," Allen wrote in regard to the Alpine folk.

*   *   *

Allen's last piece, for the *Chicago Tribune*, was published posthumously. Suggested by my attorney friend Forrest D. Concannon, it had to do with a collection of characters living in the little southern Illinois town of Olney, which claimed to be the Belly Button of the United States population.

Concannon, who was raised in this hamlet of ten thousand, told us about the peculiar Olney characters who fit into Smith's equally peculiar essays. "One," said Concannon as we three sat on my patio, "was old Poke Field. He lived in the Olney Hotel and was watching a Saturday afternoon rain develop into a healthy hailstorm. Another storm came over old Poke. He rushed to the water cooler at the end of the hall, swiped a twenty-pound block of ice and threw it out his second-story window. Hearing a crashing sound, the storekeep below hurried into the street armed with a tin pan covering his head [so he wouldn't get his brains knocked loose by hailstones]. Grunting, he picked up the chunk and weighed and measured it in front of witnesses. 'The biggest hailstone ever to fall in Richland County!' he cried. Chicago newspapers carried the story," Concannon added. "And if Poke could have kept his mouth shut, they'd still be talking about it."

One of Olney's principal attractions was its white squirrels. The brazen little critters hopped all over town and around the courthouse lawn. Then the albino rodents became threatened when their little gray cousins began visiting — and *mating*.

Citizens called an emergency town hall meeting. One concerned chamber of commerce officer cried, "We've got to keep those animals exclusive-like and pure, else we're liable to end up with a lousy bunch of off-gray squirrels." The motion was carried and the town got squirrel racial conscious overnight. From then on, a watch was kept for intruding gray squirrels, which from then on hurried through the city limitts under the protective shade of night and away from buckshot.

The other attraction bringing visitors to Olney was the fact that, between 1950 and 1960, the government census bureau geographically placed the country's population center in a vacant field just eight miles northwest of town. Folks would come up in great numbers to have their pictures taken on the very spot, then swipe a chunk of dirt to place on their mantelpieces back home. But, when the 1960 census came out, citizens of Olney were shocked to find that the new population center had been placed a helluva lot farther west in Centralia. Centralians were called dirty things by Olneyites who claimed that the country's Belly Button, not to mention their pride, had been stolen outright.

Allen was put in touch with Allen W. Otis, who lived a few miles south of Olney. Otis wasn't interested in *anything* about

Olney, with the exception of a game the boys used to play with the girls, which was played only in the falling-off-places swimming holes. It was known thereabouts as "Plumbsocket and Butterass." A half-dozen boys would line up on one side of the creek, and the same number of girls would be on the other. All in the nude, and at one time, they would swing on ropes atatached to trees. On the signal "Go!" they would swing over the water and meet halfway. If the proper contact was made, the boy would holler, "Plumbsocket!" If it wasn't, the girl would cry, "Butterass!" I hope to travel there one day to see if they are still playing it.

* * *

When Smith sobered up, readying to hit the typewriter in earnest once again, he would first catch up on his correspondence. He would keep a glass of ice water at his elbow, a substitute for the beer he craved. He would start writing short magazine pieces until a book took form in his head. "He wrote, cooked, exercised, gardened, visited friends and researched at Sul Ross," said Dr. Elton Miles, the university's English professor.

"Then, full of vitality before burrowing into his library to face the long push on his typewriter, he would drive about town in his red sports car, and once meeting an English professor friend (not me) out for a walk, the boy H. Allen Smith leaned out the car window and yelled, 'Fuck Shakespeare!' "

19

The Real McCoy and Gentleman Jim

In his youth, Fowler refereed many fights in Denver. A number
were world's championship fights. He refereed for Ad Wolgast,
Battling Nelson, Sam Langford and Norman Selby, better
known the world over as Kid McCoy, "The *Real* McCoy."

McCoy became the world's welterweight champion in 1896,
fought James J. Corbett in 1900, and held claim to the world's
middleweight championship. With violence and trickery,
McCoy had fought more than two hundred professional fights
and lost only six. He possessed a great vanity, and although cruel
in the ring, he owned a corner on wit. He was married to eight
women eleven times. When Pop met Norman Selby (the Kid) in
1916, the boxer had hung up his gloves. But Fowler and McCoy
shared the same girlfriend, a newspaper artist for the *Denver
Post* named Faye King. Therefore, whenever McCoy hit Denver, he invariably insisted that he and Pop have a sparring session at the local gym. "I used to keep away from 'the Kid' for the
first few rounds until he got a bit winded," Pop said, "then I'd
get in for the following two rounds to get back at him for the
previous beating he had given me. I guess this was sort of his way
to tell me that he knew that Faye and I were sparking."

One day in 1939, when I was finishing up a piece of music for
piano and orchestra which was to be published by Jack Robbins
in New York, there was a knock at the door. It was a weekend
and Pop was home from the studio, working on his novel, *Illu-
sion in Java.*

Pop opened the door and cried out to the visitor, "Well, for God's sake! Norman Selby!"

It's impossible to believe that four years later I would marry Kid McCoy's great-niece, Beverly Blanchard.

Some weeks earlier, Pop had returned to his studio scripting following an auto accident which had been nearly fatal to the driver, director Leo McCarey (*Going My Way* and *The Bells of St. Mary's*). They were returning from McCarey's Lake Arrowhead villa where the two were working on a scenario. The last thing Pop recalled before impact was McCarey saying, as he noticed a car's lights far ahead of them, "That's all right. He can see us."

Pop, still walking around with a cane, told McCoy that he had awakened in a hearse and asked for a cigarette. "You can't have a cigarette, sir," said the morgue attendant as the vehicle changed course and headed for the nearest hospital. "You're drenched in gasoline, sir."

"Well, every time I write a movie script for a dying actor," Pop related to McCoy, "I always have him ask for a cigarette."

"You can't, sir. The gasoline," said the attendant.

"Then," Pop said to McCoy, "I asked if someone could piss down my back and put out the damned fire!"

"Well, at least your friends must have been concerned when they heard of your accident," said McCoy.

"As soon as they knew I was going to make it," said Pop, "hundreds of telegrams started coming in at the Good Samaritan Hospital, razzing me. The only ones that were serious came from my old fighter pals."

"We fighters pursue such a body-punishing career," said McCoy, "that when we hear a friend has been hurt, we just can't seem to joke about it."

"I guess you read in the papers how many times the car was supposed to have rolled over," said Pop.

"I did."

Pop picked up a telegram by his easy chair, where he was waiting out some aches. "Here's a for instance. It's from W.C. Fields. He's as sensitive as hell and I think he really masked his concern with this one." It read:

GOOD PUBLICITY, YES. BUT DON'T YOU THINK YOU WERE
TAKING AN AWFUL CHANCE? ONCE OVER WOULD HAVE
BEEN ENOUGH. BUT WHY THREE TIMES? THINK OF YOUR
MRS. AND THE NIPPERS. I LIKE THE PART WHERE YOU SAID
'TAKE CARE OF LEO . I AM ALL RIGHT.' AND HE REPEATED
VERBATIM WORDS TO YOU. WAS THAT AN ECHO? COME
CLEAN. I AM OFFERED FIVE THOUSAND DOLLARS FROM
SATURDAY EVENING POST TO EXPOSE THIS HOE-AX.
YOUR DEAREST UNCLE WILLIE FIELDS

Laughing it off, Fowler said, "I suppose you're married. You usually are."

"Not at the present," said McCoy.

"If you have time," said Fowler, "I'd like to put a few things straight in my mind because I plan in the near future to write extensively about you."

"What do you want to know?" McCoy asked.

"I heard a welterweight named Jack Wilkes kind of bothered you. You were sort of worried he might outclass you in the ring."

"As a matter of fact," said McCoy, "when I climbed into the ring — it was in Boston — my face was as white as a sheet. I had dark hollows under my eyes, and I was coughing like a consumptive. When we shook hands before the first round began, I said, 'Take it easy on me, Jack. I'm awful sick, but I need the money for the fight.' I caught an opening in the second round," said McCoy, "and gave Wilkes the hardest right hand I had. I knocked him cold."

"But you were sick," said Fowler.

"Not exactly," said McCoy. "I'd made up my face with talcum powder and put black pencil under my eyes. The cough, hell, anyone can cough."

"When I was a kid," said Fowler, "I remember you fought a huge guy from Holland named Plaacke. You were yelling at him in the second round about something. History has it that you were telling him that his shoelace was untied. Is that true?"

"That story's had a lot of versions," said McCoy, "but what I was doing was pointing to his waistband and saying, 'Your pants are falling off.' And when he looked down, that's all I needed.

Wham! And as I stood over him on the canvas, I told him if he got up, I'd tear his head off. . . . So he stayed down."

Even "Gentleman" Jim Corbett had to admit that McCoy, for a man never heavier than 170 in the ring, was "a marvel, a genius of scientific fighting."

The Kid stood up to leave. As Fowler showed him to the door, he asked McCoy, "What's the story behind the fight you had with that 250-pound man you fought in South Africa? There are so many conflicting yarns about that one, too."

"Yes," said McCoy. "This was when I developed the 'corkscrew punch,' where I added an extra turn to the wrist when I delivered a left hook — got the idea from the barreling of a gun."

"What about the fight?" Fowler asked. "This was another man you played some tricks on to beat."

"Had to," McCoy added. "It was at Bulawayo in South Africa that I met this black monster. He was known as the King of the Kaffirs, and he was 'unbeatable.' I was worried about my chances until I was tipped off that this man never wore shoes. That's all I needed. When I stepped into the ring," McCoy went on, "I had a glove filled with tacks. And, as we went to the middle of the ring for instructions just before the first round, I dropped all these tacks on the canvas at my corner. Well, as soon as I could, I steered this ox over to my corner, and he started picking up tacks in his bare feet. He began hopping around, picking at his feet and I waded in on him, hit him about a half-dozen times until I knocked him senseless."

As he drove away, McCoy promised he would visit Fowler the following year. "The Real McCoy" never did make it. He died a few months latter in his Detroit home.

* * *

The oldest champion I met was "Gentleman" James J. Corbett, who had won the heavyweight title from John L. Sullivan in twenty-one rounds at New Orleans. It was the first title fight in which gloves were used. Prior to this, it was bare knuckles.

Corbett told my father about his most difficult match, in 1891, the year before he won the title from the Boston Strong Boy. "He was Peter Jackson," said Corbett, a black man born in the West Indies in 1861. He was six and a half feet tall." After sixty-one rounds, the fight was called a draw because the two were too exhausted to continue.

"Jim was one of the very few pugilists who could really act," Pop told me. "I remember Sullivan was horrible. He used to star in a terrible play titled *Honest Hearts and Willing Hands.* He was, oh, horrible."

Pop recalled one time when heavyweight Tom Sharkey was appearing with somebody in New York vaudeville. Sharkey was the man to beat before you were allowed a crack at the heavyweight title.

Sharkey was not doing very well on the boards, and Jim Corbett was asked if he couldn't visit old Tom, appear on the stage, and sort of bolster up the act. Corbett agreed, so they stayed backstage to rehearse. Tom was not the most gigantic intellect in the world.

"Now, Tom," said Corbett, "I'm going to come in on the stage and I'll ask you how you are, and then you'll reply, 'Fit as a fiddle.' Do you get that?"

Tom nodded, "Yeah, yeah. Feet as a fiddle. Yeah, feet as a fiddle."

Then Jim said, "I'll ask you, 'What are you doing?' and you'll say, 'Well, I opened a saloon here on Herald Square.' And I'll say, 'Oh, good, good. That's fine and what are your plans for the future?' And then you'll tell me, 'Well, I want to keep in shape. I'll meet all comers. I'm a fine fighter and have a lot of friends.' So," Corbett concluded, "we'll go on from there and talk a little bit and just give me plain answers, and now, remember . . ."

"Yeah, yeah," said Tom.

Sharkey was standing on stage when the curtain went up. Then Corbett entered as blithe and debonair as ever, and said, "Well, Tom Sharkey. How are you?"

"Feet as a fiddle," Sharkey answered.

"What are you doing now, Tom?"

"Feet as a fiddle."

"I understand you are at a place of business. Where is it?" Corbett went on.

"Feet as a fiddle," Sharkey kept repeating.

Trying to cover for him, Corbett went on, "Well, now look. What are your plans for the future? I understand you have a *lot* of plans for the future. You're going to get some rematches with the best heavyweights. Tell me about it, Tom."

Tom looked him over, then said, "Feet as a fiddle."

Corbett bowed out of the show following the first performance.

* * *

When he was champion, Corbett used to train down in Lakewood, New Jersey. This man, who gave boxing a push toward respectability because of his gentlemanly behavior, told Fowler of a time during a Lakewood training period when Isidor Straus, of the internationally known Abraham and Straus department store, took a fancy to Corbett and invited him to ride in a kind of tallyho with twelve prominent persons.

Lakewood was quite a fancy place in those days, and they were on the road, and one of Mr. Straus' guests, a beautiful young girl, said to Gentleman Jim, "You know, Mr. Corbett, until I had met you, I always believed that prizefighting of course was brutal. It still think it must be brutal."

"Oh, no, no," Corbett tried to reassure her. "It's not brutal. It's a game of skill and endurance. It's really an art, a physical art, *but* an art."

"Well," she said, "whatever it is, having met you, I wonder that a man such as you, with your charm and manners, would be in that business."

And he said, "A lot of people have the wrong idea of fighting. We fight. It's in a sense brutal, yes. The impetus of fists against flesh. But really, fighters and men in the pugilistic game are gentlemen, actually."

At this moment, one of Jim's sparring partners came running alongside the coach. He was a mean monster named Ed Dunkhorst. Dunkhorst looked up at the tallyho, spying Corbett, who was busy giving this discourse on the gentlemanly aspects of pugilism to his newly found lady friend. Then Dunkhorst shouted so all could hear, "Well, you dirty son-of-a-bitch! There you are, up there with all them swell pricks, an' here I am down here runnin' my ass off!"

20

Who Would Wish
to Entertain the Devil?

A Letter to a Recent Bride

* * *

Mrs. Randall F. Geddes, III
McCall, Idaho

My dear Virginia:

I am grateful to your parents Jean and Peter Sales for having been invited to your wedding last November. It had a special meaning for me because I, myself, had been married to Beverly in that very same Westwood United Methodist Church nearly forty years ago. I remember that Jean and Pete, too, had.

But more than herein rendering my wishes for happy years ahead for you and Randall, I must confess it has always been my policy never to attend my friends' children's weddings. I suppose it is because the first three of my five children have already collectively visited the altar nine times. I do not wish to place an anathema on what I believe will be your first and only espousal.

Usually, when being accommodated by my handsome mother-in-law, Bess Blanchard, we seem always to arrive early at any event. That held true on this day.

Before the ceremonies began, I found time to meditate on what my father had advised me about marriage so long ago. When I told him that I wished to wed Beverly, he had said:

* * *

Two intelligent persons — with possible reservations in-

volving youth and the age-old anesthesia of Venus Aphrodite — are concerned in your present particular case. . . . No one is keener than I to see, know, and understand your predicament. I have not entirely forgotten my own youth. . . . You must know in advance that all is not rose petals floating on cream. . . . Marriage must be regarded with earnest honesty on both sides of the bed. . . . Who am I or anyone else to defy an urge which an inscrutable God has placed in the souls and bodies of his children? . . . I try in the first stages of my reasoning to objectify the case, to state things not found in the Lived Happily Ever After *school of thought. Then, when I have done with my little urinations against the wind, I abdicate.*

* * *

Of the hundreds present, I peered over a sea of gray hair, then recalled what an old woman had told me shortly after my own nuptual ceremony. She seemed as old as I am today. "Enjoy every day of your young married life," she said as though warning me of the Ides of March. "Time has a habit of passing all too quickly."

What a stale thing to say! I thought as I nodded and pretended to take her admonition to heart. *I'm twenty. And when one is twenty, like the amaranth — the flower that never fades — there is no thing such as growing old.*

Well, that was the first incorrect thought of my married life.

* * *

Before I leave you to continue the enjoyment of your honeymoon, I have a few thoughts to pass on to you, Virginia.

You see, yesterday was a small town. When I was your age, it was not the habit for men to masquerade with long locks, high heels and purses, and use hair dryers. Nor yet had women began to neutralize themselves by placing "Ms." before their enchantingly feminine names. There was no political pressure put upon us to exclude the sounds and sights of our primary heritage such as the Lord's Prayer, the National Anthem and the American

Who Would Wish to Entertain the Devil?

Flag. But perhaps these basic factions shall return once we have fought on our own country's continental home grounds.

The historic persons I have written about here lived with me in a safer time when the population was aloof to the present dangers of pollution and atomic destruction. Yes, yesterday *was* a small town when the Barrymores, W.C. Fields, Dempsey, Lardner, Faulkner, Ben Hecht and the rest abounded. Those were the times when it was unnecessary to lock the front door and a woman could walk the streets in safety.

As ink has always been the embalming fluid of civilization, I wonder what Damon Runyon, Pegler, Rice, Baer, Winchell, H.G. Wells, yes, and even Sadakichi Hartmann, would write if they descended upon us from Heaven to chronicle our way of life today. I say "Heaven" simply because I do not believe in hell. When I think of these friends who have left me, I say, "After all, who would wish to entertain the devil?"

Personally, Virginia, I should like to find repose at night, knowing that neither starvation nor hunger persists either at home or far away, and that all creatures of greed, intolerance, and suppression have been caged in an international zoo.

I do believe that tomorrow's great chronicler will bring us a revolutionary message. It should be founded upon the word "for." We now move upon, and long have been motivated by, the word "against." Our leverage has been exercised on the propositional fulcrum "against." Man against Fate. . . . Man against Man. . . . Man against Enlightenment. The new generation should be taught that Man was intended to stand *for* the things that mean a whole heart and a tolerant mind. Man, indeed, was created in God's image; but he has been loitering for centuries in front of distorting mirrors. . . .

Some day, I desire and hope to write of Faith, although ours does not yet seem to be an age of Faith. Still, I look upon writing and Art as a priestly vestment, and not as a crying towel. Whatever I am in fact or by reputation, and however lax and remiss I may be as a person among persons, I have within me a Faith that sustains me. Faith in my country, notwithstanding the lard-assed politicans and dung-grabbers. Faith in the destiny of mankind, though a million million years must go past the sun before they

Who Would Wish to Entertain the Devil?

will learn to give and forgive, to live and let live, be big and
don't belittle, and not merely get and forget, grab and be
grabbed, slave and be enslaved. Then let us all go out and cru-
cify somebody. It is the thing, you know. And we must be in the
fashion. Horse-hockey!

But in all, it is a great country in other ways; must be. Everybody's been trying to steal it, rob it, betray it. Not everybody, but
a whole lot of people. And the country still endures. In my small
way I think it will make it once we finally decide to all get together and pull the oars in cadence.

I'm not one who thinks that we — our country — is "going to
the dogs." we were always going to the dogs, according to what I
have heard through the years. But I still do not believe it. I don't
think we should demean dogs. Dogs are superior to a great many
persons. I think it's a compliment if we're "going to the dogs." If
we are, at least we're assured of a more loyal group of comrades
then we might be if we were *going to the men* . . . *or going to
the people. . .*

*   *   *

We shall all die. No Supreme Court injunction can prevent it.
But, meanwhile, let us live in the areas of love, loyalty and decency. May I timidly inquire: Are you laying a wreath on your
own three meals a day?

As for Fowler, well, Fowler is fifty-seven (as we go to press),
slightly disabused, but never cynical; possessed of fine animal
spirits, with not one gland given out, and with not one vital organ limping — except for a confounded liver that must look like
Plymouth Rock, which prevents him from a workmanlike handling of modern toddies.

*   *   *

If I felt like that, I'd get a gun and shoot myself.

Sometimes I *do* sit and stew and look upon death as man's last
and greatest luxury. But the cup soon passes. I am still raw-boned
and swarthy although my hair, what there is left of it, is now as
white as the feathers on a seagull's outspread wings.

I am still pulsing with Life, ebullient, defiant, eager, careless, confused, naïve, timid in soul but bold in address, twitchy (on account of a nose thrice broken), big-footed, big-hearted, sensitive, given to nightmares, jealous of solitude after a life of gadding about, incapable of sustained drudgeries, forgiving of the bad, in love with children, an adorer of women, tactless, a blundering *moujik* — in short, it has not bored me to live with this scoundrel for fifty-seven years.

I was a guest of the world, I am of the Earth, and tomorrow *in* the Earth.

* * *

Many persons look down their noses upon the physical urges. They exalt the spiritual. For me, I sing the "What is!"

The body — so widely demeaned — is to me the Taj Mahal of the present.

God created the sinews, the muscles, the glands!

Bravo, God!

Most sincerely yours,
Will Fowler

So far, so good.

Index

Index